FAVORITE RECIPES
WITH
HERBS

FAVORITE RECIPES
WITH
HERBS

DAWN J. RANCK
AND
PHYLLIS PELLMAN GOOD

Good Books

Intercourse, PA 17534

Cover design and illustration by Cheryl Benner
Design by Dawn J. Ranck
Illustrations by Cheryl Benner

FAVORITE RECIPES WITH HERBS
Copyright © 1997 by Good Books, Intercourse, Pennsylvania, 17534
International Standard Book Number: 1-56148-225-0
Library of Congress Catalog Card Number: 97-42052

Library of Congress Cataloging-in-Publication Data
Ranck, Dawn J.
  Favorite recipes with herbs / Dawn J. Ranck and Phyllis Pellman Good.
    p. cm.
  Includes index.
  ISBN 1-56148-225-0
  1. Cookery (Herbs) 2. Herbs. I. Good, Phyllis Pellman. II. Title
TX819.H4R35   1997
641.6'57--dc21   97-42052
                                                                      CIP

Table of Contents

About This Cookbook

Cooking with herbs is like being part of a small rebellion. The pleasure of growing our own food—even a few stalks of basil or rosemary—helps many of us withstand our too-full lives and concrete and macadam worlds.

The satisfaction of cooking with fresh ingredients—perhaps some lemon thyme or apple mint—brings energy both to preparing food and to eating it. We are not—we will not be—completely captive to packaging and advertising and carry-in speed meals!

Herbs, with all their personality, liven up any dish, yet don't require a major cooking production. They are, in fact, humble ingredients in what they ask of a cook. But they sing out when they are put in place—either mixed in early, or added impromptu at the end of preparing a dish.

Herbs do their part, whether fresh or dried, albeit with somewhat different effect. So you don't need your own pot or garden, or even supermarket-fresh varieties, to add herbs to your meals. We give suggested portions of both fresh and dried herbs in most recipes in this book.

Favorite Recipes with Herbs is a *cookbook.* Herbs have medicinal and cosmetic and aromatic properties, but we do not cover those uses here.

Instead, we offer cooking recipes using 14 herbs within easy reach of most of us who live within temperate or subtropical climates. These herbs are not exotic plants. They are good for beginning herb growers; they are favorites of veteran herb farmers.

We have also tapped the knowledge and experience of herb shopkeepers across the country. What a wonderful variety of recipes has resulted! What downright useful and imaginative tips!

Join this growing group of cooks. **Favorite Recipes with Herbs** will give you many recipes and ideas to follow—and will likely lead you to experimenting happily on your own, freed from bland cooking forever!

—Dawn J. Ranck and Phyllis Pellman Good

Appetizers and Snacks

Baked Herb Cheese Spread

Danielle Vachow
Busha's Brae Herb Farm
Suttons Bay, MI

Makes 24 small wedges

8-oz. pkg. cream cheese, softened
2 eggs, beaten
$1/2$ cup sour cream
1 tsp. Dijon mustard
$1/4$ cup chopped fresh herbs
 (5 tsp. dried): choose one, or any
 combination of, thyme, oregano,
 rosemary, dill, tarragon, basil, parsley
1 clove garlic, minced
$1/4$ tsp. coarsely ground pepper

1. Beat together cream cheese and eggs
 until smooth. Add sour cream and
 mustard.
2. Fold in herbs, garlic, and pepper.
3. Spread mixture into greased 2-2$1/2$ cup
 mold or 2 8"-springform pans.

4. Bake at 350° for 30 minutes, or until
 center is firm.
5. Cool. Unmold onto serving dish. Cut
 each round into 12 pie-shaped wedges.
6. Garnish with fresh herbs or edible
 flowers. Serve with whole wheat or
 wafer crackers.

Herbal Cheese Spread

Lynn Redding
Redding's Country Cabin
Ronda, NC

Makes 20 servings

8-oz. pkg. cream cheese, softened
1/4 cup margarine, softened
1 1/2 Tbsp. milk
1/4 tsp. garlic powder
3/4 tsp. chopped fresh savory
 (1/4 tsp. dried)
1/2 tsp. chopped fresh oregano
 (1/8 tsp. dried)
1/2 tsp. chopped fresh dill (1/8 tsp. dried)
1/2 tsp. chopped fresh basil (1/8 tsp. dried)
1/8 tsp. black pepper

1. Beat together cream cheese and margarine until fluffy. Add milk and mix well.
2. Stir in seasonings and herbs. Mix well.
3. Serve with crackers or on hot vegetables or hot pasta.

Garden Party Herb Terrine

Nancy J. Reppert
Sweet Remembrances
Mechanicsburg, PA

Makes 20 servings

2 8-oz. pkgs. cream cheese, softened
1/2 cup crumbled feta cheese
1/2 tsp. garlic powder
1/4 tsp. ground red pepper
1/2 cup sour cream
2 eggs
2 1/2 tsp. shredded lemon peel
1/2 cup fresh garden herbs
 (any combination), chopped

1/4 cup thinly sliced green onion
1/2 cup chopped pimento
1/3 cup chopped black olives
1/2 cup chopped parsley
fresh edible flowers

1. Beat cream cheese until smooth. Add feta cheese, garlic powder, and red pepper. Beat well.
2. Stir in sour cream, eggs, and lemon peel. Beat just until blended.
3. Stir in 1/2 cup herbs, onion, pimento, and olives.
4. Pour into 8" x 4" loaf pan, with its sides greased and its bottom lined with foil.
5. Place loaf pan into large baking pan. Fill larger pan to a depth of 1" with boiling water.
6. Bake at 325° for 50 minutes, or until center is soft set. Remove from water bath and cool on wire rack for 1 hour. Cover and chill for at least 8 hours.
7. Gently remove from pan. Press chopped parsley around edges and garnish with edible flowers.
8. Serve with crackers.

Herbal Cream Cheese

Jacoba Baker & Reenie Baker Sandsted
Baker's Acres
Groton, NY

Makes 2 cups spread

2 8-oz. pkgs. cream cheese, softened
2 Tbsp. cream
1 Tbsp. fresh dill (1 tsp. dried)
2 tsp. fresh basil leaves (2/3 tsp. dried)
1-2 cloves garlic

1. Mix together all ingredients in food processor. Process until herbs and garlic are chopped.
2. Chill for 8 hours. Use with fresh vegetables or crackers.

Homestyle Boursin

Jacoba Baker & Reenie Baker Sandsted
Baker's Acres
Groton, NY

Makes 25-30 servings

2 8-oz. pkgs. cream cheese, softened
$1/4$ cup light mayonnaise
2 tsp. Dijon mustard
2 Tbsp. fresh chives, finely chopped
   (2 tsp. dried)
2 Tbsp. fresh dill, finely chopped
   (2 tsp. dried)
1 clove garlic, minced

1. Beat cheese, mayonnaise, and mustard until thoroughly blended.
2. Stir in chives, dill, and garlic. Mix well. Chill for 8 hours.
3. Serve as spread on crackers.

Boursin-Style Cheese Spread

Mary Ellen Wilcox
South Ridge Treasures Herb Shop
Scotia, NY

Makes 1$1/2$ cups

8-oz. pkg cream cheese, softened
1 stick unsalted butter, softened
$1/4$ tsp. red wine vinegar
$1/2$ tsp. Worcestershire sauce
1 clove garlic, minced
1$1/2$ tsp. chopped fresh parsley
   ($1/2$ tsp. dried)
1$1/2$ tsp. chopped fresh dill ($1/2$ tsp. dried)
$3/4$ tsp. chopped fresh basil ($1/4$ tsp. dried)
$3/8$ tsp. chopped fresh marjoram
   ($1/8$ tsp. dried)

$3/8$ tsp. chopped fresh thyme
   ($1/8$ tsp. dried)
$1/4$ tsp. chopped fresh rosemary
   (dash of dried)
dash of cayenne pepper

1. Combine cream cheese and butter. Mix well.
2. Stir in vinegar and Worcestershire sauce. Blend well.
3. Add garlic, herbs and cayenne. Blend well.
4. Refrigerate for several hours or overnight before serving.
5. Use as a spread for crackers, a topping for sandwiches, or spread for bagels.

Note: This will keep several weeks in the refrigerator.

Fool's Boursin

Maryland Massey
Maryland's Herb Basket
Millington, MD

Makes 2$1/2$ -3 cups

2 8-oz. pkgs. cream cheese, softened
8-oz. unsalted butter, softened
2 garlic cloves, minced
1 tsp. fresh marjoram ($1/4$ tsp. dried)
1$1/2$ tsp. fresh dill ($1/2$ tsp. dried)
1$1/2$ tsp. fresh basil ($1/2$ tsp. dried)
$3/4$ tsp. fresh thyme ($1/4$ tsp. dried)
$1/4$ tsp. pepper
1 tsp. Worcestershire sauce

1. Combine all ingredients.
2. Serve on crackers, toast, or muffins.

Note: Keeps for weeks in refrigerator.

Rosemary's Garlic Cheese Spread

Bertha Reppert
The Rosemary House
Mechanicsburg, PA

Makes 1³/₄ cups

8 oz. cream cheese, softened
¹/₂ cup butter, softened
¹/₂ tsp. Worcestershire sauce
1 clove garlic, minced
1¹/₂ tsp. chopped fresh dill (¹/₂ tsp. dried)
1¹/₂ tsp. chopped fresh basil
  (¹/₂ tsp. dried)
1¹/₂ tsp. chopped fresh oregano
  (¹/₂ tsp. dried)
³/₄ tsp. chopped fresh thyme
  (¹/₄ tsp. dried)
³/₄ tsp. chopped fresh rosemary
  (¹/₄ tsp. dried)

1. Mix together all ingredients.
2. Spread on crackers, bagels, or sandwiches.

Variation: *Eliminate butter; mix together all other ingredients.*

Kim's Herbed Cheese Spread

Kim Snyder
Kim's Kakes, Kutting, and Kandles, too!
Ivesdale, IL

Makes 1 cup

8 oz. cream cheese, softened
1 Tbsp. chopped fresh thyme
  (1 tsp. dried)
2 tsp. chopped fresh chives
  (²/₃ tsp. dried)
1-2 Tbsp. herbed vinegar

1. Mix together all ingredients. Blend well.
2. Refrigerate for 1-2 hours before serving.
3. Serve with assorted crackers or bread.

Sweet Herbed Cheese

Bertha Reppert
The Rosemary House
Mechanicsburg, PA

Makes approximately 2 cups

8 oz. cream cheese, softened
8 oz. ricotta cheese
2 Tbsp. chopped orange zest
orange juice, enough to thin cheese to
  desired consistency
3 Tbsp. honey
¹/₄ cup coarsely chopped nuts
2 Tbsp. chopped peeled fresh ginger
4 Tbsp. chopped fresh herbs (rose
  geranium, mint, lemon verbena, rose
  petals, lemon balm, or a combination
  of any of those)

1. Combine all ingredients until smooth.
2. Serve with fresh fruit or vanilla wafers.

Veggie Dill Dip

Donna Treloar
Harmony
Gaston, IN

Makes 2 cups

1 cup mayonnaise
1 cup sour cream
1 1/2 Tbsp. minced onion
1 Tbsp. chopped fresh parsley
1 tsp. chopped fresh dill
1/2 tsp. seasoned salt
1/4 tsp. garlic powder
3/4 cup finely diced and seeded cucumber
(optional)
dash of hot pepper sauce (optional)

1. Mix together mayonnaise and sour cream.
2. Add remaining ingredients. Mix well.
3. Cover and chill for several hours.
4. Serve with raw vegetables or crackers.

Garlic-Dill Dip

Gerry Janus
Vileniki—An Herb Farm
Montdale, PA

Makes 1 pint

1 cup sour cream
3/4 cup plain yogurt
2 small cloves garlic, finely minced, or
put through garlic press
1 Tbsp. minced fresh dill (1 tsp. dried)
4 Tbsp. minced fresh parsley
(1 1/2 tsp. dried)
2 Tbsp. minced fresh chives (2 tsp. dried)
1/2 tsp. finely minced fresh lovage
1/2 tsp. celery salt
dash of cayennne pepper

1. Blend together sour cream and yogurt.
2. Add garlic, herbs, and seasonings, and blend well.
3. Refrigerate for several hours to allow flavor to develop. Serve with raw vegetables, chips, or crackers.

Dill-Radish Dip

Kathleen Brown
Brown Horse Herb Farm
Lakewood, CO

Makes 2 cups

8-oz. pkg. cream cheese, softened
1 Tbsp. lemon juice
3/4 tsp. chopped fresh dill (1/4 tsp. dried)
1/2 - 3/4 tsp. salt
1 clove garlic, minced
1 cup chopped radishes

1. Mix together cream cheese, lemon juice, dill, salt, and garlic.
2. Stir in chopped radishes. Mix until blended. Cover. Refrigerate for at least 2 hours before using.
3. Serve with crackers or fresh vegetables.

Sesame Dill Dip

Connie Johnson
Heartstone Herb Farm
Loudon, NH

Makes 10-12 servings

3 Tbsp. fresh dill (1 Tbsp. dried)
3 Tbsp. sesame seeds
3 Tbsp. dried chopped onion
16-oz. container sour cream

1. Mix together all ingredients.
2. Use as a dip or to top baked potatoes or baked haddock.

Dip with Dill

Robin Giese
Riverview Farm
Fall City, WA

Makes 1 cup

1/2 cup mayonnaise
1/2 cup plain yogurt
1/4 cup chopped fresh dill
1 tsp. soy sauce
1 Tbsp. lemon juice

1. Mix together all ingredients.
2. Serve with fresh vegetables.

Dill Dip

Ernestine Schrepfer
Herbal Scent-sations
Trenton, MO

Makes 2 cups

1/2 cup dried onion
8 Tbsp. dried dill
8 Tbsp. dried parsley
4 Tbsp. garlic powder
2 Tbsp. sugar
4 Tbsp. celery seed
1/2 tsp. white pepper
1/2 tsp. sea salt

1 cup mayonnaise
1 cup sour cream or plain yogurt

1. Mix together all dry ingredients. Store in jar in cool, dry, dark area.
2. To serve, mix together mayonnaise and sour cream. Stir in 2 Tbsp. dry mix (or more if you like a zippy taste).

Note: Use as a dip, salad dressing, or to top baked potatoes.

Chive-Dill Spread

Linda Hangren
LinHaven Gardens
Omaha, NE

Makes 1 cup

8-oz. cream cheese, softened
1/4 cup finely chopped fresh dill
  (1 1/2 tsp. dried)
2 Tbsp. finely chopped fresh chives
  (2 tsp. dried)

1. Mix cream cheese and herbs until well blended.

2. Refrigerate in tightly covered container.
3. Use to stuff celery or cherry tomatoes, or to spread on crackers or toast squares.

Herb Garden Dip
"No Salt, All Herbs"

Carol Vaughn
Healthy Horse Herb Farm
Onley, Va

Makes 12 servings

8-oz. pkg. cream cheese, softened, or
   sour cream
2 Tbsp. fresh rosemary (2 tsp. dried)
2 Tbsp. fresh sage (2 tsp. dried)
2 Tbsp. fresh lovage (2 tsp. dried)
2 Tbsp. fresh parsley (2 tsp. dried)
2 Tbsp. fresh basil (2 tsp. dried)
1 Tbsp. dried minced onion, or
   1 tsp. garlic powder

1. Chop herbs; then mix together all ingredients.
2. Chill for several hours before serving.
3. Serve with crackers or fresh vegetables.

Green Dip

Jacoba Baker & Reenie Baker Sandsted
Baker's Acres
Groton, NY

Makes 2 cups

3 cups Swiss chard leaves, packed
3/4 cup fresh basil leaves
3 cloves garlic
1/2 cup olive oil
1 cup feta cheese, crumbled
1/2 cup walnuts, coarsely chopped
3/4 cup whipping cream

1/4 cup minced green onion
freshly ground pepper to taste

1. In blender, mix together chard leaves, basil leaves, garlic, olive oil, feta cheese, and walnuts until a paste forms.
2. Stir in whipping cream, onions, and pepper.
3. Use as a dip for fresh vegetables.

Variation: Substitute fresh spinach leaves for Swiss chard leaves.

Onion Chive Dip

Stephanie L. Distler
Sweet Posie Herbary
Johnsonburg, PA

Makes 2 cups

1 cup sour cream
1 cup mayonnaise
1 Tbsp. vinegar
1 tsp. minced garlic
1 Tbsp. chopped onion
1 1/2 cups fresh chives (1/2 cup dried)
1/2 tsp. cracked black peppercorns
2 tsp. sugar
1. Combine all ingredients with whisk or spoon. Let mixture sit in refrigerator for at least 4 hours.
2. Serve with your favorite dippers.

Herbed Cheese Dip

Barbara Steele and Marlene Lufrin
Alloway Gardens & Herb Farm
Littlestown, PA

Makes 12 servings

8 oz. cottage cheese
3-oz. pkg. cream cheese, softened
1 Tbsp. chopped fresh parsley
    (1 tsp. dried)
1½ Tbsp. chopped fresh chives
    (1½ tsp. dried)
2 tsp. fresh thyme or lemon thyme
    (⅔ tsp. dried)
2 tsp. chopped fresh basil (⅔ tsp. dried)

1. Press cottage cheese through a large strainer.
2. Add cream cheese and beat until smooth.
3. Stir in remaining ingredients. Cover and refrigerate several hours.
4. Serve with crackers or fresh vegetables.

Basil Dip

Jacoba Baker & Reenie Baker Sandsted
Baker's Acres
Groton, NY

Makes 10 servings

16 oz. sour cream
1 pkg. ranch seasoning
⅓ cup fresh basil (2 Tbsp. dried)

1. In blender, mix together all ingredients until well blended.
2. Serve with raw vegetables or crackers.

Black Bean Dip

Eone Riales
Fogg Road Herb Farm
Nesbit, MS

Makes 2½ cups

15-oz. can black beans, rinsed, drained
⅓ cup mayonnaise
½ cup sour cream
4-oz. can chopped green chilies, drained
2 Tbsp. chopped fresh cilantro
3 tsp. chili powder
1½ tsp. hot pepper sauce of your choice
1 tsp. garlic powder
1 tsp. salt (optional)
1 Tbsp. cilantro

1. Mash beans with fork.
2. Stir in all remaining ingredients except 1 Tbsp. cilantro until well blended.
3. Refrigerate. Garnish with 1 Tbsp. cilantro and serve with tortilla chips.

Olive Spread

Marian E. Sebastiano
Salt Box Gallery Herbs
Hubbard, OH

Makes 8 servings

1 cup Greek olives, pits removed
2 cloves garlic
2 tsp. lemon juice
1 tsp. capers
1 tsp. Dijon mustard
2 tsp. fresh parsley (⅔ tsp. dried)
2 tsp. fresh thyme (⅔ tsp. dried)
3-4 Tbsp. olive oil
baguette, or toasted pita bread
4-6 Tbsp. butter
¼ cup Parmesan cheese

1. In food processor, mix together olives, garlic, lemon juice, capers, mustard, parsley, and thyme. Process until mixed but not smooth.
2. Blend in olive oil to hold mixture together.
3. Cut baguette into 3/4" slices. Spread with butter and then with olive mixture. Sprinkle with Parmesan cheese. Toast under broiler until lightly browned.
4. Serve bread with additional Olive Spread.

Antipasto Cheese and Olives

Shari Jensen
Crestline Enterprises
Fountain, CO

Makes 6-8 servings

1/2 cup medium or large pitted black olives
1/4 cup medium sharp cheddar cheese, cut into strips to stuff black olives
1/2 lb. mozzarella cheese, cut in 1/2" cubes
1/2 red or green bell pepper, cut in 3/4" pieces
1/2 cup stuffed green olives
1/2 cup white wine vinegar
1/3 cup olive oil
1/2 tsp. minced garlic
1 Tbsp. fresh oregano (1 tsp. dried)
1 tsp. crushed red pepper flakes
1 1/2 tsp. fresh thyme (1/2 tsp. dried)

1. Stuff cheddar sticks into black olives.
2. Combine mozzarella cubes, bell pepper pieces, and black and green olives. Set aside.
3. In saucepan, combine vinegar, oil, garlic, oregano, red pepper, and thyme.

Cook until heated, but not boiling. Pour over olive and cheese mixture. Cool to room temperature.
4. Marinate in refrigerator for 1-3 days. Let stand at room temperature for 30 minutes before serving.
5. Drain and serve with mushrooms, salami, and/or good bread.

Goat Cheese and Tomato Flatbread

Arlene Shannon
Greenfield Herb Garden
Shipshewana, IN

Makes 6-8 servings

4 or 5 6"-flat flour tortillas
1/4 cup basil pesto (see pages 57-60)
1 small log (3 1/2 oz.) goat cheese
1/4 cup julienne-cut, sun-dried tomatoes
4 cloves roasted garlic
small bunch of basil (thai, sweet, or lemon), chopped

1. Brush pesto onto tortillas so entire surface has a light coat.
2. Place small pieces of cheese and tomatoes over tortillas.
3. Slice roasted garlic into small slivers and scatter over cheese and tomatoes.
4. Top with chopped basil.
5. Broil until lightly browned. Cut into wedges and serve.

Grilled Bread with Onions and Cheese

Arlene Shannon
Greenfield Herb Garden
Shipshewana, IN

Makes 2 servings

4 slices good Italian bread, cut 1/2" thick
flavored olive oil
1 red onion, sliced thin
1/4 cup chopped fresh thyme, oregano, or
  rosemary
1 tomato, sliced thin
4 thin slices Romano or Parmesan cheese

1. Broil bread until lightly browned.
2. Brush both sides of browned bread with olive oil.
3. Lightly saute onion slices in flavored oil until limp but not crispy. Drain onion.
4. Layer each piece of bread with onion, chopped herb, and tomato. Top with cheese.
4. Broil until cheese melts. Serve immediately.

Mustard and Herbs with French Bread

Judith M. Graves
Lambs & Thyme at Randallane
Richmond, NH

Makes 6 servings

1/2 cup butter or margarine, softened
1/4 cup snipped fresh parsley
  (4 tsp. dried)
2 Tbsp. chopped fresh chives
  (2 tsp. dried)
2 Tbsp. prepared mustard

1 Tbsp. sesame seeds
1 tsp. lemon juice
loaf of French bread

1. Blend together butter, parsley, chives, mustard, sesame seeds, and lemon juice. Mix well.
2. Cut a loaf of French bread into slices, not quite cutting through bottom crust.
3. Spread herb mixture on both sides of slices. Wrap loosely in foil.
4. Heat at 350° for 10-15 minutes.

Pesto Pizza Rounds

Kathleen Brown
Brown Horse Herb Farm
Lakewood, CO

Makes 15-20 servings

2 cups fresh basil
2 large garlic cloves
1/2 cup Parmesan cheese
1/4 cup pine nuts
1/2 cup olive oil
salt to taste
pepper to taste
2 baguettes, sliced 1/2" thick
1/2 cup pizza sauce
1/2 cup Parmesan cheese

1. To make pesto, blend together basil, garlic, 1/2 cup Parmesan cheese, and pine nuts in food processor or blender. Process until smooth. Slowly add olive oil. Add salt and pepper. Process until well blended.
2. Lay slices of bread on cookie sheet. Spread a little pizza sauce and a dollop of pesto on each slice of bread. Top with a sprinkle of the remaining 1/2 cup Parmesan.
3. Place under broiler about 3 minutes, or until cheese is bubbly and bread is toasted. Serve hot or at room temperature.

Herb Toastettes

Maryland Massey
Maryland's Herb Basket
Millington, MD

Makes 8 servings

1/2 **cup butter or margarine, softened**
2 **Tbsp. sesame seeds**
3/4 **tsp. fresh marjoram (**1/4 **tsp. dried)**
3/4 **tsp. fresh basil (**1/4 **tsp. dried)**
3/4 **tsp. fresh rosemary (**1/4 **tsp. dried)**
3/4 **tsp. fresh chives (**1/4 **tsp. dried)**
8-oz. **loaf of party rye or other flavored**
bread

1. Mix together butter, sesame seeds, and chopped herbs.
2. Spread on bread slices. Place on cookie sheet.
3. Bake at 350° for 6-8 minutes, until slightly browned.

Herb Melba

Jacoba Baker & Reenie Baker Sandsted
Baker's Acres
Groton, NY

Makes 20 servings

1/3 **cup butter or margarine, softened**
1 **Tbsp. fresh parsley leaves (1 tsp. dried)**
1 **Tbsp. fresh basil leaves (1 tsp. dried)**
2 **tsp. fresh oregano (**2/3 **tsp. dried)**
2 **tsp. fresh tarragon (**2/3 **tsp. dried)**
1 **tsp. fresh marjoram leaves**
    (1/3 **tsp. dried)**
8-oz. **sliced party rye bread**

1. Mix together all ingredients, except bread, in food processor until herbs are finely chopped.

2. Spread on bread slices. Arrange on baking sheets.
3. Bake at 350° for 10-15 minutes, until light brown and crisp.
4. Serve immediately, or store in tightly covered container for a few days, or freeze.

Herbal Garlic Bread

Lynn Redding
Redding's Country Cabin
Ronda, NC

Makes 10 servings

2 **cloves garlic, minced**
2 **tsp. olive oil**
2 **Tbsp. chopped fresh parsley**
    (2 tsp. dried)
2 **Tbsp. chopped fresh thyme**
    (2 tsp. dried)
1/2 **tsp. paprika**
2 **Tbsp. grated Parmesan cheese**
2 **small loaves (4-oz. each) Italian or**
French bread

1. Combine garlic and oil. Mix well.
2. Combine parsley, thyme, and paprika. Stir in cheese. Mix well.
3. Angle your knife on the diagonal and slice bread into 1/2 inch slices, without cutting all the way through bottom crust.
4. Brush cut sides of slices with garlic mixture. Sprinkle herb mixture between slices. Wrap bread in foil and place on baking sheet.
5. Bake at 350° for 10-15 minutes. Open the foil and place loaves under broiler for a minute or two to brown the tops. Serve immediately.

Hot Herb Bread

Cassius L. Chapman
Mr. C's Cooking Castle
Tucker, GA

Makes 4 servings

1 loaf French bread
$1/2$ cup butter at room temperature
1 large clove garlic, minced
$1/4$ cup chopped fresh parsley
   (5 tsp. dried)
$1^1/2$ tsp. chopped fresh oregano
   ($1/2$ tsp. dried)
2 Tbsp. chopped fresh chives
   (2 tsp. dried)
salt to taste
pepper to taste

1. Cut bread into slices $1^1/2$" thick, but do not cut the whole way through the loaf so the bread slices remain attached at the bottom.
2. Cream together butter and remaining ingredients. Spread mixture on each side of the slices. Wrap bread in foil, leaving top open.
3. Bake at 375° for 10 minutes. Serve hot.

Herb Cheese Log

Toni Anderson
Cedarsbrook Herb Farm
Sequim, WA

Makes 10-12 servings

1 log Montrachet goat cheese
4 cloves garlic, minced
$1/2$ cup olive oil
2 large fresh or dried bay leaves, torn in several pieces
2 Tbsp. chopped fresh thyme
   (2 tsp. dried thyme)

2 Tbsp. butter, melted
1 Tbsp. olive oil
2 cloves garlic, minced
sourdough baguettes, sliced thin
fresh thyme

1. In mixing bowl combine 4 cloves garlic, $1/2$ cup olive oil, bay leaves, and thyme.
2. Place cheese log in bread pan and baste well with oil mixture. Refrigerate for 24 hours, basting occasionally.
3. Mix together butter, 1 Tbsp. olive oil, and 2 cloves garlic.
4. Brush on sliced baquettes. Place on cookie sheet.
5. Bake at 325° for 15-20 minutes, until toasted.
6. To serve, place cheese log on serving dish. Remove bay leaves. Garnish with fresh thyme. Serve with baguettes.

Layered Cheese Torte with Pesto

Jacoba Baker & Reenie Baker Sandsted
Baker's Acres
Groton, NY

Makes 14-16 servings

Pesto Filling:
$2^1/2$ cups lightly packed fresh basil
1 cup freshly grated Parmesan or
   Romano cheese
$1/3$ cup olive oil
$1/4$ cup pine nuts, chopped
salt to taste
pepper to taste

1 lb. cream cheese, softened
1 lb. unsalted butter, softened
fresh basil sprigs

1. In blender or food processor, whirl basil leaves, Parmesan cheese, and olive oil until a paste forms. Stir in pine nuts, salt, and pepper. Set pesto aside.
2. Cream together cream cheese and butter until smoothly blended.
3. Cut 2 18" squares of cheesecloth or unbleached muslin. Moisten with water and ring dry. Use cloth to line a 5-6 cup loaf pan. Drape excess cloth over rim of mold.
4. Spread 1/6th of cheese mixture in prepared mold. Cover with 1/5th of pesto filling. Repeat until mold is filled, finishing with cheese.
5. Fold ends of cloth over top and press down lightly with hands to pack the mixture together..
6. Chill until firm, about 1-1½ hours. (If the torte is allowed to stand longer in the pan, the cloth will act as a wick and cause the filling color to bleed onto the cheese.)
7. Invert onto serving dish and remove cloth. (The torte can be wrapped in plastic and refrigerated up to 5 days.)
8. Before serving, garnish with basil sprigs.
9. Spread on bread or vegetables.

Basil Tapenade

Ary Bruno
Koinonia Farm
Stevenson, MD

Makes 1 pint

1 cup packed fresh basil
1/2 cup fresh Italian parsley
3 cloves garlic, minced
4 Tbsp. lemon juice
4 Tbsp. ground pine nuts or almonds
sea salt to taste
3/4 cup olive oil
crusty French bread

1. In blender or food processor combine basil, parsley, garlic, lemon juice, nuts, and sea salt. Process until finely chopped. Slowly add oil until well blended.
2. Spread on bread and serve.

Variation 1: *Pack into pint jar. Cover with thin layer of olive oil. Will keep in refrigerator for up to 1 month.*

Variation 2: *Add a bit more oil and serve with hot pasta, or as a sauce for shrimp or scallops.*

Fresh Tomato Salsa

Kathy Mathews
Heavenly Scent Herb Farm
Fenton, MI

Makes 2 cups

4 large plum tomatoes
1/4 cup chopped scallions
1/4 cup chopped fresh cilantro
1 Tbsp. chopped fresh oregano
(1 tsp. dried)
2 cloves garlic, minced
1 tsp. minced jalapeno pepper, or to taste
1 Tbsp. olive oil
2 tsp. fresh lime juice
salt to taste
fresh black pepper to taste

1. Cut tomatoes in half lengthwise and remove the seeds. Cut halves into 1/4" pieces. Place in bowl.
2. Add remaining ingredients. Cover loosely and let stand at room temperature for 4 hours before serving.

Ralph's Salsa

Ralph Tissot
Cottage Herbs
Albuquerque, NM

Makes 4 cups

2 15-oz. cans stewed tomatoes, chopped
4 cloves garlic, minced
1 large onion, chopped
2 Tbsp. crushed red chilies
1/2 tsp. Tabasco sauce (optional)
1 Tbsp. chopped fresh cilantro
1/2 tsp. salt
1/4 tsp. pepper
1 Tbsp. chopped fresh lemon thyme
1/2 tsp. Worcestershire sauce

1. Mix together all ingredients.
2. Refrigerate for serveral hours before serving.
3. Serve with warmed corn tortilla chips.

Cucumber Salsa

Jan Becker
Becker's Cottage Garden Herb Farm
Akron, OH

Makes 1 cup

1 cucumber, diced
1 small onion, diced
juice of half a fresh lime
1/4 cup sour cream
2 Tbsp. fresh cilantro, chopped
1 tsp. seasoning blend
   (see recipe on page 37)

1. Mix together all ingredients. Allow to stand for 1 hour before serving.
2. Serve with nacho chips as a dip, or as a salad.

Mango Salsa

Kelly Stelzer
Elderflower Farm
Roseburg, OR

Makes 8 servings

1 cup plum tomatoes, diced
1 cup mangoes, peeled and diced
1/4 cup sweet red or green bell peppers, diced
1 fresh jalapeno pepper, seeded and minced
1/4 cup chopped scallions
1 Tbsp. chopped fresh cilantro
   (1 tsp. dried), or 2 Tbsp. chopped fresh mint leaves, slightly mashed
   (2 tsp. dried)
2/3 cup fresh lime juice
   (about 2 or 3 limes)
1/8 tsp. salt
1/8 tsp. pepper
1/2 tsp. zest of lemon or lime

1. Mix together all ingredients. Stir well. Let stand at room temperature for 30 minutes.
2. Keeps in refrigerator for up to a week.
3. Serve with grilled chicken, fish, black beans and rice, or any jerked dish.

Variation: Mix salsa into 2 8-oz. packages of softened cream cheese and serve with crackers.

Salsa to Can

Lee A. Good
Lititz, PA

Makes several pints

6 cups diced onion
4 cups diced bell pepper
4 jalapeno peppers
8 large cloves garlic
2 Tbsp. ground cumin
3 Tbsp. oil
15 cups peeled, cored, and chopped
   tomatoes
5 cups tomato juice
2 Tbsp. chopped fresh oregano
1 Tbsp. sugar
1 tsp. salt
1/2 cup cornstarch
11/2 cups white vinegar
2 cups chopped fresh cilantro

1. In large, non-aluminum soup kettle,
   saute the onion, peppers, garlic, and
   cumin in the oil until the onions are
   translucent.
2. Add tomatoes, tomato juice, oregano,
   sugar, and salt. Bring to a boil.
3. Lower heat and simmer uncovered for
   1-2 hours. Stir frequently to prevent
   sticking. The vegetables should become
   soft but not mushy.
4. Mix together cornstarch and vinegar.
   Stir into salsa and mix well.
5. Stir in the cilantro. Mix well.

*Note: This recipe is best when all fresh
ingredients are used. Increase or decrease
the jalapeno to your liking. I can this
recipe by pouring the hot salsa into
sterilized jars, covering with lids and
rings, and inverting until sealed
(1-2 hours).*

Tomato-Basil Tart

Maryanne Schwartz and Tina Sams
The Herb Basket
Landisville, PA

*Makes 8 appetizer servings
or 4 main dish servings*

9" pie crust
11/2 cups shredded mozzarella cheese
   (6 oz.)
4 medium-sized tomatoes
1 cup loosely packed basil leaves
   (1/3 cup dried)
4 cloves garlic
1/2 cup mayonnaise
1/4 cup grated Parmesan cheese
1/8 tsp. ground white pepper
fresh basil leaves

1. Bake pie crust. Remove from oven.
   Sprinkle with 1/2 cup mozzarella. Cool
   on wire rack.
2. Dice tomatoes. Drain on paper towels.
   Arrange tomato chunks on melted
   cheese in baked pie shell.
3. Combine basil and garlic in food
   processor. Cover and process until
   chopped. Sprinkle over tomatoes.
4. Mix together remaining mozzarella,
   mayonnaise, Parmesan cheese, and
   pepper. Spoon cheese mixture over
   basil mixture, covering evenly.
5. Bake at 375° for 35 to 40 minutes, or
   until top is golden and bubbly. Garnish
   with fresh basil. Serve warm.

Mary's Mexican Munchies

Mary Peddie
The Herb Market
Washington, KY

Makes 8-10 servings

3 cups freshly shredded head lettuce
8-oz. pkg. cream cheese, softened
5 Tbsp. mayonnaise, milk, buttermilk,
    sour cream, or salsa juice
1 Tbsp. chopped fresh garlic chives
1/2 cup thinly sliced green onions
16-oz. can refried beans
few drops of oil
2 cloves garlic, minced
1 cup fresh tomatoes, finely chopped
1/2 cup chopped avocado (optional)
1/2 cup diced jicama, or cucumber
1 tsp. salt
16-oz. jar taco salsa, whatever strength
    you prefer
1 cup sour cream
1 cup shredded sharp cheddar cheese
3 Tbsp. chopped fresh cilantro
1/2 cup chopped black olives
corn chips or tortilla chips

1. Line a deep platter with a bed of freshly
   shredded head lettuce.
2. Mix together cream cheese, mayonnaise,
   or other liquid, and chives. Spread over
   lettuce.
3. Sprinkle onions over cream cheese
   mixture.
4. Mix together beans, oil, and garlic.
   Spread over onions.
5. Sprinkle tomatoes and avocado over
   beans.
6. Layer jicama or cucumbers over
   tomatoes and avocado. Salt lightly.
7. Pour salsa over jicama or cucumbers.
8. Top with a thin layer of sour cream.
   Cover with plastic wrap and chill for
   several hours before serving.
9. Before serving, garnish with cheese,
   cilantro, and black olives.
10. Serve with corn chips or tortilla chips.

Guacamole

Barbara Sausser
Barb's Country Herbs
Riverside, CA

Makes 3 cups

2 medium-sized, very ripe avocados
1 small onion, grated fine
1 Tbsp. olive oil
dash of paprika
freshly ground pepper to taste
2 medium-sized ripe tomatoes, chopped
2 Tbsp. chili powder
2 tsp. lime juice
2 tsp. lemon juice
1 tsp. salt
1 tsp. ground coriander
1/2 cup shredded Jack cheese

1. Cut avocados in half, lengthwise.
   Remove pit or seed. Peel each half.
   Place in bowl and mash with a fork.
2. Stir in remaining ingredients, except
   cheese. Mix well.
3. Stir in cheese. Serve immediately.
4. Serve as a dip with tortilla chips, or as a
   condiment on enchiladas or tacos.

Jeanette's Spring Rolls

The Backdoor Store, Herbs-n-More
Oak Ridge, TN

Makes 4 servings

2 "nests" of mung bean vermicelli*
1 pkg. spring rolls*
1 cup chopped fresh cilantro
1 cup chopped fresh basil
2 cups shredded cabbage
2 cups grated carrots
1 cucumber, finely diced
1/2 small green bell pepper, finely diced
1/2 small yellow bell pepper, finely diced
1/2 small red bell pepper, finely diced

Dipping Sauce:
1 cup rice vinegar
2 Tbsp. peanut butter
1 Tbsp. sugar
2 Tbsp. sweet chili sauce

1. Bring 4 cups water to a boil. Remove from heat and add vermicelli. Allow to sit in water for 3 minutes. Drain. Rinse in cold water. Drain again and chop.
2. Mix together vermicelli, cilantro, basil, cabbage, carrots, cucumber, and peppers.
3. Open spring rolls. Keep covered with a damp towel while working with them so they don't dry out.
4. Spread 1/4 cup of vegetable mixture on center of one spring roll sheet. Fold up the bottom corner, tucking the stuffing in. Next fold over the left corner and then the right corner, and then roll up towards the top. Spread a little water on the edge of the top fold and press to seal.
5. Cut in half and serve with dipping sauce.
6. To make dipping sauce, whisk together all ingredients.

Ingredients can be found at Asian food markets.

Ham, Cream Cheese, and Chive Squares

Mary Ellen Warchol
Stockbridge Herbs & Stitches
South Deerfield, MA

Makes 8 servings

8-oz. pkg. cream cheese, softened
1/4 cup chopped fresh chives
 (5 tsp. dried)
8 slices imported ham (1/8" thick)

1. Mix together cream cheese and chives.
2. Spread 1-2 Tbsp. cheese mixture on slice of ham. Cover with another. Repeat until you have 4 slices of ham and 3 layers of cheese mixture. Make a second stack with remaining ham and cheese mixture.
3. Wrap in foil and place in freezer.
4. One hour before serving, remove from freezer. Defrost for half an hour. While still partially frozen, cut each into 16 squares. Place a toothpick through the center of each square. Place on serving dish and allow to defrost completely.

Tip for Drying Herbs

Lucy Scanlon
Merrymount Herbs
Norris, TN

If you need dried but colorful herbs quickly, wrap 1-2 oz. of herbs in a paper towel and place them in the microwave. To provide a full load for the machine, you must also place a covered container of water beside the herbs; then microwave on high for 3-4 minutes, until the leaves turn crunchy.

Easy Swiss-Bacon Squares

Judy and Don Jensen
Fairlight Gardens
Auburn, WA

Makes 12-15 servings

8-oz. pkg. refrigerated crescent roll
  dough
8-10 slices bacon, fried, drained,
  crumbled
12-oz. shredded Swiss cheese
3 eggs, beaten
3/4 cup milk
1 Tbsp. minced chives
  (or any herb you wish)
1/2 tsp. salt

1. Press dough into a 9" x 13" pan.
2. Combine remaining ingredients and
   pour over dough.
3. Bake for 30 minutes at 375°. Remove
   from oven. Let stand for 5 minutes,
   then cut into squares to serve.

Cucumber Appetizers

Marty Mertins & Clarence Roush
Woodstock Herbs
New Goshen, IN

Makes 20 servings

8-oz. pkg. cream cheese, softened
7-oz. pkg. Italian Dry Dressing Mix
8-oz. loaf party rye bread
1 large cucumber, sliced
1 1/2 Tbsp. fresh dill 1 1/2 tsp. dried)

1. Mix together cream cheese and dressing
   mix.
2. Spread on slices of rye bread.

3. Top each slice of bread with a slice of
   cucumber. Sprinkle with dill and serve.

Dilled Green Beans

Marty Mertens & Clarence Roush
Woodstock Herbs
New Goshen, IN
Kathy Hertzler
Lancaster, PA

Makes 7 pints

4 lbs. fresh green beans, washed
1 3/4 tsp. crushed red chile pepper
3 1/2 tsp. whole yellow mustard seed
7 heads fresh dill,
  or 3 1/2 tsp. dried dill seed
7 cloves garlic
5 cups vinegar
5 cups water
1/2 cup salt

1. Cut beans into lengths to fit into pint
   jars. Pack beans into clean, hot jars.
2. To each jar add 1/4 tsp. pepper, 1/2 tsp.
   mustard seed, 1 head fresh dill, or 1/3
   tsp. dill seed, and a garlic clove.
3. Combine vinegar, water, and salt. Heat
   to boiling.
4. Pour liquid over beans, leaving 1/4"
   headspace. Seal and process in boiling
   water bath for 10 minutes.
5. Serve cold.

*Note: The beans' flavor improves in time,
so let sealed pints sit for several days
before serving.*

Basil Vinegar Mushrooms

Brandon Brown
Brown's Edgewood Gardens
Orlando, FL

Makes 4-5 servings

1/4 cup basil vinegar
  (see recipe on page 54)
1 quart fresh mushrooms, sliced

1. Pour vinegar over mushrooms. Cover.
2. Refrigerate for at least 8 hours before serving.

Stuffed Mushrooms

Judy and Don Jensen
Fairlight Gardens
Auburn, WA

Makes 8 servings

1/2 cup ricotta cheese
1/3 cup pesto sauce (see pages 57-60)
1/2 cup Parmesan cheese
1/2 box spinach, drained and squeezed dry
24 large mushrooms, stems removed
1/4 cup Parmesan cheese
1/4 cup Italian bread crumbs

1. Mix together ricotta cheese, pesto, 1/2 cup Parmesan cheese, and spinach.
2. Stuff mushrooms with cheese mixture.
3. Sprinkle with 1/4 cup Parmesan cheese and bread crumbs. Place stem-side up in greased baking dish.
4. Bake at 350° for 10 minutes, or until brown.

Herbs-Liscious Mushrooms

Carol Lacko-Beem
Herbs-Liscious
Marshalltown, IA

Makes 6 servings

1 large shallot, or 2 small ones, sliced
3 cloves garlic, cut in quarters
2 Tbsp. butter
16 oz. fresh mushrooms, whole
2 Tbsp. chopped fresh marjoram
  (2 tsp. dried)
1 Tbsp. chopped fresh oregano
  (1 tsp. dried)
1 1/2 tsp. chopped fresh basil
  (1/2 tsp. dried)
1 1/2 tsp. chopped fresh thyme
  (1/2 tsp. dried)
3/4 tsp. chopped fresh summor savory
  (1/4 tsp. dried)
1/4 cup dry red wine

1. Saute shallots and garlic in butter until tender. Add mushrooms. Stir and cook until tender and beginning to darken.
2. Add herbs and wine. Stir well. Continue to cook for 3-4 minutes. Serve immediately.

Thyme-Mushroom Canapes

Carolee Snyder
Carolee's Herb Farm
Hartford City, IN

Makes 40 pieces, or about 10-12 servings

8-oz. pkg. cream cheese, softened
2 egg yolks
1 small onion, grated
4-oz. can mushrooms, drained, chopped
salt to taste
pepper to taste
dash of Worcestershire sauce
10 slices white bread
2 Tbsp. chopped fresh thyme
   (2 tsp. dried)

1. Mix together cream cheese, egg yolks, onion, mushrooms, salt, pepper, and Worcestershire sauce. Stir well. Chill 30 minutes. Sir in half of thyme.
2. Cut crusts from bread. Cut each slice into 4 small squares. Place on cookie sheet. Broil until lightly toasted. Remove from oven and turn each square over.
3. Spread cheese mixture on each untoasted side, being careful to cover the bread completely, so there are no exposed edges to burn in the broiler. Sprinkle with remaining thyme.
4. Broil until bubbly.

Note: These can be made ahead and frozen. Follow directions, except do not broil after spreading cheese mixture on bread. To serve, defrost for 15-20 minutes, then broil and serve.

Marinated Mushrooms with Thyme

Martha Gummersall Paul
Martha's Herbary
Pomfret, CT

Makes 8-10 servings

1 cup olive oil
1/2 cup red wine vinegar
7 sprigs fresh thyme (1 tsp. dried)
2 tsp. Dijon mustard
dash of Tabasco sauce
3 cloves garlic, minced
salt to taste
pepper to taste
1/2 tsp. Worcestershire sauce
3/4 lb. small mushrooms

1. Mix together all ingredients except mushrooms. Heat to boiling point.
2. Add mushrooms and bring to boil again. Remove from heat. Refrigerate until ready to use. Serve with toothpicks. This makes a good addition to antipasto.

Salmon-Stuffed Mushrooms

Kathy Little Star
Indian River Herb Co.
Millsboro, DE

Makes 20 pieces

20 large, fresh, button mushrooms
1 Tbsp. hazelnut oil
1/4 cup chopped wild onions
2 Tbsp. chopped hazelnuts, walnuts, or pecans
1/4 tsp. chopped fresh dill
1/2 tsp. Worcestershire sauce

1/4 tsp. sea salt
4-oz. smoked or steamed salmon
salmon roe (optional)
minced, fresh, flat-leaf parsley (optional)

1. Clean mushrooms and remove stems. Place stem-side up in glass pie pan. Cover with foil.
2. Bake at 350° for 10 minutes, or until mushrooms are almost tender. Turn mushrooms over onto paper towels to drain.
3. Stir together oil, onions, nuts, dill, Worcestershire sauce, and salt. Stir in salmon. Let sit for 20 minutes.
4. Fill mushroom caps with salmon mixture. Return to glass pie plate.
5. Bake at 350° for 3-5 minutes, or until salmon mixture is bubbly.
6. Garnish with salmon roe and minced parsley. Serve immediately.

Quick Salmon Mousse

Mary "Auntie M" Embler
Auntie M's Enchanted Garden
Clayton, NC

Makes 10 appetizer servings
or 4 salad servings

7 3/4-oz. can red salmon
3-oz. pkg. cream cheese, softened
2 Tbsp. lemon juice
6 drops Tabasco sauce
1/4 tsp. dry mustard
1/4 tsp. curry powder
1 tsp. chopped fresh dill (1/3 tsp. dried)

1. Drain salmon. Remove any bones or skin.
2. Combine all ingredients. Mix well and chill for 8 hours.
3. Serve with crackers.

Note: This mousse may be molded into any shape and nestled on a bed of fresh greens for an elegant salad presentation. Garnish with fresh parsley and dill.

Crabmeat Nibblers

Elaine Seibel
Scents and Non-Scents
Hill, NH

Makes 12 servings

12 oz. crabmeat, cleaned
1 cup grated cheddar cheese
1/4 cup mayonnaise
1 tsp. prepared mustard
1 Tbsp. fresh dill (1 tsp. dried)
6 English muffins, split in half
paprika

1. Combine crabmeat, cheese, mayonnaise, mustard, and dill. Mix until well blended.
2. Spread on English muffins. Place on baking sheet and sprinkle with paprika.
3. Broil 5" from heat for 2-5 minutes, or until golden brown and bubbly. Cut into quarters. Serve warm.

Crabmeat Spread

Gerry Janus
Vileniki—An Herb Farm
Montdale, PA

Makes 6 servings

6-oz. can crabmeat, rinsed and drained
8-oz. pkg. cream cheese, softened
1 Tbsp. chopped fresh dill
1 Tbsp. chopped fresh tarragon

1. Beat cream cheese until fluffy. Stir in crab and herbs. Mix well.
2. Stuff into nasturtium blossoms, or spread on toast or on cucumber rounds and garnish with edible flowers.

Karozott

Shatoiya de la Tour
Dry Creek Herb Farm
Auburn, CA

Makes 3 cups

2 8-oz. pkgs. cream cheese, softened
1/4 cup butter, softened
1/2 lb. blue cheese, softened
1/2 tsp. caraway seeds, or
    1 1/2 tsp. chopped, fresh caraway thyme
2 tsp. anchovy paste
1 cup chopped fresh chives
    (1/3 cup dried)
2 tsp. paprika

1. Mix together cream cheese, butter, and blue cheese. Blend well.
2. Stir in caraway seeds or thyme, anchovy paste, chives, and paprika.
3. Serve with crackers or stuffed in celery or olives.

Note: Karozott is a traditional Hungarian cheese dip— rich, but loved!

Cheddar Crisps

Sheryl Lozier
Summers Past Farms
El Cajon, CA

Makes 40 servings

8-oz. cheddar cheese, grated
1/2 cup butter or margarine, softened
1/2 tsp. Tabasco sauce
1/2 tsp. prepared mustard
1 cup flour
2 Tbsp. chopped fresh purple opal basil
1 1/2 cups crispy rice cereal

1. Mix together cheese, butter, Tabasco sauce, and mustard.
2. Blend in flour and basil.
3. Stir in cereal. Blend carefully and shape into small balls.
4. Place on greased baking sheet and flatten with bottom of lightly floured glass.
5. Bake at 350° for 15 minutes. Serve hot.

Note: Crisps may be made several days ahead and stored in an airtight container, or frozen. Reheat for 5 minutes before serving.

Rosemary Cheese Twists

Gerry Janus
Vileniki—An Herb Farm
Montdale, PA

Makes about 5 dozen twists

1 cup unbleached flour
1/4 tsp. cayenne pepper
2 Tbsp. chopped fresh rosemary
  (4 tsp. dried)
1/4 cup cold butter, cut into chunks
1/2 cup shredded sharp cheddar cheese
1 egg yolk
ice water

1. Mix together flour, cayenne pepper, and rosemary. Cut in butter until mixture is crumbly.
2. Stir in cheese and egg yolk. Mix well. Add ice water a teaspoon at a time until a stiff dough is formed.
3. Roll dough to 1/4" thickness between two sheets of wax paper. Cut into strips 3" x 1/2". Twist strips several times and place on greased baking sheet.
4. Bake at 400° for 9 minutes, or until lightly browned. Cool on rack. Store in tightly covered tin.

Pecans Rosemary

Mary Ellen Warchol
Stockbridge Herbs & Stitches
South Deerfield, MA

Makes 8-12 servings

2 Tbsp. melted butter
1/8 tsp cayenne pepper
1 1/2 Tbsp. finely chopped fresh rosemary
  (1 1/2 tsp. dried)
2 cups pecan halves
salt to taste

1. Mix together butter, pepper, and rosemary. Add pecans and toss well.
2. Spread pecans in baking pan.
3. Bake at 350° for 8-10 minutes, stirring once or twice while baking. Cool.
4. Sprinkle with salt if desired.

Rosemary House Walnuts

Bertha Reppert
The Rosemary House
Mechanicsburg, PA

Makes 2 cups

4 Tbsp. butter or margarine, melted
4 Tbsp. finely chopped fresh rosemary
  (4 tsp. dried)
1/2 tsp. salt (optional)
1 tsp. paprika
1 lb. walnut halves

1. Mix together butter and seasonings in shallow baking pan. Stir in nuts. Mix until well coated.
2. Bake at 350° for 8 minutes. Nuts crisp as they cool.

Variation: Substitute cayenne pepper for paprika.

Spicy Peanut Dip

Kathleen Brown
Brown Horse Herb Farm
Lakewood, CO

Makes 1 cup

1/2 cup smooth peanut butter
1/4 cup minced onion
1/4 cup fresh lemon juice
1 Tbsp. soy sauce
2 cloves garlic, minced
1 tsp. ground coriander
1/4 cup chopped fresh parsley
  (5 tsp. dried)

1. Mix together all ingredients in blender for 1 minute.
2. Serve at room temperature. Use as dip for veggies or crackers.

Sage Tempura

Judy Kehs
Cricket Hill Herb Farm
Rowley, MA

Makes 24 pieces

1 egg
4 Tbsp. flour
1-2 Tbsp. milk
2 dozen fresh sage leaves
vegetable oil

1. Mix together egg, flour, and milk. (Amount of milk depends on size of egg. Batter should be the consistency of pancake batter.) Beat well.
2. Coat each sage leaf with batter.
3. Heat oil to 350°. Fry batter-covered leaves until golden, about 40 seconds. Remove leaves and drain well.
4. Serve while still hot.

Variation: Season batter by adding a few pinches of fresh or dried herbs, or 1/8 tsp. cayenne pepper.

Seasoned Oyster Crackers

Rachel Bell
Hummingbird Farms
Nederland, TX

Makes 4-6 servings

14-oz. pkg. oyster crackers
2-oz. pkg. Hidden Valley Ranch Dressing Mix
4 tsp. fresh dill (1 1/3 tsp. dried)
1 tsp. garlic powder
1/2 tsp. salt
1 tsp. lemon pepper
1/2 cup light oil

1. Mix together crackers, dressing mix, dill, garlic powder, salt, and pepper. Toss with oil until all crackers are coated.
2. Store in airtight container that is lined with paper towels to absorb oil.

Basiled Cracker Bites

**Jacoba Baker & Reenie Baker Sandsted
Baker's Acres**
Groton, NY

Makes 6-8 servings

10 oz. oyster crackers
1/3 cup salad oil
1 pkg. Hidden Valley Ranch House
   seasoning
3 Tbsp. chopped fresh basil (1 tsp. dried)
1 large clove garlic

1. Pour crackers into large microwave-safe
   bowl.
2. Blend remaining ingredients in blender
   until smooth. Pour over crackers. Mix
   well.
3. Microwave on High for 2 minutes. Cool
   and serve.

*Note: These will keep for several weeks in
an airtight container.*

Herbed Party Mix

Dawn Ranck
Harrisonburg, VA

Makes 8 cups

2 cups wheat chex cereal
2 cups corn chex cereal
2 cups rice chex cereal
3/4 cup nuts
1 cup little pretzels
8 Tbsp. butter, melted
4 tsp. Worcestershire sauce
1 tsp. seasoned salt
2 tsp. dried thyme
3 tsp. dried dill
4 tsp. dried chives

1. In large bowl, mix together cereal, nuts,
   and pretzels. Set aside.
2. Mix together butter, Worcestershire
   sauce, seasoned salt, thyme, dill, and
   chives. Pour over cereal and mix until
   well coated.
3. Bake at 250° for 1 hour, stirring every
   15 minutes. Cool before serving or
   storing.

Beverages

Iced Mint Tea

Donna Treloar
Harmony
Gaston, IN

Makes 2 quarts

2 cups boiling water
6 fresh mint sprigs
3 tea bags of your choice
2 cups boiling water
1 cup sugar, or less
juice of one lemon
1 qt. cold water
lemon peel, sliced
sprigs of fresh lemon balm

1. Pour 2 cups boiling water over mint and tea bags. Let steep 20 minutes.
2. Pour 2 cups boiling water over sugar and lemon juice. Let steep 20 minutes.
3. Strain mint and tea bags from tea. Add to sugar mixture. Stir in cold water. Chill.
4. Garnish with sliced lemon peel and sprigs of lemon balm.

Basil Mint Tea

Nancy T. Dickman
Cascade Country Gardens
Marblemount, WA

Makes 1 serving

2 fresh basil leaves (1/2 tsp. dried)
2 fresh spearmint or peppermint leaves
  (1/2 tsp. dried)
almost boiling water

1. Put fresh leaves in bottom of mug and mash with a spoon. (Use a tea ball for dried leaves.)
2. Pour water over leaves. Cover with a saucer and steep for 5 minutes. (Covering the mixture captures the essential oils which would otherwise evaporate.) Remove leaves and drink!

Lemon Mint Punch

Jacoba Baker & Reenie Baker Sandsted
Baker's Acres
Groton, NY

Makes 16 servings

¹/₂ gallon water
2 cups fresh mint
1 cup fresh lemon verbena
12-oz. can frozen lime-aid
2 liters lemon-lime soda

1. Heat water, mint, and lemon verbena to almost boiling. Turn off heat and let steep for half an hour.
2. Strain mint and lemon verbena from water.
3. Stir lime-aid and soda into tea.
4. Chill and serve with fresh mint sprigs, fresh lemon slices, or ice cubes with flower blossoms suspended in them.

Herbal Mint Fruit Tea

Jacoba Baker & Reenie Baker Sandsted
Baker's Acres
Groton, NY

Makes 6 quarts

³/₄ cup fresh lemon balm
¹/₂ cup fresh mint leaves
1 quart boiling water
³/₄ cup lemon juice
2 cups orange juice
1 cup apricot nectar
1 qt. strong black or green tea
1 cup sugar dissolved in ½ cup hot water (optional)
3 quarts ginger ale
mint leaves, lemon balm, and orange slices

1. Add lemon balm and mint to boiling water. Let steep for 20 minutes. Strain lemon balm and mint leaves from tea.
2. Stir in lemon juice, orange juice, apricot nectar, black or green tea, and sugar syrup, if desired.
3. Just before serving stir in ginger ale. Garnish with mint, lemon balm, and orange slices.

Mint Zinger Punch

Lynn Halstead
The Kitchen Garden
Canadensis, PA

Makes 20 servings

2 cups mint leaves—combination of orange mint, apple mint, spearmint, peppermint, etc.
4 cups boiling water
4 Tbsp. sugar
2 qts ginger ale
juice of 2 oranges
juice of 2 lemons
sprigs of fresh mint, pansies, and/or Johnny-jump-ups

1. Steep mint in boiling water for 15 minutes. Strain and cool.
2. Stir in sugar, ginger ale, orange and lemon juices. Add ice.
3. Float sprigs of fresh mint, pansies, and/or Johnny-jump-ups in punch.

Gran-Gran's Citrus Mint Refresher

Rita Holder
Holder's Herbs and Gifts
Choctaw, OK

Makes 4 cups concentrate

2 cups sugar
2¹/₂ cups water
4 oranges
6 lemons
large handful of peppermint or
   spearmint leaves

1. Bring sugar and water to boil. Reduce heat to low and simmer 5 minutes. Remove from heat.
2. Grate rinds of oranges and lemons. Then extract juice. Stir grated rinds and juice into sugar mixture.
3. Add mint while syrup is still warm. Steep 30 minutes.
4. Strain and store in refrigerator.
5. To serve, mix concentrate with equal amount of water. Serve chilled.

Orange and Lemon Iced Tea Concentrate

Eileen Ranck
Strasburg, PA

Makes 4 quarts concentrate

2¹/₂ cups water
1¹/₃ cups sugar
1 cup firmly packed fresh tea leaves
12-oz. can frozen lemonade
6-oz. can frozen orange juice

1. Boil water and sugar together for 5 minutes.
2. Pour over tea leaves. Cover tightly and allow to steep for 1 hour. Strain.
3. Stir in lemonade and orange juice concentrates.
4. Freeze until ready to use.
5. To serve, add 3 quarts water to 1 quart concentrate. Stir until well mixed.

Zesty Lemon Tea

Janette Petersen
Rose Herb Nursery
La Center, CO

Makes 8 cups

1 Tbsp. dried lemon balm
1¹/₂ tsp. dried lemon thyme
1 Tbsp. dried lemon verbena
1 Tbsp. dried lemon geranium leaves
1¹/₂ tsp. dried lemon grass
¹/₂ tsp. dried lavender flowers
8 cups boiling water

1. In large bowl, mix together herbs and lavender flowers.
2. Cover with boiling water. Let stand until cool. Strain. Sweeten to taste before serving.

Refreshing Fruit Beverage

Judy C. Jensen
Fairlight Gardens Nursery
Auburn, WA

Combine 2 Tbsp. fruity vinegar, 1 Tbsp. sugar or sweetener of your choice, and 8-oz. sparkling water. Pour over ice and drink on a hot day!

Minty Raspberry Punch

Sue Nussear
Cottage Thyme
Bay City, MI

Makes 10 servings

2 cups sugar
2 cups water
1 cup fresh mint
20-oz. pkg. frozen raspberries, whirred
 briefly in blender
2 liters lemon-lime soda
1/2 bag cracked ice
flowers, limes slices, and/or mint leaves
 for garnish

1. Boil sugar, water, and mint leaves
 together. Cool to room temperature.
2. Pour into large punch bowl; mix in
 raspberries and soda. When well
 blended, stir in ice.
3. Garnish with flowers, fruit, or mint and
 serve.

Herbal Tea from Caprilands Herb Farm

Sheryl Lozier
Summers Past Farms
El Cajon, CA

Makes 7 cups loose tea

1 cup dried mint
1 cup dried rosemary
1 cup dried sage
1 cup dried thyme
1 cup dried marjoram
1 cup dried calendula
1 cup dried chamomile

1. Mix together all ingredients. Keep in jar
 until ready to use.
2. Use one teaspoon of mixture to 1 cup
 boiling water. Allow to steep for 3-5
 minutes. Strain tea before drinking.

Rosemary Lemonade

Madeline Wajda
Willow Pond Farm
Fairfield, PA
Judy C. Jensen
Fairlight Gardens Nursery
Auburn, WA

Makes 1 1/2 quarts

3 Tbsp. fresh rosemary (1 Tbsp. dried)
1 cup water
1/4 cup sugar (optional)
12-oz. can frozen lemonade concentrate
3 cans water
sprigs fresh rosemary
borage flowers (optional)

1. Mix together rosemary, water, and sugar.
 Simmer 5 minutes. Strain.
2. Mix together lemonade concentrate and
 water. Stir into rosemary mixture. Chill.
3. Serve iced. Garnish with rosemary sprigs
 and borage flowers.

Rosemary Pineapple Punch I

Marilyn Jones
Jones Sheep Farm Bed & Breakfast
Peabody, KS

Makes 1 gallon

5 sprigs rosemary, each about 3" long
$1/2$ cup water
12-oz. can frozen lemonade concentrate
46-oz. can pineapple juice
1 liter lemon-lime soda

1. Simmer rosemary sprigs in water.
2. Place thawed lemonade in gallon jar. Add rosemary mixture and pineapple juice.
3. Fill jar with lemon-lime soda. Let stand a few hours, or overnight, to blend.
4. Serve over crushed ice.

Rosemary Pineapple Punch II

Jane Knappen Cole
The Faded Rose
Green Bay, WI

Makes 3$1/2$ quarts

5-6 sprigs fresh rosemary ($1/3$ cup dried)
46-oz. can pineapple juice
2 12-oz. cans frozen lime juice, thawed
1 liter ginger ale
rosemary flowers, borage, and/or violet flowers for garnish

1. In 3-quart saucepan, warm pineapple juice and rosemary almost to a boil. Remove from heat. Cool.
2. Remove rosemary sprigs and pour juice into punch bowl. Add lime juice and ginger ale.

3. When ready to serve, float an ice ring or ice cubes containing rosemary flowers, borage, or violet flowers in punch.

Rosemary Pineapple Punch III

Lynn Redding
Redding's Country Cabin
Ronda, NC

Makes 5-6 quarts

1 cup fresh rosemary ($1/3$ cup dried)
2 cups water
46-oz. can unsweetened pineapple juice
2 liters lemon-lime soda
1 liter ginger ale
rosemary sprigs
borage or nasturtium flowers (optional)

1. Mix together rosemary and water. Bring to boil. Remove from heat and steep for 30 minutes. Strain.
2. Stir in pineapple juice, lemon-lime soda, and ginger ale.
3. Pour liquid into punch bowl. Make a small wreath of rosemary to float in punch. Add borage or nasturtium flowers to wreath for extra color.

Variation: Use sweetened pineapple juice, or add sugar of desired amount to rosemary/water mixture.

Mulled Cinnamon Basil Punch

Madeline Wajda
Willow Pond Farm
Fairfield, PA

Makes 4 cups

4 cups apple juice
1/3 cup fresh cinnamon basil leaves
(5 tsp. dried)
1/2 tsp. whole cloves
1/4 cup sugar
1 cinnamon stick
2 small limes, or one large one, thinly
sliced

1. Heat apple juice, cinnamon basil, cloves, sugar, and cinnamon stick, stirring until mixture comes to a boil. Reduce heat.
2. Add lime slices and simmer for 5 minutes. Strain.
3. Serve hot, or cold with ice cubes added.

Floral Ice Ring

Kelly Wisner
Herbal Heaven
Wernersville, PA

Fill a bundt pan one third full with water. Layer basil leaves, lemon balm, pansies, violets, rose petals, lilac petals, day lily petals, or other edible flowers over water. Freeze. Repeat two more times, ending with a shallow layer of water.

To unmold, turn bundt pan upside down. Run warm water over pan until the ice releases. Place ring in punch bowl.

Apple Cooler

Elaine Seibel
Scents and Non-Scents
Hill, NH

Makes 12 servings

1 cup water
1/3 cup sugar
1 tsp. mulling spices
3 sprigs fresh mint
1 qt. apple juice
1/2 cup lemon juice
1 liter ginger ale
sprigs of fresh mint

1. Bring water, sugar, spices, and mint to boil. Reduce heat and simmer 10 minutes. Strain and chill.
2. Add apple juice and lemon juice to syrup. Chill.
3. When ready to serve, pour into punch bowl and add ginger ale. Garnish with fresh mint.

Refreshing Cranberry Beverage

Judy C. Jensen
Fairlight Gardens Nursery
Auburn, WA

Makes 1 glass

2 Tbsp. cranberry vinegar
(see recipe on page 55)
1 Tbsp. sugar
8 oz. sparkling water
ice

1. Mix together vinegar, sugar, and water.
2. Serve over ice.

Peach Basil Cooler

Louise Hyde
Well-Sweep Herb Farm
Port Murray, NJ

Makes 10 cups

6 cups water, boiling
3 tea bags of your choice
1 cup fresh basil leaves
1/3 cup sugar
4 cups peach nectar

1. Pour boiling water over tea bags and basil. Steep for 5 minutes. Strain.
2. Stir in sugar. Cool.
3. Add peach nectar.
4. Serve over ice. Garnish with basil sprigs.

Veggie Beverage with an Herbal Twist

Jean Argus
Jean's Greens Herbal Tea Works!
Newport, NY

Makes 20-22 servings

3 vegetable bouillon cubes
3 cups boiling water
46-oz. can vegetable juice
juice of 1 lemon
1 cup chopped scallions or chives
2 garlic cloves, minced
1/4 cup chopped fresh herbs—
combination of cilantro, dill, parsley,
tarragon, thyme, basil, and/or
oregano—or 1 1/3 Tbsp. combination of
dried herbs

1. Dissolve bouillon in water.
2. In blender, mix together vegetable juice, lemon juice, scallions, garlic, and herbs. Blend until herbs are finely minced.
3. Pour into gallon jar. Stir in dissolved bouillon. Cover. Shake and refrigerate until well chilled.

Herb Punch Bowl Ice Ring

Carol Ebbighausen-Smith
C&C Herb Farm
Spokane, WA

Makes 1 ring

1 cup mint
1 cup violets
1 cup pansies
water

1. Place 1 1/2" of water in round ice ring mold.
2. Arrange 2/3 cup violets and 2/3 cup pansies upside down in water.
3. Arrange 2/3 cup mint leaves evenly over flowers. Lightly press leaves down.
4. Place ring in freezer for 1 hour. Remove from freezer.
5. Add 1 1/2" very cold water to ring. Add remaining flowers and mint leaves in same order as before. Press down. Place in freezer for 1 hour. Remove ring from freezer.
6. Add 1"-2" very cold water. Return ring to freezer. Freeze at least 24 hours before using.

Note: Add some slightly bruised mint leaves to punch just before serving.

Condiments
Butters, Dressings, Pestos, Vinegars…

Super Seasoning

Lynea Weatherly
The Herb College
San Antonio, TX

Makes approximately 2 cups

1/4 tsp. garlic powder
2 Tbsp. dried parsley
1 1/2 tsp. dried dill
2 Tbsp. poppy seeds
2 Tbsp. celery seeds
2 tsp. paprika
1/2 tsp. black pepper
1/2 cup roasted sesame seeds
1 Tbsp. dried tarragon
1 Tbsp. dried chives
2 cups grated fresh Parmesan cheese

1. Mix together all ingredients. Store in glass jar.
2. Toss desired amount with oil and vinegar and sprinkle on salads. Sprinkle on steamed vegetables or baked potatoes.

Seasoning Blend

Jan Becker
Becker's Cottage Garden Herb Farm
Akron, OH

Makes 1/4 cup

4 tsp. ground cumin
4 tsp. dried oregano
1 tsp. cayenne pepper
2 tsp. garlic powder
2 tsp. onion powder

1. Combine all ingredients and store in airtight jar.
2. Use to season vegetables, soups, salsa, or as a popcorn topper.

Bouquet Garni

Judy and Don Jensen
Fairlight Gardens
Auburn, WA

Makes 1 bag

1 dried bay leaf
1 Tbsp. dried tarragon
1 Tbsp. dried parsley
1 tsp. dried rosemary
1 tsp. dried thyme
5-6 peppercorns

1. Put herbs in middle of coffee filter.
   Gather up into a bag and tie with white
   kitchen string. Multiply this mixture and
   make several bags at a time.
2. Store in an airtight glass jar.
3. Use to flavor your soup or stew.

No-Salt Salt

Kelly Wisner
Herbal Heaven
Wernersville, PA

Makes approximately 1/2 cup

2 Tbsp. dried basil
2 Tbsp. dried savory
2 Tbsp. dried celery seeds
2 Tbsp. dried sage
1 Tbsp. dried thyme
1 Tbsp. dried rosemary
1 Tbsp. dried marjoram

1. Grind herbs using a mortal and pestle.
2. When powdery, place in glass jar. Shake
   to blend.
3. Use instead of salt on vegetables,
   chicken, beef, salads, buttered breads,
   eggs, and fish. Blend into cream cheese
   and use as a spread.

No-Salt Herb Blend

Jeannette Page
The Backdoor Store, Herbs-N-More
Oak Ridge, TN

Makes 1/4-1/3 cup

1/4 tsp. onion powder
1/4 tsp. garlic powder
3/4 tsp. dried oregano
3/4 tsp. dried basil
3/4 tsp. dried marjoram
1/2 tsp. dried tarragon
1/4 tsp. nutritional yeast
3/4 tsp. lemon thyme
1/4 tsp. paprika
1/8 tsp. rubbed sage

1. Mix together all ingredients.
2. Store in jar.
3. Use on just about anything that can
   benefit by a little additional flavor when
   cooking.

Herbal Cheese Spread

Jeannette Page
The Backdoor Store, Herbs-n-More
Oak Ridge, TN

2 Tbsp. No-Salt Herb Blend (above)
8-oz. pkg. cream cheese, softened

1. Mix Herb Blend into cream cheese.
2. Serve on bagels or crackers.

Salt-Free Herb Mix

Suzanne Duecker
Something Different Herb & Gift Shop
Cattaraugus, NY

Makes 5 cups

2 cups dried parsley
2 cups dried chives
1/2 cup garlic powder
1/2 cup onion chips

1. Mix together all ingredients.
2. Store in airtight container.

For Appetizer:
1. Mix 2 tsp. with 16 oz. sour cream for dip. Serve with crackers.
2. Mix 2 tsp. with 8 oz. cream cheese for spread. Serve with baguette or rye bread.

For Salad: Sprinkle over your favorite chef salad or add to your pasta or potato salad.

For Soup: Sprinkle into soup or stew 10 minutes before serving.

For Bread: Roll out frozen bread dough. Spread with melted butter and sprinkle with Herb Mix. Roll and bake according to package directions.

For Vegetables: Sprinkle over hot vegetables just before serving. (Use instead of salt.)

For Eggs: Sprinkle into scrambled eggs or omelets.

Broth Blend

Sue-Ryn Burns
Northern Paradise Gift Shop
Wellesley Island, NY

Makes about 2 cups

1/4 cup celery seed
1/2 cup dried rosemary
1/2 cup dried parsley
1/4 cup dried summor savory
1/4 cup dried thyme
1 1/2 Tbsp. dried lovage
1 1/2 Tbsp. dill seed
1 1/2 Tbsp. crushed bay leaves
2 Tbsp. garlic powder
2 Tbsp. onion powder

1. Mix together all ingredients and store in jar.
2. Use to season soups or sprinkle on chicken or fish fillets.

Herb Salt

Jill Fisher
Moss' Florist and Greenhouses
Mt. Juliet, TN

Makes 1 1/2 cups

1 cup salt
1/2 cup chopped fresh parsley
1/2 cup chopped fresh chives
1/2 cup chopped fresh basil

1. Mix all ingredients in bowl for 5 minutes with your fingers, rubbing salt into herbs.
2. Spread out on tray or jelly roll pan. Let stand until herbs are dried and brittle.
3. Store in airtight container.
4. Use to season steamed vegetables or pasta dishes, hot or cold.

Many-Herbed Butter

Jacoba Baker & Reenie Baker Sandsted
Baker's Acres
Groton, NY

Makes 2 cups

1/4 cup fresh sage leaves
1/4 cup fresh marjoram leaves
1/4 cup fresh thyme leaves
1/4 cup fresh rosemary leaves
1/3 cup packed fresh parsley sprigs
1/3 cup celery leaves
1/3 cup scallions
1/2 lb. butter
freshly ground pepper to taste
salt to taste

1. In food processor, finely chop all herbs.
2. Add butter, pepper, and salt. Process until smooth and well mixed.
3. Place in refrigerator until ready to use, where it will keep well for several weeks. The butter can also be frozen.

Herbal Butter

Lynn Halstead
The Kitchen Garden
Canadensis, PA

Herb butters are one of the most wonderful treats you can make with your herbs. Mix together 1 stick butter, 1 tsp. lemon juice, and 2 Tbsp. fresh chopped herbs of your choice.

Make several batches ahead of time and store in the freezer.

Herbal butters make great gifts in little crocks or tubs. There's no end to what you can do with herb butter. It's a great starting point for novice herbal cooks.

Elaine's Herb Butter

Elaine Seibel
Scents and Non-Scents
Hill, NH

Makes 1 cup

1/2 lb. butter or margarine, softened
1 1/2 tsp. chopped fresh thyme
   (1/2 tsp. dried)
1 Tbsp. chopped fresh oregano
   (1 tsp. dried)
1 Tbsp. chopped fresh basil (1 tsp. dried)
2 Tbsp. chopped fresh parsley
   (2 tsp. dried)
1/4 tsp. garlic powder

Mix together all ingredients until well blended. Then use in any of the following ways:

1. Spread on Italian bread. Bake at 400° for 15 minutes.
2. Mix into cooked pasta. Add 1 Tbsp. Parmesan cheese.
3. Spread on fish fillets before baking.
4. Stir into steamed broccoli.
5. Spread on baked potatoes.
6. Serve on hot corn-on-the-cob.

Freezing Herbal Butter

Carol Frank
Summer Kitchen Herbs
Allenton, WI

Pack herb butter into serving-size containers, label and date, and freeze to have on hand throughout the winter months when the gardens are sleeping.

Betty's Herb Butter

Betty Summers
Herbs 'N Things
Muskogee, OK

Makes 2 1/4 cups

1/2 lb. butter, softened
8-oz. pkg. cream cheese, softened
1 tsp. finely chopped fresh basil
  (1/4 rounded tsp. dried)
1 tsp. finely chopped fresh chives
  (1/4 rounded tsp. dried)
1 tsp. finely chopped fresh dill
  (1/4 rounded tsp. dried)
1 tsp. finely chopped lemon thyme
  (1/4 rounded tsp. dried)
dash of white wine or fresh lemon juice

1. Mix together all ingredients. Refrigerate.
2. Remove from refrigerator 20 minutes
   before serving.

Basil Butter

Donna Weeks
Old Sage Farm
Laytonsville, MD

Makes 1/2 cup

1/4 lb. unsalted butter, softened
4 Tbsp. chopped fresh basil
1 tsp. lemon juice
salt to taste
pepper to taste

1. Beat butter until light and fluffy.
2. Stir in basil, lemon juice, salt, and
   pepper.
3. Refrigerate until ready to use on breads,
   vegetables, baked potatoes, and corn-
   on-the-cob.

Basil Butter

Jacoba Baker & Reenie Baker Sandsted
Baker's Acres
Groton, NY

Makes 1/2 cup

2 tsp. corn oil
1/4 lb. butter, softened
1 hard-boiled egg yolk
1 tsp. cider vinegar
dash of Tabasco sauce
1/4 cup chopped fresh basil
salt to taste

1. Mix together oil, butter, egg yolk,
   vinegar, and Tabasco sauce into a fine
   paste.
2. Blend in basil and salt. Refrigerate until
   ready to use.
3. Serve over steamed vegetables or spread
   on hearty bread.

Chive Butter
for Corn-on-the-Cob

Lynn Halstead
The Kitchen Garden
Canadensis, PA

Makes 1/2 cup

1/2 cup butter, softened
1 tsp. lemon juice
2 Tbsp. chopped fresh chives
1/4 tsp. black pepper

1. Mix together all ingredients. Cover
   tightly and refrigerate for several hours.
2. Serve on hot, fresh corn-on-the-cob.

Parsley Herb Spread

Anna L. Brown
Longfellow's Greenhouses
Manchester, ME

Makes 1 1/4 cups

8 oz. cream cheese, softened
1/4 cup butter or margarine, softened
2 Tbsp. chopped fresh chives
   (2 tsp. dried)
1 Tbsp. chopped fresh parsley
   (1 tsp. dried)
1 garlic clove, minced
1 tsp. chopped herb of your choice

1. Mix together all ingredients until well blended. Chill.
2. Serve with crackers or fresh bread.

Variation: Eliminate butter or margarine; blend all remaining ingredients.

Dill Butter

Robin Giese
Riverview Farm
Fall City, WA

Makes 1/2 cup

1/2 cup butter, softened
2 tsp. chopped fresh dill

1. Mix dill into butter.
2. Refrigerate at least 8 hours before serving.
3. Spread on bread of any kind. Serve over any steamed vegetables.

Light-As-Air Sage Butter

Kelly Wisner
Herbal Heaven
Wernersville, PA

Makes 2 cups

1 cup butter, softened
2/3 cup buttermilk
2/3 cup vegetable oil
1 Tbsp. snipped fresh sage (1 tsp. dried)

1. Mix together all ingredients. Whip until very fluffy.
2. Refrigerate at least 8 hours before serving.
3. Spread on French bread and place under broiler, or stir into mashed potatoes, vegetables, rice, or pasta.

Roasted Garlic and Herb Butter

Sue Floyd
Herb Herbert's Herbs
Tahlequah, OK

Makes 1/2 cup

1 medium-sized garlic bulb
1/4 lb. butter, softened
1 Tbsp. chopped fresh chives
1 Tbsp. chopped fresh tarragon
   (1 tsp. dried)
1 Tbsp. chopped fresh dill (1 tsp. dried)
1 Tbsp. chopped fresh thyme
   (1 tsp. dried)
1 Tbsp. chopped fresh parsley
   (1 tsp. dried)
1 Tbsp. chopped fresh basil (1 tsp. dried)

1. Roast garlic at 350° for 25-30 minutes, until soft. Test doneness by gently squeezing. Cool.
2. Peel each clove. Place in bowl and mash until smooth.
3. Stir in butter and herbs. Beat until smooth and evenly combined.
4. Refrigerate in a container with a lid, or shape into a roll, chill until firm, and slice to serve.
5. Place slices over grilled beef, chicken, or fish, or spread on warm French bread.

Roasted Garlic

Sheryl Lozier
Summers Past Farms
El Cajon, CA

Makes 8 servings

8 whole garlic heads
4 Tbsp. unsalted butter
1 tsp. dried thyme
1 tsp. coarsely ground black pepper
1/2 tsp. coarse kosher salt
3/4 cup chicken stock or canned broth

1. Carefully remove outer papery skin from garlic heads, leaving the whole heads intact.
2. Arrange garlic heads in small baking dish. Dot with butter, thyme, pepper, and salt. Pour stock into the dish. Cover dish with foil.
3. Bake at 350° for 1 hour, basting frequently. Uncover and bake 15 minutes more.
4. Spread on French baguette, bread, or crackers, or toss with pasta.

Sweet Posie Herbary's Basic Mustard

Stephanie L. Distler
Sweet Posie Herbary
Johnsonburg, PA

Makes 2 quarts

4 cups cider, white wine, or red wine vinegar
2 cups mustard flour
2 cups bleached, unbleached, or wheat flour
1 1/2 cups sugar
1/4 cup dried herbs (your choice)

1. Whisk together vinegar, mustard flour, flour, and sugar until lump-free.
2. Stir in herbs. Let mixture stand for at least 8 hours. If mustard is too thin, add more flour.
3. Pour into covered jars. Store in cool place.

Golden Sauce

Suzanne Duecker
Something Different Herb & Gift Shop
Cattaraugus, NY

Makes 1 cup

1/2 cup prepared mustard
1/2 cup honey
1 tsp. salt (optional)
1/2 tsp. dried rosemary

1. Mix ingredients in small jar. Shake well.
2. Marinate lamb chops, pork chops, chicken, or ham steak in sauce for several hours in the refrigerator.
3. Grill or bake meat. Baste with sauce while cooking.

Hot Trio-Herb Mustard

Stephanie L. Distler
Sweet Posie Herbary
Johnsonburg, PA

Makes 2 quarts

4 cups cider vinegar
2 cups oriental mustard flour
2 cups wheat flour
1 cup honey
1/4 cup dried herbs—a mixture of thyme,
  chives, and parsley
2 cloves garlic, minced
2 tsp. mustard seeds, processed in
  blender for a few pulses (don't
  pulverize)

1. Whisk together vinegar, mustard flour,
   wheat flour, and honey until lump-free.
2. Stir in herbs, garlic, and mustard seeds.
   Let mixture stand for at least 8 hours. If
   mustard is too thin, add more flour.
3. Pour into covered jars. Store in cool
   place.

Rosemary and Wine Mustard

Martha Gummersall Paul
Martha's Herbary
Pomfret, CT

Makes 2+ cups

1 cup powdered mustard
1/2 cup warm water
1 cup white wine
4 Tbsp. flour
4 Tbsp. sugar
1 tsp. salt
2 tsp. crushed rosemary
1/2 cup warm water

1. Combine mustard with 1/2 cup warm
   water. Set aside for 10 minutes.
2. Combine wine, flour, sugar, salt, and
   rosemary. Add mustard mixture and
   remaining water. Put in saucepan.
3. Bring to boil. Cook and stir until
   thickened, about 2-3 minutes. Cool and
   whisk until smooth. Cover and let age.

Dijon Tarragon Mustard

Stephanie L. Distler
Sweet Posie Herbary
Johnsonburg, PA

Makes 2 quarts

2 cups white wine vinegar
2 cups infused tarragon vinegar
2 cups mustard flour
2 cups white flour
1 1/2 cups sugar
1/4 cup dried tarragon

1. Whisk together vinegars, mustard flour,
   flour, and sugar until lump-free.
2. Stir in tarragon. Let mixture stand for at
   least 8 hours. If mustard is too thin, add
   more flour.
3. Pour into covered jars. Store in cool
   place.

Tarragon White Wine Mustard

Martha Gummersall Paul
Martha's Herbary
Pomfret, CT

Makes 1-1½ cups

1 cup powdered mustard
1½ cups white wine
½ cup red wine vinegar
6 Tbsp. fresh tarragon
2 tsp. salt
½ tsp. ground allspice
2 Tbsp. sugar
1 Tbsp. oil

1. Combine mustard and wine. Set aside for 10 minutes.
2. Combine vinegar, tarragon, salt, allspice, sugar, oil, and mustard mixture in small saucepan. Bring to boil over medium heat, stirring constantly. Cook until thickened.
3. Remove from heat and whisk until smooth. Pour into covered container and let age.

Creole Herbal Mustard

Barbara Corrales
Honeysuckle Farm Herbs
Lafayette, LA

Makes 1 cup

1 cup Dijon or yellow mustard
⅓ cup fresh herbs, used singly or mixed (5 tsp. dried)—dill, basil, tarragon, and/or oregano
1 tsp. garlic powder or 1 Tbsp. minced raw garlic (blanche one minute in boiling water before adding)
1 tsp. onion powder, 1 Tbsp. minced raw onion, or ¼ cup sliced chives
¼-½ tsp. cayenne pepper

1. Combine all ingredients in blender or food processor. Puree until thoroughly blended into a paste.
2. Stored in refrigerator, this mustard will keep at least one month.

To use as a sandwich spread: Spread onto bread or combine with equal parts of mayonnaise for a milder flavor.

To use as a marinade: Prick meat or fish with the tines of a fork. Liberally coat fish or meat with herbal mustard. (Tarragon and dill work especially well with fish and chicken.) Salt and pepper as desired. Marinate fish 30-45 minutes; chicken or pork for at least 4 hours. All meat or fish can be broiled, baked, grilled, deep- or pan-fried.

Basil Cream

Judy C. Jensen
Fairlight Gardens
Auburn, WA

Makes 2 1/2 cups

1/2 cup fresh basil leaves
1-2 cloves garlic
1/3 cup olive oil
2 1/2 Tbsp. white wine vinegar
2 Tbsp. Dijon mustard
1 cup nonfat plain yogurt
salt to taste
pepper to taste

1. In food processor or blender, chop basil and garlic.
2. Pour in oil, vinegar, and mustard. Process.
3. Stir in yogurt. Season with salt and pepper.
4. Serve over pasta, chicken, or as a vegetable dip.

Dill Sauce I

Jane D. Look
Pineapple Hill Herbs and More
Mapleton, IL

Makes 1+ cup

2 Tbsp. butter or margarine
2 Tbsp. flour
1/2 tsp. salt
1 Tbsp. chopped fresh dill (1 tsp. dried), or 1/2 tsp. dried dill seeds
1 cup milk

1. Melt butter over low heat. Stir in flour.
2. Add salt, dill, and milk. Slowly bring to boil, stirring constantly. Reduce heat and cook until thickened, about 5 minutes.

3. Serve over rice, noodles, macaroni, boiled potatoes, or fish.

Dill Sauce II

Charlotte Chandler
Honey of an Herb Farm
Walton, WV

Makes 1 3/4 cups

1 cup mayonnaise
1/4 cup chopped fresh dill
1 garlic clove, minced
2 Tbsp. lemon juice
1/2 tsp. salt
2 Tbsp. oil
1/2 cup sour cream

1. Mix together all ingredients.
2. Serve with fish or as a dip.

Variation: Eliminate mayonnaise; mix other ingredients as directed above.

Elaine's Dill Sauce

Elaine Seibel
Scents and Non Scents
Hill, NH

Makes 1 cup

1/4 cup chicken broth
1 Tbsp. flour
dash of pepper
3 Tbsp. chopped fresh dill (1 Tbsp. dried)
1 cup sour cream or plain yogurt

1. Combine chicken broth and flour. Stir constantly over low heat until thickened. Stir in pepper and dill. Remove from heat.

2. Stir in sour cream. Mix well.
3. Pour over cooked broccoli, cauliflower, chicken, or fish.

Dill Sauce for Fish

Anna L. Brown
Longfellow's Greenhouses
Manchester, ME

Makes 1/2 cup

1/2 cup mayonnaise
1 Tbsp. fresh lemon juice
1 Tbsp. chopped fresh dill (1 tsp. dried)
black pepper to taste

1. Mix together all ingredients.
2. Serve with grilled, baked, poached, or broiled fresh fish. It is especially good with salmon.

Variation:
Add 1/2 cup mustard to the above ingredients.

Robin Giese
Riverside Farm
Fall City, WA

Lizard Sauce

Barb Perry
Lizard Lick Organic Herbs
Huron, TN

Makes approximately 2 cups

1 cup cayenne peppers or a mixture of
    hot red peppers, with stems removed
1 medium red or yellow onion, chopped
6 cloves garlic
1 cup apple cider vinegar

2 tsp. salt
1/2 cup honey

1. Put peppers, onion, and garlic in blender. Chop finely.
2. Heat vinegar, salt, and honey until well mixed.
3. Pour hot vinegar mixture over peppers, onions, and garlic. Cover and process on high speed until smooth. If too thick to pour, add more vinegar.
4. Store in glass shaker bottles.

Note: This is a hot and lively pepper sauce to use anytime you want a peppery flavor.

Herbal Mustard Vinaigrette

Barbara Corrales
Honeysuckle Farm Herbs
Lafayette, LA

Makes 3/4 cup

Creole Herbal Mustard makes an excellent base for salad dressing, particularly when combined with dill or a Mediterranean herbal blend (oregano, thyme, basil, marjoram, etc.).

1 Tbsp. Creole Herbal Mustard (page 45)
1 tsp. sugar or honey (more if you want a
    sweet dressing)
1 tsp. black pepper or 1/4 tsp. cayenne
1/4 cup vinegar of choice (do not use
    balsamic)
1/3 cup plus 1 Tbsp. olive oil

Whisk or blend all ingredients until combined. This is excellent in pasta salads to which additional minced fresh herbs have been added.

Irish Chicken Sauce

Jill Fisher
Moss' Florist and Greenhouses
Mt. Juliet, TN

Makes 1¹/₄ cups

2 Tbsp. unsalted butter
1 Tbsp. flour
1 cup half-and-half
¹/₄ cup chicken broth
1 Tbsp. Irish whiskey (optional)
³/₄ tsp. chopped fresh rosemary
   (¹/₄ tsp. dried)
1 bay leaf
1 tsp. black pepper
1¹/₂ tsp. chopped fresh basil (¹/₂ tsp. dried)
1¹/₂ tsp. chopped fresh chervil
   (¹/₂ tsp. dried)
1¹/₂ tsp. chopped fresh thyme
   (¹/₂ tsp. dried)

1. Melt butter in saucepan. Add flour and stir for 2 minutes.
2. Gradually whisk in half-and-half, broth, and whiskey. Reduce heat.
3. Add herbs and seasoning. Stir until thickened, about 8 minutes.
4. Serve over baked chicken or on the side for dipping.

Herbal Seasoning Oil

Barbara Corrales
Honeysuckle Farm Herbs
Lafayette, LA

half a blender jar packed with fresh herb leaves (no stems or stalks) of your choice, rinsed and air-dried
olive or canola oil
juice of 1 lemon
2 peeled garlic cloves
1 Tbsp. black pepper

1. Begin pureeing herb leaves, and then add oil in a steady stream until a thick paste forms.
2. Store the paste in the refrigerator or freeze in jars, making sure oil covers the pureed herbs. (Fresh herbs will last many weeks if kept covered with oil and properly refrigerated. Frozen herbs will last for years.)
3. Before using the paste, puree lemon juice, garlic cloves, and black pepper. Add to herb/oil mixture.

To use:
With meat: Score chicken pieces, beef, or pork with a fork; then coat with herb/oil mix. Marinate overnight and then bake, broil, or saute as usual. Add salt shortly before cooking to prevent meat from drying.

Making Herbal Oils

Jeanette Page
The Backdoor Store, Herbs-n-More
Oak Ridge, TN

I use only dried herbs when making herbal oil because many herbs contain a high level of water which can contaminate the oil.

Use 1 Tbsp. of chopped herb to 1 cup of oil. Heat oil gently to almost boiling. Stir in herbs. Turn off heat and allow to cool.

Pour mixture into container and let steep for 1 month. Stir daily. Strain.

Let oil sit for 1 day to allow sediment to settle on bottom. Strain again through a cheese cloth into a bottle. Label oil by placing a dried spring of herb in oil.

With pasta:
1. Add herb/oil, fresh garlic or garlic powder, and grated Romano or Parmesan cheese to cooked pasta.
2. Add herb/oil to inexpensive commercial spaghetti sauces for a homemade taste.

With bread: Spread French bread with herb/ oil, grated cheese, and salt, then broil until toasty.

With tomatoes: Add one tablespoon herb/oil to 1/4 cup balsamic vinegar and pour over freshly sliced, home-grown tomatoes.

With salad: Use herb/oil as salad dressing, or add to commercial brands for enhanced flavor.

Herbed Salad Dressing

Lynea Weatherly
The Herb College
San Antonio, TX

Makes 3/4 + cup

2 Tbsp. dried tarragon
2 Tbsp. dried dill seeds
1 Tbsp. dried rosemary
3 Tbsp. dried chives
3 Tbsp. dried parsley
1 Tbsp. dried mustard
1 Tbsp. vege-sal (optional)
1 Tbsp. dried basil

1. Mix together all ingredients until well blended.
2. To serve, add 1 Tbsp. herb mix to 6 Tbsp. olive oil and 2 Tbsp. apple cider vinegar. Spray on or pour over salad greens or sliced tomatoes.

Sage Oil

Gerry Janus
Vileniki-An Herb Farm
Montdale, PA

Add a handful of fresh sage leaves to a pint of olive oil. Let stand in refrigerator for about 10 days. Remove sage leaves. Place oil in small containers and store in freezer. Use as a dressing for pasta, a dip for bread, or as an ingredient in your favorite recipes.

Herbed Cream Cheese Salad Dressing

Judy and Don Jensen
Fairlight Gardens
Auburn, WA

Makes 2 1/2 cups

8-oz. pkg. cream cheese, softened
1/2 cup sour cream
1/2 cup chopped fresh parsley leaves (3 Tbsp. dried)
1/2 cup chopped fresh dill sprigs without stems (3 Tbsp. dried)
1/2 cup chopped fresh chives (3 Tbsp. dried)
1 Tbsp. white wine vinegar
1/4 cup vegetable oil
2 tsp. Worcestershire sauce
1/2 cup milk
salt to taste
pepper to taste

1. Blend together all ingredients in food processor or mixer. Process until smooth.
2. Add more milk if needed to use as salad dressing.

Basil Salad Dressing

Gerry Bauman
The Farmhouse
Grimes, IA

Makes 1+ cup

1 cup loosely packed fresh basil leaves,
   washed and patted dry
2 cloves garlic
1¹/2 Tbsp. fresh oregano
³/4 cup olive oil
¹/4 cup fresh lemon juice
¹/2 cup fresh Parmesan cheese
1 tsp. grated lemon rind,
   or 1 tsp. lemon basil

Process all ingredients in food processor
   or blender. Store in refrigerator.

Creamy Basil Dressing

Wendy Harrington
Harvest Herb Company
Malone, NY

Makes 2 cups

¹/4 cup firmly packed fresh basil leaves
1 cup mayonnaise
¹/2 cup sour cream
3 green onions, chopped
1 clove garlic, minced
3 Tbsp. herbal vinegar
2 Tbsp. chopped fresh chives
1 tsp. Worcestershire sauce
¹/2 tsp. dry mustard
freshly ground pepper to taste

1. Combine all ingredients in blender or
   food processor. Blend until smooth.
   Refrigerate for up to one week.
2. Spread over fresh tomatoes, pour over
   mixed green salads, or use as a dip.

Harmony Italian Dressing

Donna Treloar
Harmony
Gaston, IN

Makes 1¹/2 cups

1 cup olive oil
¹/2 cup red wine vinegar, or your choice
1¹/2 tsp. chopped fresh basil
   (¹/2 tsp. dried)
1¹/2 tsp. chopped fresh oregano
   (¹/2 tsp. dried)
1 clove garlic, minced,
   or ¹/2 tsp. garlic powder
freshly ground pepper to taste

1. Mix together all ingredients in jar with
   lid. Shake well.
2. Let stand for several days before using
   to allow flavors to blend.
3. Store in refrigerator.

Dill Salad Dressing

Jane D. Look
Pineapple Hill Herbs and More
Mapleton, IL

Makes 2 cups

4 eggs
¹/4 cup vegetable oil
1 cup sour cream
2 Tbsp. vinegar
1 Tbsp. chopped fresh dill (1 tsp. dried),
   or to taste
1 tsp. salt
1 tsp. garlic powder
1 tsp. onion powder
1 tsp. ground pepper

1. Mix together all ingredients in blender.
2. Refrigerate until ready to use.

Creamy Dill Dressing

Mary Ellen Warchol
Stockbridge Herbs & Stitches
South Deerfield, MA

Makes 8 servings

1 cup buttermilk
3 Tbsp. mayonnaise
4 Tbsp. chopped fresh dill (4 tsp. dried)
3 Tbsp. chopped fresh chives
  (3 tsp. dried)
1 Tbsp. chopped fresh parsley leaves
  (1 tsp. dried)
1 Tbsp. lemon juice
1 tsp. prepared Dijon mustard
salt to taste
pepper to taste

1. Combine all ingredients in blender.
   Blend until smooth.
2. Let stand for at least 1 hour before
   serving. Store refrigerated for 4-5 days.
3. Serve on salad greens or over sliced,
   seeded cucumbers.

Dilled Cucumber Salad Dressing

Charlotte Chandler
Honey of an Herb Farm
Walton, WV

Makes 2 cups

1 large cucumber, seeded and chopped
2 Tbsp. chopped fresh dill
1 Tbsp. extra-virgin olive oil
2 tsp. lemon juice
1 tsp. white wine Worcestershire sauce
2/3 cup plain low-fat yogurt
1/4 tsp. salt
1/4 tsp. ground white pepper

1. In food processor, blend cucumber, dill,
   olive oil, lemon juice, and
   Worcestershire until cucumber is finely
   chopped.
2. Add yogurt, salt, and pepper. Process
   until smooth.
3. Refrigerate until ready to serve.
4. Use as a dip for steamed or raw
   vegetables or pour over salad greens.

Quick Vinaigrette

Carol Ebbighausen-Smith
C&C Herb Farm
Spokane, WA

Makes 1 cup

1 Tbsp. chopped fresh basil (1 tsp. dried)
1 Tbsp. chopped fresh chives
  (1 tsp. dried)
1 Tbsp. chopped fresh parsley
  (1 tsp. dried)
1 Tbsp. chopped fresh tarragon
  (1 tsp. dried)
1 Tbsp. chopped fresh lemon thyme
  (1 tsp. dried)
1/4 cup cider vinegar
1/4 cup water
1/2 cup olive oil

1. Mix together basil, chives, parsley,
   tarragon, and lemon thyme.
2. Mix together vinegar and water. Heat
   just to boiling point.
3. Pour over herbs. Whisk together. Let
   stand for 5 minutes.
4. Whisk in olive oil. Allow to cool.
5. Serve over salads, roasted vegetables,
   fresh fruit, or baked fish.

Rosemary Dressing

Jacoba Baker & Reenie Baker Sandsted
Baker's Acres
Groton, NY

Makes 3 cups

1 cup wine vinegar
1 large clove garlic, crushed
black pepper to taste
2 Tbsp. lemon juice
1$^{1}/_{2}$ cups olive or vegetable oil
$^{1}/_{2}$ tsp. salt
3 tsp. fresh rosemary

1. Mix together all ingredients.
2. Refrigerate until ready to use.
3. Let stand for one or two weeks so that flavors can blend.

Tarragon-Mustard Vinaigrette

Elaine Seibel
Scents and Non-Scents
Hill, NH

Makes 2 cups

1 cup olive oil
1 cup tarragon vinegar
6 Tbsp. chopped fresh tarragon
   (2 Tbsp. dried)
1 Tbsp. Dijon-style mustard

1. Combine all ingredients in jar with tightly fitting lid. Shake well.
2. Use as salad dressing or as basting sauce.

Lemon Thyme Vinaigrette

Judy Kehs
Cricket Hill Herb Farm
Rowley, MA

Makes approximately $^{1}/_{2}$ cup

6 Tbsp. extra virgin olive oil
1$^{1}/_{2}$ Tbsp. white vinegar
$^{1}/_{8}$ tsp. dry mustard
$^{1}/_{4}$ tsp. sugar
1 tsp. salt
$^{1}/_{8}$ tsp. freshly ground pepper
3 tsp. chopped fresh lemon thyme
   (1 tsp. dried)

1. Process all ingredients in blender at low speed for 1 minute.
2. Serve over favorite salad, or brush over chicken while grilling or broiling.

Note: In this recipe lemon thyme can be replaced with thyme, oregano, marjoram, basil, lemon basil, dill, or lemon mint.

Italian Vinegar

Karen Sanders
Your Flower Basket
Robinson, IL

Makes 1 quart

1 quart white wine vinegar
mixture of fresh basil, oregano, Italian parsley, thyme

1. Heat vinegar just to boiling point.
2. Place herbs into sterilized clean glass container with secure lid. Pour vinegar over herbs.
3. Seal and store for up to 7 days before using.

Basic Herb Vinegar

Brenda Moss
Moss' Florist & Greenhouses
Mt. Juliet, TN

Makes 1 quart

2 sprigs fresh basil
2 sprigs fresh tarragon
2 sprigs fresh oregano
2 cloves garlic
1 quart red or white wine vinegar

1. Bruise herbs. Place in sterilized glass bottle or jar.
2. Heat vinegar almost to boiling. Pour over herbs. Seal.
3. Set in a warm, sunny spot for 2 weeks.
4. Strain vinegar into fresh bottle and discard the herbs. Add fresh sprig of an herb for identification.
5. Use in salad dressings, sauces, and marinades.

Applemint Vinegar

Carol Vaughn
Healthy Horse Herb Farm
Onley, VA

applemint leaves
   (or other varieties of mint)
distilled white vinegar

1. Loosely fill a quart glass jar with rinsed and dried applemint leaves.
2. Pour vinegar over mint until jar is full.
3. Put on lid and let steep in dark, cool place for 2 weeks.
4. Strain, cap, and store in cool place. Keeps for a year or more.

Italian Balsamic Vinegar

Deborah S. Thorp
Thorp's Igloo Grown Herbs
Atlantic, PA

Makes 1 bottle

1 bottle balsamic vinegar
3 Tbsp. chopped fresh parsley
   (3 tsp. dried)
2 Tbsp. chopped fresh fennel leaves
   (2 tsp. dried)
3 Tbsp. chopped fresh basil (3 tsp. dried)
3 Tbsp. chopped fresh Greek oregano
   (3 tsp. dried)
1 Tbsp. chopped fresh summer savory
   (1 tsp. dried)
1 sage leaf, chopped
1 whole hot pepper (optional)
1 coffee filter

1. Heat vinegar to between 100° and 120°.
2. If using fresh herbs, place all herbs in wide mouth jar. Add whole pepper (do not chop so you can remove it more easily). Pour heated vinegar over herbs. Cover. Allow to steep for 1-2 weeks. Taste periodically to determine strength of mixture. Remove pepper whenever vinegar is hot enough for your taste buds.
3. Strain vinegar when the flavors are blended to your liking.
4. If using dried herbs, crush them and tie them into a coffee filter. Place in jar. Proceed as with fresh herbs.
5. Use as a salad dressing, meat marinade, or a soup spicer-upper. Or slice tomatoes, crumble feta cheese over them, and top with vinegar.

Basil Vinegar

Brandon Brown
Brown's Edgewood Gardens
Orlando, FL

Makes 1 quart

handful of clean, fresh, coarsely torn
   basil
1 quart white wine vinegar
sprig of basil

1. Place handful of basil in quart jar.
2. Fill jar with vinegar.
3. Set in a warm, sunny spot for 2 to 3
   weeks.
4. Strain vinegar into fresh bottle and
   discard the herbs. Add a fresh sprig of
   basil to bottle for identification.

Sweet Basil with Blueberry Vinegar

Judy and Don Jensen
Fairlight Gardens
Auburn, WA

Makes 1¹/2 -2 quarts

1 lb. fresh or frozen blueberries,
   pulverized or ground in blender with
   1/3 cup of the vinegar
1 handful of sweet purple or green basil,
   chopped
1 quart white wine vinegar

1. Place blueberries and basil in sterilized
   glass jars.
2. Cover with vinegar.
3. Store in cool dark place for 4 weeks.
4. Strain through layers of cheesecloth.
   Bottle and cap with corks, or cover with
   screw-on lids.

Opal Basil Vinegar

Diane T. Morris
The Morris Farm
Seaboard, NC

Makes 1 gallon

6-8 cups coarsely torn, fresh opal basil
   (this dark burgundy colored herb
   makes a rich garnet red vinegar)
1 gallon distilled white vinegar or white
   wine vinegar
sprigs of fresh opal basil

1. Place basil in plastic gallon jug.
2. In large enamel pan, heat vinegar just to
   boiling point. Pour into jug, making
   sure basil is covered. Cover jug tightly.
   Store in cool dark place. Shake every
   day for about a week.
3. When vinegar has steeped, place a sprig
   of fresh basil into freshly sterilized
   decorative bottles. Using a funnel with a
   coffee filter inside, pour the herb
   vinegar into the bottles.
4. Seal and tie with a raffia bow.

*Note: Once the level of herb vinegar has
dropped so that the herb sprig is not
under liquid, discard the sprig so mold
will not form.*

*Variations: Almost any herb or herb
combination makes a good vinegar. Try
combining thyme and basil, sage and
oregano, or cilantro and lemon thyme.
   Use your herb vinegars to make salad
dressings, marinate meats, and add
flavor to barbecued or roasted cooked
meats, cooked greens, and vegetables.*

Basil Marinade

Elaine Seibel
Scents and Non-Scents
Hill, NH

Makes 1/3-1/2 cup

3 Tbsp. olive oil
2 Tbsp. basil vinegar
2 Tbsp. finely chopped fresh basil
1/8 tsp. black pepper

1. Combine all ingredients in jar with tightly fitting lid. Shake until well mixed. Allow to stand for several days until flavors are well blended.
2. Use as a marinade for chicken or as a basting sauce while barbecuing meats.

Cranberry Vinegar

Judy C. Jensen
Fairlight Gardens Nursery
Auburn, WA

Makes 1 quart

1 quart white wine vinegar
2 cups fresh or frozen cranberries
1/2 cup light clover or herb-flavored honey
1/4 cup whole cloves
4 small cinnamon sticks
4 sprigs fresh lemon thyme

1. Combine vinegar and 1 cup cranberries in saucepan. Bring to boil. Reduce heat and simmer for 2 minutes. Remove from stove.
2. Stir in honey. Mix well. Pour through strainer into a large measuring cup.
3. Divide remaining cranberries, cloves, cinnamon, and thyme between 4 8-oz. decorative bottles.

4. Pour warm vinegar mixture into bottles, to within 1" of top. Allow to stand for 7 days.
5. Use as salad dressing. Pour vinegar into a spray bottle and spray over greens, so that it clings and more fully covers the salad greens.

Use to make Refreshing Cranberry Beverage (see page 35).

Rosemary Vinegar

Irene L. Weidenbacher
Herbs in the Woods
Hollidaysburg, PA

Makes 1 pint

2 sprigs fresh rosemary
1 pint white wine vinegar

1. Place rosemary in vinegar. Leave in cool dark place for 2 weeks.
2. Use as marinade for chicken.

Dill Vinegar

Dorothy Weaver & Pat Dyer
Village Herb Shop
Blue Ball, PA

Makes 1 bottle

bottle of good white wine vinegar
fresh dill leaves, stems, and flowers

1. Fill canning jar with dill. Pour vinegar over dill and cap. Let stand for 24 hours, shaking several times.
2. Strain vinegar and pour back into original bottle.

Hot Pepper Vinegar

Ellen Barker
Ellen's Delights
Maryville, TN

Makes 5-6 cups

2 haberno peppers
2 chili peppers
2 red bell peppers
2 jalapeno peppers
2 green onions
2 garlic cloves
10-15 stems fresh cilantro
1 quart red wine vinegar

1. Distribute peppers, onions, garlic cloves, and cilantro among small glass bottles and pack down.
2. Cover with vinegar. Seal and let stand for at least 1 week before using.
3. Use in chili or soups, over greens or steamed vegetables, as a salad dressing or salsa.

Lemon Zest Vinegar

Donna Weeks
Old Sage Farm
Laytonsville, MD

Makes 2 cups

2 cups rice wine vinegar or white wine
   vinegar
8 sprigs fresh lemon thyme
3 sprigs fresh parsley
3" piece of fresh gingerroot, cut up, or
   5 slices pickled gingerroot
half a lemon, cut into thin slices

1. Pour vinegar into sterilized wide mouth jar.
2. Add lemon thyme, parsley, ginger, and

lemon to vinegar. Cover top with piece of plastic wrap, and put on lid.
3. Place jar in strong light (sun or artificial) and let it age for 4 weeks.
4. Using a coffee filter, pour the vinegar through the filter into a new bottle. (You may need to do this several times until the vinegar clears.) Add fresh sprigs of thyme, a slice of lemon, and a slice of pickled ginger.
5. Serve with salads, steamed vegetables, chicken, and fish.

Mint Vinegar

Judith M. Graves
Lambs and Thyme at Randallone
Richmond, NH

Makes 1 quart

mint leaves
1 quart white wine vinegar,
   or apple cider vinegar
fresh mint sprig

1. Fill quart jar with mint leaves. Fill with vinegar.
2. Let stand in unlit area for 2-3 weeks.
3. Strain vinegar into fresh bottle. Discard mint leaves. Add a fresh sprig of mint to bottle for identification.

Herbal Vinegar Vegetables

Carol Vaughn
Healthy Horse Herb Farm
Onley, VA

When cooking steamed or boiled vegetables, splash 1-2 Tbsp. of an herbal vinegar into the cooked vegetables just before serving.

Basic Basil Pesto

Charles R. Fogleman
Ashcombe Farm and Greenhouses
Mechanicsburg, PA
Judy C. Jensen
Fairlight Gardens
Auburn, WA

Makes 1 cup

2 cups fresh basil leaves
2 cloves garlic
1/2 cup freshly grated Parmesan cheese
1/4 cup pine nuts or walnuts
1/2 cup olive oil
salt and pepper to taste

1. Place basil in food processor or blender and chop.
2. Add garlic, cheese, and nuts. Process to mix.
3. Add olive oil, salt, and pepper and process to desired consistency.
4. Allow to stand for 5-10 minutes before serving on your favorite crackers, pasta, or raw vegetables.

Note: Can be kept in refrigerator for up to 1 week. Freezes best when you leave the garlic out and add it just before serving.

Basil Mint Pesto

Charles R. Fogleman
Ashcombe Farm and Greenhouses
Mechanicsburg, PA

Makes 1 cup

1 cup fresh mint
1 cup fresh basil
2 cloves garlic
1/2 cup freshly grated Parmesan cheese
1/4 cup pine nuts

1/2 cup olive oil
salt and pepper to taste

1. Place mint and basil in food processor or blender and chop.
2. Add garlic, cheese, and nuts. Process to mix.
3. Add olive oil, salt, and pepper and process to desired consistency.
4. Allow to stand for 5-10 minutes before serving on your favorite crackers, pasta, or raw vegetables.

Basil Mint Pesto

Flo Stanley
Mililani Herbs
Mililani, HI

Makes approximately 1 cup

3-4 cloves garlic
3 cups fresh basil leaves
1 cup fresh mint leaves
2 Tbsp. pine nuts, almonds, or walnuts
2 Tbsp. grated Parmesan cheese
2 Tbsp. olive oil
1 Tbsp. fresh lemon juice, or balsamic vinegar
2-3 Tbsp. plain yogurt
2-3 Tbsp. buttermilk, or more
salt to taste
pepper to taste

1. Chop garlic in food processor.
2. Add half the basil and process until coarsely chopped.
3. Add mint, nuts, cheese, remaining basil, olive oil, and lemon juice. Process.
4. Add yogurt and buttermilk and process until of desired consistency.
5. Add salt and pepper.
6. Will keep in refrigerator for 1-2 weeks. Freezes well.

Basil Parsley Pesto

Harriette Johnson &
Dianna Johnson-Fiergola
Mustard Seed Herbs & Everlastings
Spring Valley, WI
Linda Hangren
LinHaven Gardens
Omaha, NE

Makes 2-3 cups

3 cups loosely packed fresh basil
1/2 cup loosely packed fresh parsley
3-5 large garlic cloves
1/2-3/4 cup pine nuts
1 cup olive oil
11/2 cups freshly grated Parmesan cheese

1. Add basil and parsley to food processor or blender. Chop until fine.
2. Add garlic and pine nuts. Chop well.
3. Slowly add olive oil. Process until smooth.
4. Stir in cheese.
5. Use immediately or freeze in small jars. Serve on pasta or rice. Spread on breads. Fold into omelets. Spread on fresh tomatoes.

Cilantro Pesto

Deborah S. Thorp
Thorp's Igloo Grown Herbs
Atlantic, PA

Makes 1-11/2 cups

2 cups fresh cilantro leaves
1/4 cup parsley leaves
1/3-1/2 cup olive oil
1 Tbsp. lime or lemon juice
1 clove garlic
1/4 cup walnuts

1-2 jalapeno peppers, diced, seeded, and finely chopped
1/2 red pepper, diced, seeded, and finely chopped

1. Add cilantro and parsley leaves to food processor or blender. Chop until fine.
2. Add oil until mixture becomes consistency of whipped cream.
3. Add lemon juice and garlic. Puree for 30 seconds.
4. Add walnuts and puree for 30 seconds.
5. Remove from blender. Add peppers.
6. Use immediately, or place in jars or bags and freeze. Do not store in refrigerator.
7. Use as soup garnish. Spread on taco shells. Use as base for Mexican pizzas. Mix into black beans.

South of the Border Pesto

Carol Frank
Summer Kitchen Herbs
Allenton, WI

Makes 11/2 cups

3 cups fresh cilantro leaves
1/2 cup fresh parsley
1/2 cup olive oil
1 jalapeno pepper, seeded
3 cloves peeled garlic
1/2 cup salted peanuts, chopped coarsely
1 cup Parmesan cheese

1. Mix together all ingredients and process until well blended and almost smooth.
2. Serve immediately, or pack into small containers and freeze until needed.
3. Serve with corn bread, tortilla chips, or as a topping on refried beans.

Oregano Pesto

Charles R. Fogleman
Ashcombe Farm and Greenhouses
Mechanicsburg, PA

Makes 1 cup

1/2 **cup fresh oregano leaves**
11/2 **cups fresh parsley leaves**
2 **cloves garlic**
1/2 **cup freshly grated Parmesan cheese**
1/2 **cup walnuts**
1/2 **cup olive oil**
salt and pepper to taste

1. Place oregano and parsley leaves in food processor or blender and chop.
2. Add garlic, cheese, and nuts. Process to mix.
3. Add olive oil, salt, and pepper and process to desired consistency.
4. Allow to stand for 5-10 minutes before serving on your favorite crackers, pasta, or raw vegetables.

Sage Pesto

Charles R. Fogleman
Ashcombe Farm and Greenhouses
Mechanicsburg, PA

Makes 1 cup

1/2 **cup fresh sage leaves**
11/2 **cups fresh parsley leaves**
2 **cloves garlic**
1/2 **cup freshly grated Parmesan cheese**
1/2 **cup pine nuts**
1/2 **cup olive oil**
salt and pepper to taste

1. Place sage and parsley leaves in food processor or blender and chop.

2. Add garlic, cheese, and nuts. Process to mix.
3. Add olive oil, salt, and pepper and process to desired consistency.
4. Allow to stand for 5-10 minutes before serving on your favorite crackers, pasta, or raw vegetables. Or add the pesto to mashed potatoes. Use it in an omelet along with a mild cheese. Spread it on pizza dough in place of tomato sauce. Mix it with softened cream cheese: 1 part pesto to 3 parts cheese.

Rosemary Pesto

Charles R. Fogleman
Ashcombe Farm and Greenhouses
Mechanicsburg, PA

Makes 1 cup

1/2 **cup fresh rosemary leaves**
11/2 **cups fresh parsley leaves**
2 **cloves garlic**
1/2 **cup freshly grated Parmesan cheese**
1/2 **cup walnuts**
1/2 **cup olive oil**
salt and pepper to taste

1. Place rosemary and parsley leaves in food processor or blender and chop.
2. Add garlic, cheese, and nuts. Process to mix.
3. Add olive oil, salt, and pepper and process to desired consistency.
4. Allow to stand for 5-10 minutes before serving on your favorite crackers, pasta, or raw vegetables.

Thyme Pesto

Charles R. Fogleman
Ashcombe Farm and Greenhouses
Mechanicsburg, PA

Makes 1 cup

1/2 cup fresh thyme leaves
1 1/2 cups fresh parsley leaves
2 cloves garlic
1/2 cup freshly grated Parmesan cheese
1/2 cup walnuts
1/2 cup olive oil
salt and pepper to taste

1. Place thyme and parsley leaves in food processor or blender and chop.
2. Add garlic, cheese, and nuts. Process to mix.
3. Add olive oil, salt, and pepper and process to desired consistency.
4. Allow to stand for 5-10 minutes before serving on your favorite crackers, pasta, or raw vegetables.

Nut-Free Pesto

Myra Bonhage-Hale
La Paix Farm Shop
Alum Bridge, WV

12 cups fresh basil leaves
3 cups fresh parsley leaves
1/2 cup virgin olive oil
1 cup freshly grated Parmesan cheese
6 garlic cloves, peeled
salt to taste
pepper to taste
1 cup sunflower seeds

1. Place in blender or food processor 4 cups basil, 1 cup parsley, and 3 Tbsp.

oil. Process. Slowly add remaining basil, parsley, and oil. Process to make a moist, almost smooth, mixture.
2. Add cheese, garlic cloves, salt, and pepper. Process.
3. Stir in sunflower seeds.
4. Mix into hot, cooked pasta, along with cottage or ricotta cheeses, or with plain yogurt. Serve with vegetables as a dip. Add to tuna or egg salad. Or freeze in freezer bags for a winter delight!

All-Purpose Freezer Blend Pesto

Jan Becker
Becker's Cottage Herb Farm
Akron, OH

Makes 3/4 cup,
or 3 medium-sized ice cubes

1/2 cup fresh basil leaves
1 Tbsp. fresh marjoram leaves
1 Tbsp. fresh thyme leaves
1 tsp. fresh rosemary leaves
1 Tbsp. fresh savory leaves
1 Tbsp. fresh oregano leaves
1/4 cup olive oil

1. Combine all ingredients in blender or food processor. Chop well.
2. Pour into ice cube trays and freeze.
3. Use by thawing 3 cubes in microwave. Combine with 1/2 cup freshly grated Parmesan cheese.
4. Add to basic muffin mix for great herb muffins. Or combine 2 thawed cubes with 1/4 cup melted butter and 1/4 cup olive oil to spread on crusty bread, or pour over popcorn. Or add 2-3 frozen cubes to season spaghetti sauce.

Tomato Basil Jam

Ernestine Schrepfer
Herbal Scent-sations
Trenton, MO

Makes 5 8-oz. jars

3¹/2 cups fresh tomatoes, peeled, cored,
   seeded, chopped
3 Tbsp. chopped fresh basil
   (1 Tbsp. dried)
¹/4 cup fresh lemon juice
11³/4-oz. box powdered fruit pectin
3 cups sugar

1. Measure 3¹/2 cups tomatoes in heavy
   pan. Simmer for 10 minutes.
2. Stir in basil and lemon juice.
3. Combine pectin with ¹/4 cup sugar. Add
   to tomato mixture. Bring to rolling boil,
   stirring occasionally.
4. Add remaining sugar. Return to rolling
   boil. Boil for 1 minute, stirring
   constantly.
5. Remove from heat. Skim. Pour into hot
   sterilized jars, leaving ¹/4" head space.
   Screw on lid.
6. Process in boiling water for 15 minutes.

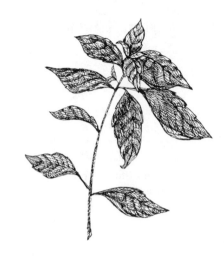

Basil Tomato Jelly

Madeline Wajda
Willow Pond Farm
Fairfield, PA

Makes about 3 cups

1 cup packed fresh basil leaves
1³/4 cups tomato juice
¹/2 cup lime juice
4 cups sugar
¹/2 tsp. butter
3-oz. pkg. liquid pectin

1. Simmer basil and tomato juice for 15
   minutes. Strain through a sieve into a
   large pot.
2. Stir in lime juice, sugar, and butter.
   Bring to full boil.
3. Add pectin. Boil for 1 minute.
4. Remove from heat and pour into
   sterilized jars. Top with lids. Invert jars
   for 5 minutes to facilitate sealing.

Tip for Using Herbs

Marian E. Sebastiano
Salt Box Gallery Herbs
Hubbard, OH

To learn the individual flavor of an
herb, finely chop a few teaspoons of it
and mix it with a bland base such as
sour cream, cream cheese, butter, or
plain yogurt. Let the mixture set in the
refrigerator for several hours. Use as a
dip or spread for raw vegetables, bread,
or crackers.

Lemon Thyme Herbal Jelly

Danielle Vachow
Busha's Brae Herb Farm
Suttons Bay, MI

Makes 2+ cups

3 cups boiling distilled water
3/4 cup fresh lemon thyme
1/4 cup lemon juice
4 cups sugar
3-oz. pkg. liquid pectin

1. Pour water over lemon thyme. Cover. Let stand for 20 minutes. Strain through clean muslin cloth.
2. Measure 2 cups lemon thyme juice into 6-quart pot. Stir in lemon juice and sugar. Mix well. Bring to full boil, stirring constantly.
3. Stir in pectin. Bring to rolling boil that cannot be stirred down. Boil 1 minute, stirring constantly. Remove from heat.
4. Skim foam. Pour into sterilized jars. Store in refrigerator for up to 1 month.

Variations: This recipe can be used as a base recipe for any herb jellies. Instead of lemon thyme use lavender blossoms, scented geranium leaves, rosemary, or other herbs.

Use fruit juices such as apple, raspberry, cranberry, or orange juice instead of distilled water.

Substitute cider vinegar in place of lemon juice.

Seasoned Croutons

Judy and Don Jensen
Fairlight Gardens
Auburn, WA

Makes 2 cups

1/3 cup butter or margarine
1 1/2 tsp. chopped fresh rosemary
  (1/2 tsp. dried)
1/2 tsp. garlic powder
3/4 tsp chopped fresh thyme
  (1/4 tsp. dried)
1/4 tsp. mace
2 cups spoon-size shredded wheat, halved

1. Melt butter in 9" x 13" pan.
2. Stir in herbs and shredded wheat. Stir well to mix.
3. Bake at 400 deg for 12-15 minutes, until golden brown, stirring twice.
4. Serve in soups or salads.
5. Store in airtight container. Refrigerate if not used within a week.

Breads, Rolls, and Muffins

Herb Bread

Diane T. Morris
The Morris Farm
Seaboard, NC

Makes 2 large or 3 small loaves

2 cups milk
1¹/₂ cups water
5 Tbsp. sugar
2 pkgs. dried yeast
4 Tbsp. butter or margarine, softened
**1-2 Tbsp. mixed dried herbs—oregano,
   thyme, and basil**
7-8 cups all-purpose flour

1. Combine milk and water. Heat until very warm but not hot.
2. Stir in sugar and yeast. Let stand for 5 minutes.
3. Stir in margarine, herbs, and 4 cups flour. Mix well.
4. Work in 3-4 cups flour until dough becomes thick and is no longer sticky.
5. Place on floured board and knead for 5 minutes, adding more flour if needed.

Dough should be elastic and should not stick to your board or work table.
6. Place dough in greased bowl, turning to grease top. Cover and let rise in a warm area until double in size, approximately 1 hour.
7. Punch down. Divide into 2 or 3 pieces. Roll out each into a rectangle and then roll up, jelly-roll fashion. Seal ends by pinching. Place in greased bread pans. Let rise just until dough reaches the top of the pans.
8. Bake at 375° for 25 minutes. Remove bread from pans. Let cool on rack or slice and eat hot.

Variation 1: Use 5 cups bread flour and 3 cups whole wheat flour instead of 7-8 cups all-purpose flour.

Variation 2: Used dried dillweed and dill seeds instead of herbs listed.

Ready-for-Lunch Herb Bread

Quailcrest Farm
Wooster, OH

Makes 2 loaves

1 cup milk
1½ Tbsp. sugar
1 Tbsp. salt
2 Tbsp. butter
2 pkgs. dry yeast
1 cup warm water
2 Tbsp. chopped fresh dill (2 tsp. dried),
   or your choice of herb
4½ cups flour

1. Scald milk. Add sugar, salt, and butter. Stir until dissolved.
2. Dissolve the yeast in warm water. Allow to stand for 5 minutes.
3. Add yeast to cooled milk mixture. Stir in dill.
4. Stir in flour to make a stiff batter.
5. Lightly grease top of dough. Cover and let stand in a warm area until double in size, approximately 45 minutes.
6. Stir down and mix well. Turn into 2 greased casseroles or bread pans. Let rise again.
7. Bake at 350° for 50-60 minutes, covering with aluminum foil if bread begins to become too dark.
8. When cooled, slice and serve.

Easy French Bread

Ann Marie Wishard
Sweet Annie Herbs, Inc.
Centre Hall, PA

Makes 2 loaves

1 pkg. dry yeast
1²/₃ cups warm water
4 cups flour
1 Tbsp. sugar
1 tsp. salt
1 tsp. dried parsley
3/4 tsp. dried sage
1 tsp. dried rosemary
1 tsp. dried thyme

1. Dissolve yeast in ²/₃ cup warm water. Let stand for 5 minutes.
2. Mix together flour, sugar, salt, and herbs. Add one cup of warm water. Add yeast/water mixture and stir. Dough should be sticky. Add more flour if necessary.
3. Cover the bowl with a towel and place in warm place to rise. Let rise until double in size, about an hour.
4. Punch down. Place in two greased and floured bread pans. Cover with towel and let rise until double in size, approximately 45 minutes.
5. Place pans in cold oven and turn to 400°. Bake for 30 minutes.
6. Remove bread from pans immediately and place on rack to cool.

Herb Peel-Away Bread

Verna Schrock
Salem, Oregon

Makes 8-10 servings

2 pkgs. dry yeast
1 cup warm water
1 egg
1/3 cup sugar
1 tsp. salt
2 Tbsp. Parmesan cheese
3 Tbsp. chopped fresh parsley
  (1 Tbsp. dried)
1 Tbsp. chopped fresh basil (1 tsp. dried)
1 Tbsp. chopped fresh thyme
  (1 tsp. dried)
1 1/2 tsp. chopped fresh dill (1/2 tsp. dried)
1 1/2 tsp. chopped fresh rosemary
  (1/2 tsp. dried)
1/4 cup butter or margarine, melted
3 1/2 cups flour
2 Tbsp. butter or margarine, melted

1. Dissolve yeast in warm water.
2. Mix together yeast mixture, egg, sugar, salt, Parmesan cheese, herbs, 1/4 cup butter, and half the flour.
3. Mix in remaining flour and knead for 5 minutes. Let rise until double, about 60-90 minutes.
4. Roll into a 12-inch square. Brush with 2 Tbsp. butter. Cut into 25 squares.
5. Overlap squares, butter side down, in greased bundt pan. Let rise until double.
6. Bake at 375° for 20-25 minutes.

Herb Bread

Nancy Raleigh
HBB
Belcamp, MD

Makes 1 loaf

1 cup whole wheat flour
1 1/2 cups flour
1 cup rolled oats
1/4 cup wheat germ
1 tsp. baking powder
1 tsp. baking soda
1/2 tsp. salt
1 1/2 Tbsp. fresh rosemary (1 1/2 tsp. dried)
1 1/2 Tbsp. fresh oregano (1 1/2 tsp. dried)
1 1/2 Tbsp. fresh thyme (1 1/2 tsp. dried)
2 Tbsp. dried minced onion
1/2 cup sunflower seeds
1/3 cup vegetable oil
1 1/2 cups buttermilk

1. Combine flours, oats, wheat germ, baking powder, baking soda, salt, and herbs.
2. Stir in onion and sunflower seeds.
3. Whisk together oil and buttermilk. Add to dry ingredients. Mix well.
4. Knead dough on lightly floured surface until smooth and elastic, about 8-10 minutes. Add more flour if needed.
5. Shape dough into ball and place in a greased baking dish or pie pan. Cut a cross in the top with a sharp knife.
6. Bake at 375° for 40-50 minutes. Remove and cool on rack.

Herb Whole Wheat Bread

Jacoba Baker & Reenie Baker Sandsted
Baker's Acres
Groton, NY

Makes 1 loaf

1/4 cup warm water
1 pkg. dry yeast
1/2 tsp. sugar
1 cup whole wheat flour
1 1/2 cups flour
1 Tbsp. fresh basil (1 tsp. dried)
2 tsp. fresh marjoram (2/3 tsp. dried)
1 tsp. fresh thyme (1/3 tsp. dried)
1 Tbsp. fresh chives (1 tsp. dried)
1 tsp. salt
approximately 3/4 cup warm water
1 egg yolk
1 Tbsp. cold water

1. Dissolve yeast and sugar in 1/4 cup warm water. Let stand for 5 minutes.
2. Mix together flours, herbs, and salt. Add yeast mixture to flour mixture.
3. Stir in enough warm water to form a ball. Add more warm water to make a dough that is soft and smooth but not sticky.
4. Place dough in greased bowl. Let rise until double in size, approximately 1 hour.
5. Punch down dough and shape into loaf. Place in greased 8" x 5" pan. Cover and let rise until double, approximately 45 minutes.
6. Mix together egg and 1 Tbsp. cold water and brush over top of bread.
7. Bake at 375° for 25 to 30 minutes, until loaf sounds hollow when thumped.

Dark Herb Bread I

Jane D. Look
Pineapple Hill Herbs & More
Mapleton, IL

Makes 1 loaf

2 pkgs. dry yeast
1 1/2 cups warm water
2 cups whole wheat flour
1 cup rye flour
1 1/2 cups flour
1/4 cup wheat germ
1 Tbsp. sugar
1 tsp. salt
1/4 tsp. powdered garlic
1 Tbsp. chopped fresh rosemary
   (1 tsp. dried)
1/4 tsp. caraway seeds
1/2 tsp. chopped fresh oregano
   (1/8 tsp. dried)
3/4 tsp. chopped fresh dill (1/4 tsp. dried)
1/4 cup butter or margarine, melted and cooled

1. Dissolve yeast in water. Let stand for 5 minutes.
2. Combine flours, wheat germ, sugar, salt, garlic, rosemary, caraway seeds, oregano, and dill. Gradually stir in yeast mixture and melted butter.
3. Beat mixture until stiff.
4. Place dough on floured bread board and knead 8-10 minutes, or until smooth in texture.
5. Place dough in greased bowl. Cover with damp cloth and place in a warm location. Let rise until double in size, 45-60 minutes.
6. Punch down and put into greased loaf pan. Grease top of dough. Cover with waxed paper. Let rise until dough rises an inch above pan.
7. Bake at 400° until done, 35-40 minutes.
8. Cool, slice, and serve.

Dark Herb Bread II

Jacoba Baker & Reenie Baker Sandsted
Baker's Acres
Groton, NY

Makes 2 loaves

2 pkgs. dry yeast
1 Tbsp. sugar
1/2 cup warm water
3 cups whole wheat flour
1 cup rye flour
1 1/2 cups bread flour
1/4 cup olive oil
1 Tbsp. salt
1 tsp. freshly ground pepper
1-1 1/2 cups warm water
3 small cloves garlic
2 Tbsp. fresh parsley, finely chopped
   (2 tsp. dried)
2 tsp. fresh rosemary (2/3 tsp. dried)

1. Dissolve yeast and sugar in warm water. Let stand for 5 minutes.
2. Mix together whole wheat flour, rye flour, and 1 cup bread flour.
3. Stir in olive oil, salt, and pepper, and mix well.
4. Add yeast mixture and 1 cup warm water. Stir well. Add more water if necessary to make a firm, slightly sticky dough.
5. Grind garlic, parsley, and rosemary to a paste with a mortar and pestle. Work into dough.
6. Knead dough on lightly floured surface until smooth and elastic, about 8-10 minutes. Add flour as needed to prevent sticking.
7. Place in greased bowl, turning to grease top. Cover and let rise in a warm place until double in size, about 1 hour.
8. Punch down dough and knead again. Form into 2 loaves and place in greased 5" x 9" pans. Cover and let rise again, about 30-45 minutes.
9. Bake at 400° for 20 minutes; then at 350° for about 30 minutes, or until done.

Tip for Drying Herbs

Judy Kehs
Cricket Hill Herb Farm
Rowley, MA

Many herbs can be effectively preserved by a salt-drying method. Cover a cookie sheet with salt and sprinkle it with fresh leaves of any herb. Cover with more salt. Place cookie sheet in oven on low heat. Remove from heat when leaves are brittle. Separate herbs and salt using a sifter. Save the salt which will be lightly herb-flavored for cooking. Seal dried herbs in jars. The herbs will be lightly salted and ready for cooking.

Whole Wheat Pesto Bread

Mark Silber
Hedgehog Hill Farm
Sumner, ME

Makes 1 loaf

1/2 cup lukewarm water
1 pkg. dry yeast
1 Tbsp. honey
1/2 cup lukewarm water
1/4 cup olive oil
1 egg
1 cup rolled oats
1/2 tsp. salt
2 1/2-3 cups whole wheat flour

Filling:
2 packed cups fresh basil leaves
1/4 cup grated Parmesan cheese
1/4 cup pine nuts or walnuts
3 cloves garlic
3 Tbsp. olive oil
1 egg beaten with 1 Tbsp. water

1. Combine 1/2 cup water, yeast, and honey in large mixing bowl. Let stand for 10 minutes.
2. Stir in 1/2 cup water, oil, egg, oats, and salt. Stir in flour, half a cup at a time, until a kneadable dough is formed.
3. Turn onto lightly floured surface and knead for 10-15 minutes until dough is smooth and elastic. Use only enough additional flour to keep dough from sticking.
4. Transfer to oiled bowl. Turn to coat the dough. Cover and set in a warm place to rise until doubled in size, about an hour. While dough is rising, make filling.
5. In a food processor or blender, combine the basil, Parmesan cheese, pine nuts, and garlic. Blend until finely chopped. Add oil and continue blending until a thick, fine paste is formed. Set filling aside.
6. Punch down dough. Roll out on a lightly floured surface to form a rectangle, 9" from side to side.
7. Spread pesto on dough, leaving a 1" border on all sides. Roll up, starting at one 9" side. Pinch seams closed and tuck side seams under.
8. Place seam side down in buttered 8 1/2" x 4 1/2" loaf pan. Cover and let rise in warm place until doubled, about 45 minutes. Brush top with egg beaten with 1 Tbsp. water.
8. Bake at 375° for 35-40 minutes, or until top is golden and loaf sounds hollow when tapped.

Variation: Substitute 1/2 cup fresh basil leaves and 2 Tbsp. fresh parsley leaves for the 2 cups fresh basil leaves. Reduce olive oil to 2 Tbsp.

Jacoba Baker & Reenie Baker Sandsted
Baker's Acres
Goton, NY

Parmesan Chive Biscuits

Gerry Janus
Vileniki—An Herb Farm
Montdale, PA

Add 1 Tbsp. grated Parmesan cheese and a handful of chive blossoms to your favorite biscuit mix. Serve with herbal butter.

Pesto Bread

Barbara Sausser
Barb's Country Herbs
Riverside, CA

Makes 1 loaf

1 loaf frozen bread dough, wheat or
    white, or your own favorite bread
    recipe, mixed and brought through
    one rising
1 cup firmly packed fresh basil leaves
1/2 cup torn fresh spinach leaves
1/4 cup grated Parmesan or Romano
    cheese
1/4 cup pine nuts, walnuts, or almonds
2 cloves garlic, quartered
1/4 tsp. salt
2 Tbsp. olive oil
2 Tbsp. water

1. Thaw bread according to package
   directions, or prepare your own recipe
   as described above. Set aside.
2. In a blender or food processor, combine
   basil, spinach, cheese, nuts, garlic, and
   salt. Process until a paste forms.
3. Gradually add oil and water. Blend or
   process to the consistency of soft butter.
   Can be refrigerated for up to 2 days, or
   frozen for 1 month.
4. Roll dough on floured board until you
   have a rectangle about 12" x 10".
5. Pour pesto onto bread dough and
   spread to edges.
6. Begin rolling dough at the short side.
   Pinch together at seam and at ends.
   Place on lightly greased cookie sheet.
7. Bake at 350° for 30 minutes. Remove
   from oven and place on rack to cool.
   Slice when cool.

Quick Basil Beer Bread

Nancy Raleigh
HBB
Belcamp, MD

Makes 1 loaf

3 cups self-rising flour
3 Tbsp. sugar
12-oz. beer, at room temperature
1/2 cup chopped fresh basil
    (3 Tbsp. dried),
        or 1 Tbsp. dried oregano,
            1 Tbsp. dried basil,
            and 1 Tbsp. dried rosemary,

        or 1 Tbsp. dried dill and
            1 Tbsp. dried lemon balm,

        or 1 Tbsp. dried tarragon and
            1 Tbsp. dried parsley,

        or 1 Tbsp. dried thyme and
            1 Tbsp. dried oregano

1. Mix together all ingredients. Pour into
   greased 9" x 5" loaf pan.
2. Place in unheated oven. Set temperature
   to 350°. Bake for 50 minutes.
3. Remove from pan, cool, and slice.

Herb Beer Bread

Betty Summers
Herb Garden & Greenhouse
Muskogee, OK

Makes 20 servings

3 cups self-rising flour
1/4 cup sugar
12-oz. can beer, at room temperature
3 Tbsp. chopped fresh dill (1 Tbsp. dried)
3 Tbsp. chopped fresh basil
   (1 Tbsp. dried)
1/4 cup melted butter

1. Lightly mix together all ingredients except butter.
2. Pour batter into greased loaf pan. Do not smooth top. Pour melted butter over loaf.
3. Bake at 350° until brown on top.
4. Cool on bread rack. Cut thin slices the length of the loaf. Then slice each long slice in half to serve.

Dilly Cottage Bread

Janet Piepel
The Herb Pantry
East Wenatchee, WA

Makes 1 loaf

1/4 cup warm water
1 pkg. dry yeast
1 Tbsp. sugar
1 cup creamed cottage cheese
2 Tbsp. finely chopped onion
2 Tbsp. melted butter or margarine
1 egg
1 tsp. salt
2 1/4 cups flour
1/4 cup wheat germ
3 Tbsp. fresh dill (1 Tbsp. dried)

1. Pour water into blender or food processor. Stir in yeast and sugar and let stand for 5 minutes. Process or blend for 10 seconds.
2. Add cottage cheese, onion, butter, egg, and salt and mix 20 seconds.
3. Combine flour, wheat germ, and dill. Stir in cottage cheese mixture, stirring until dough pulls away from sides of bowl.
4. Knead dough on lightly floured surface until smooth and elastic, 8-10 minutes.
5. Place in greased bowl, turning to grease top. Cover and let rise in a warm area until double in size, approximately 1 1/4 hours.
6. Punch down and shape into loaf. Place in greased 5" x 8" pan. Cover and let rise until double, approximately 1 hour.
7. Bake at 375° for 30 minutes.

Variation:

1. Dissolve yeast and sugar in warm water. Let stand for 5 minutes.
2. Stir in cottage cheese, onion, butter, egg, and salt. Mix well.
3. Combine flour, wheat germ, and dill. Add to cottage cheese mixture, stirring until dough pulls away from sides of bowl.
4. Follow steps 4-7 above.

Dill Bread

Marty Mertens and Clarence Roush
Woodstock Herbs
New Goshen, IN
Jane D. Look
Pineapple Hill Herbs & More
Mapleton, IL

Makes 10-12 servings

1 pkg. dry yeast
1/4 cup very warm water
1 cup cream-style cottage cheese
2 Tbsp. chopped onion
2 Tbsp. sugar
2 Tbsp. dill seeds
1 tsp. salt
1 egg, lightly beaten
1 Tbsp. butter or margarine, softened
2 1/2 cups flour
1/4 tsp. baking soda

1. Dissolve yeast in water. Let stand for 5 minutes.
2. Beat together cottage cheese, onion, sugar, dill, salt, egg, and butter.
3. Stir in yeast. Work in flour and baking soda.
4. Cover and let rise in warm place until double in size, approximately 1 hour.
5. Punch down dough and place in a greased 2-quart casserole dish. Allow to rise until double, about 35 minutes.
6. Bake at 350° for 45 minutes, or until golden brown. Remove immediately and cool slightly on rack. Cut into wedges to serve.

Garlic Dill Bread

Jacoba Baker & Reenie Baker Sandsted
Baker's Acres
Groton, NY

Makes 1 loaf

1/4 cup warm water
4 tsp. dry yeast
1 tsp. honey
6 cloves garlic, minced
1 cup cottage cheese, pureed until smooth
2 Tbsp. butter or margarine, softened
3 Tbsp. chopped fresh dill (1 Tbsp. dried)
1 egg
2 1/2-3 cups whole wheat flour
1 egg, beaten
1 tsp. milk

1. Dissolve yeast and honey in warm water. Let stand for 10 minutes.
2. Mix together garlic, cottage cheese, butter, dill, and egg. Beat until smooth.
3. Stir yeast mixture into cottage cheese mixture.
4. Stir in 1 cup flour. Beat well. Add remaining flour, 1/2 cup at a time, beating continuously until dough can be kneaded.
5. Knead dough on lightly floured surface until smooth and elastic, about 15 minutes. Add flour as needed to prevent sticking.
6. Place in greased bowl, turning to grease top. Cover and let rise in a warm place until double in size, about 1 hour.
7. Punch down dough. Knead briefly and form into a loaf. Place in greased 9" x 5" pan. Cover and let rise until double, approximately 45 minutes.
8. Mix together egg and milk. Brush over top of loaf.
9. Bake at 350° for 40-50 minutes.

Parsley Bread

Jacoba Baker & Reenie Baker Sandsted
Baker's Acres
Groton, NY

Makes 1 loaf

1/2 cup warm water
1 pkg. dry yeast
1 tsp. honey
1/2 cup sour cream or plain yogurt
1 egg
1 cup minced fresh parsley
   (5 Tbsp. dried)
2 cloves garlic, minced
2-2 1/2 cups whole wheat flour

1. Dissolve yeast and honey in warm water. Let stand for 10 minutes.
2. Combine sour cream, egg, parsley, and garlic. Add to yeast mixture.
3. Beat in 1 cup flour. Gradually beat in enough additional flour to make a soft, kneadable dough.
4. Knead dough on lightly floured surface until smooth and elastic, 8-10 minutes. Add flour as needed to prevent sticking.
5. Place ball of dough in greased bowl, turning to grease top. Cover and let rise in a warm place until double in size, about 1 hour.
6. Punch down and pat into a rectangle about 8" wide. Roll up like a jelly roll. Pinch the seam tightly. Place dough, seam side down, in buttered 8" x 5" loaf pan. Cover and let rise until double in bulk, approximately 45 minutes.
7. Bake at 375° for 40-45 minutes, or until the loaf is golden on top and sounds hollow when tapped.

Sage Beer Bread

Wendy Harrington
Harvest Herb Company
Malone, NY

Makes 1 loaf

3 cups self-rising flour
2 Tbsp. honey
12-oz. beer at room temperature
2 Tbsp. chopped fresh sage (2 tsp. dried)
1 Tbsp. chopped fresh parsley
   (1 tsp. dried)
1 Tbsp. chopped fresh chives
   (1 tsp. dried)
4 Tbsp. melted butter
1 Tbsp. sesame seeds

1. Combine flour, honey, beer, and herbs. Mix until dry ingredients are moistened.
2. Spoon into a well greased loaf pan.
3. Bake at 375° for 50 minutes. Remove from oven and brush with melted butter. Sprinkle with sesame seeds.
4. Return to oven and bake for 10 more minutes, or until bread sounds hollow when thumped.
5. Remove bread from pan. Cool on rack.

Batter Bread with Sun-Dried Tomatoes, Cheese, and Herbs

Connie Johnson
Heartstone Herb Farm
Loudon, NH

Makes 1 loaf

1 cup sun-dried tomatoes
warm water to cover tomatoes
1 pkg. dry yeast
1 Tbsp. sugar
1 1/4 cups warm water
2 Tbsp. vegetable oil
1 tsp. salt
3 cups unbleached flour
1 cup grated Parmesan cheese
1/4 tsp. garlic powder
1 1/2 tsp. chopped fresh oregano
  (1/2 tsp. dried)
1 1/2 tsp. chopped fresh basil
  (1/2 tsp. dried)

1. Soak tomatoes in warm water for 10 minutes. Drain. Chop tomatoes and set aside.
2. Dissolve yeast and sugar in 1 1/4 cups warm water. Let stand for 5 minutes.
3. Stir in oil, salt, 2 cups flour, Parmesan cheese, garlic powder, oregano, and basil. Mix well; then beat with electric mixer for 3 minutes on medium speed.
4. Stir in remaining 1 cup flour. Cover and let rise in warm area until double in size, approximately 1 hour.
5. Stir batter down. Place in greased 9" x 5" pan. Cover and let rise until double, approximately 45 minutes.
6. Bake at 375° for 35-40 minutes, or until loaf sounds hollow when tapped. Cool on rack before slicing.

Herb and Cheese Biscuits

Harriette Johnson
Mustard Seed Herbs & Everlastings
Spring Valley, WI

Makes 6-8 biscuits

1 cup whole wheat flour
1 cup flour
3 tsp. baking powder
2 Tbsp. chopped mixed fresh herbs
  (2 tsp. dried)—thyme, parsley, oregano, marjoram
1/2 tsp. garlic powder
1 tsp. salt
5 Tbsp. butter or margarine, softened
1/2 cup grated sharp cheddar cheese
1/2 cup milk

1. Mix together flours, baking powder, herbs, garlic powder, and salt.
2. Work in butter and cheese. Stir in milk. Knead 5-6 times.
3. Roll out to 1/2-3/4" thick. Cut with a small round cutter. Place biscuits 1/2" apart on greased cookie sheet.
4. Bake at 400° for 10-12 minutes.

Tip for Drying Herbs

Mary Peddie
The Herb Market
Washington, KY

Remove leaves of herbs from their stems. Place on paper towels on a cookie sheet. Put into a self-defrosting refrigerator. Leave for 5-10 days until crisp and dry. Put into 250° oven for a few minutes to insure leaves have no moisture. Store in jar.

Dilly Corn Muffins

Paula Winchester
Herb Gathering Inc.
Kansas City, MO

Makes 24 muffins

1 cup flour
1 cup cornmeal
4 tsp. baking powder
1/2 cup sugar
1 tsp. salt
1 cup fresh, frozen, or canned corn,
    drained
1/2 cup snipped dill (2 1/2 Tbsp. dried)
2 eggs
2/3 cup milk
1/3 cup oil

1. Stir together flour, cornmeal, baking
   powder, sugar, salt, corn, and dill. Make
   a well in the center.
2. Combine eggs, milk, and oil. Mix well.
3. Pour liquids into well in dry ingredients.
   Stir until just moistened. Batter should
   be lumpy.
4. Fill greased muffin tins 2/3 full.
5. Bake at 400° for 15 minutes. Serve
   warm.

Dilly Cheese Muffins

Nancy J. Reppert
Sweet Remembrances
Mechanicsburg, PA

Makes 12 muffins

2 cups flour
3 tsp. baking powder
1 Tbsp. sugar
1/2 tsp. salt
1 1/2 Tbsp. fresh dill (1 1/2 tsp. dried)
1 cup grated cheddar cheese
1 egg
1 cup milk
2 Tbsp. oil

1. Mix together flour, baking powder,
   sugar, salt, and dill. Stir in cheese.
2. Beat together egg, milk, and oil. Add to
   flour mixture. Stir just to moisten.
3. Pour into greased muffin tins.
4. Bake at 425° for 18-20 minutes.

Sage-Cheese Muffins

Eone Riales
Fogg Road Herb Farm
Nesbit, MS

Makes 12 muffins

2 cups self-rising flour
3 eggs
1 cup milk
4 cups shredded cheddar cheese
2 Tbsp. chopped fresh sage (2 tsp. dried)

1. Mix together flour, eggs, and milk until
   well blended. Fold in cheese and sage.
2. Pour into greased muffin tins.
3. Bake at 425° for 15 minutes.

Pesto Biscuits

Jim O'Toole
O'Toole's Herb Farm
Madison, FL

Add 1/2 cup shredded sharp cheddar
cheese plus 1-2 Tbsp. pesto to standard
biscuit mix for an easy herb biscuit.

Grandma's Savory Muffins

Carol Vaughn
Healthy Horse Herb Farm
Onley, VA

Makes 12 muffins

1 cup flour
1/4 cup sugar
3 tsp. baking powder
1/2 tsp. salt
1 Tbsp. chopped fresh rosemary
   (1 tsp. dried)
1 Tbsp. chopped fresh sage (1 tsp. dried)
1 Tbsp. chopped fresh lovage leaves
   (1 tsp. dried)
1 cup whole wheat flour
1/4 cup shortening or oil
1 egg
1 cup milk

1. Sift together 1 cup flour, sugar, baking powder, and salt.
2. Add rosemary, sage, lovage, and whole wheat flour. Mix well.
3. Mix shortening or oil into dry ingredients with pastry blender.
4. Stir in egg and milk until ingredients are just blended. Batter will be lumpy.
5. Fill greased muffin tins 2/3 full.
6. Bake at 400° for 20-25 minutes. Serve warm.

Mint Muffins

Jan Mast
The Herb Shop
Lititz, PA

Makes 12 muffins

1 cup sugar
1/3 cup butter or margarine, softened
2 eggs, beaten
2 tsp. baking powder
1/2 tsp. salt
1 cup whole wheat flour
1 cup flour
1/4 cup chopped fresh mint leaves
1 cup milk

1. Cream together sugar and butter. Add eggs. Mix well.
2. Mix together baking powder, salt, wheat flour, white flour, and mint leaves. Stir into creamed mixture alternately with milk.
3. Pour into greased muffin tins.
4. Bake at 375° for 20 minutes.

Sheriann's Tarragon Potato Rolls

Betty Leonard
Hampton Herbs
New Carlisle, OH

Makes 4 dozen rolls

1¹/₂ cups mashed potatoes,
    or 2-oz. pkg. instant potato flakes
1 cup milk
²/₃ cup shortening
¹/₂ cup sugar
1 tsp. salt
1 pkg. dry yeast
¹/₂ cup lukewarm water
2 eggs, beaten
7 ¹/₂ cups flour
¹/₃ cup chopped fresh tarragon
    (2 Tbsp. dried)

1. Prepare potatoes.
2. Scald milk. Remove from heat. Stir in potatoes, shortening, sugar, and salt. Stir until shortening is melted. Cool to lukewarm.
3. Dissolve yeast in water. Let stand 5 minutes.
4. Stir in milk mixture and eggs.
5. Beat in 2 cups flour and tarragon. Add remaining flour to form stiff dough.
6. Turn dough onto lightly floured surface. Knead.
7. Place in greased bowl, turning the dough to grease its top. Cover and let stand in warm place for 1¹/₂ hours.
8. Punch down. Shape into 1¹/₂" balls. Arrange in greased pan.
9. Cover and let stand in warm place for 1 hour.
10. Bake at 350° for 20-25 minutes. Brush tops with butter.

Tea Thyme Rolls

Pat Dyer
Village Herb Shop
Blue Ball, PA

Makes 2¹/₂ dozen rolls

4¹/₂ to 5¹/₂ cups bread flour
1 cup rye flour
2 tsp. chopped fresh sage (³/₄ tsp. dried)
2 Tbsp. chopped fresh thyme
    (2 tsp. dried)
¹/₂ cup sugar
1¹/₂ tsp. salt
2 pkgs. yeast
1 cup water
³/₄ cup milk
¹/₃ cup butter
2 eggs, room temperature

1. In large mixing bowl combine 1 cup bread flour, rye flour, herbs, sugar, salt, and yeast.
2. In saucepan, combine water, milk, and butter. Heat over low heat until liquids are very warm (120-130°).
3. Gradually add liquid to dry ingedients and beat 2 minutes at medium speed.
4. Add eggs and ¹/₂ cup bread flour. Beat 2 minutes on high speed. Stir in additional bread flour until dough is workable (about 3 cups).
5. Turn onto floured board and knead until smooth and elastic, about 6-8 minutes. Cover with plastic wrap and a towel. Allow to stand for 20 minutes in warm place.
6. Punch down and shape as you wish. Roll dough between your palms to form 6" x ³/₄" thick ropes. Form into figure eights or coils. Or pinch off chunks and form into small balls.
7. Place on greased cookie sheet and let rise until double in size, about 40 minutes.

8. Bake at 350° for 10-20 minutes, or until golden brown.

Note: Dough can be frozen and baked later. Follow instructions through step 6; then place shaped dough on greased cookie sheet. Cover with plastic wrap and freeze. When rolls are frozen, remove from cookie sheet and store in plastic bag in freezer. To bake, place frozen rolls onto a cookie sheet and allow to thaw for 1 hour. Bake at 350° for 10-20 minutes, or until golden brown.

Sheriann's Butterhorn Thyme Rolls

Betty Leonard
Hampton Herbs
New Carlisle, OH

Makes 32 rolls

1 cup shortening
1 cup boiling water
3/4 cup sugar
2 tsp. salt
2 pkgs. dry yeast
1 cup water
2 eggs, beaten
6 cups flour
1 1/2 Tbsp. chopped fresh thyme
   (1 1/2 tsp. dried)

1. In large mixing bowl, pour boiling water over shortening, sugar, and salt. Beat until shortening is dissolved. Cool to lukewarm.
2. Stir in yeast, 1 cup water, eggs, flour, and thyme. Mix until smooth.
3. Put in greased bowl and refrigerate.
4. When ready to use, divide dough in half. Roll out each half to an 18" circle. Cut

into 16 pie-shaped wedges. Roll up each piece, starting at the wide end of the wedge.
5. Put on greased baking sheet. Let rise until double in size.
6. Bake at 350° for 12-15 minutes.

Southwest Cornbread

Jennifer Shadle
The Spice Hunter, Inc
San Luis Obispo, CA

Makes 9 servings

1 cup cornmeal
1 cup flour
1 Tbsp. baking powder
1/2 tsp. salt (optional)
1 1/2-2 Tbsp. chopped fresh cilantro
1 egg, beaten
1 cup milk
1 cup creamed corn
1 small onion, chopped
1-2 jalapeno peppers, seeded and minced
1/4 cup butter or margarine
1/2 cup grated cheddar cheese

1. Mix together cornmeal, flour, baking powder, salt, and cilantro.
2. Mix together egg, milk, and corn until thoroughly combined.
3. Saute onion and jalapeno in butter until onion is transparent.
4. Add milk mixture, onion mixture, and cheese to dry ingredients. Stir until mixed.
5. Pour into greased 8" square pan.
6. Bake at 400° for 35-40 minutes, or until a toothpick inserted in center comes out clean.

Corn Dilly Bread

Judith Defrain
Eye of the Cat
Long Beach, CA

Makes 4 servings

1 box corn bread mix
1 1/2 tsp. sugar
1 1/2 tsp. dill seeds
4 tsp. poppy seeds
1 egg
1/2 cup milk

1. Combine all ingredients. Mix well.
2. Bake at 425° for 25-30 minutes.

Dilly Cheese Bread

Mary Ellen Wilcox
South Ridge Treasures Herb Shop
Scotia, NY

Makes 3 small loaves

2 cups flour
1 Tbsp. sugar
1 1/2 tsp. baking powder
1/2 tsp. salt
1/4 cup unsalted butter
2 cups shredded cheddar cheese
1 1/2 Tbsp. minced fresh dill
   (1 1/2 tsp. dried)
1 egg
1 cup milk

1. Sift together flour, sugar, baking powder, and salt.
2. Cut in butter. Stir in cheese and dill.
3. Combine egg and milk. Add to flour mixture. Be sure to stir just until moistened.
4. Divide batter into 3 greased 3" x 6" loaf pans.

5. Bake at 400° for 35 minutes, or until toothpick inserted in center comes out clean.
6. Cool 10 minutes before removing from pans.

Note: This bread keeps well in the freezer for up to six months. The recipe works well if doubled.

Sage Sticks

Kelly Wisner
Herbal Heaven
Wernersville, PA

Makes about 20 sticks

1 cup flour
1 1/2 tsp. baking powder
1/2 tsp. salt
1 Tbsp. finely snipped fresh sage
   (1 tsp. dried)
1 tsp. finely snipped fresh rosemary
   (1/3 tsp. dried)
1/2 cup grated cheddar cheese
2 Tbsp. butter, softened
1/3 cup water

1. Sift together flour, baking powder, and salt.
2. Stir in sage, rosemary, and cheddar cheese.
3. Cut butter into mixture until crumbly.
4. Sprinkle water over top. Mix lightly with a fork until pastry holds together.
5. On lightly floured surface, roll dough out to a 12" x 15" rectangle. Divide in half lengthwise, and then cut in 1/2" wide strips. Place an inch apart on ungreased cookie sheet.
6. Bake at 425° for 10 minutes. Watch carefully so sticks do not burn. Cool on rack.

Mint Tea Bread

Kim Snyder
Kim's Kakes, Kuttings, and Kandles, too!
Ivesdale, IL

Makes 2 loaves

minted sugar*
1 cup brown sugar
2½ cups flour
3½ tsp. baking powder
3 Tbsp. oil
1½ cups milk
1 egg
1 cup chopped walnut pieces
1 cup chopped fresh peppermint
   (⅓ cup dried)

1. Grease two loaf pans; then sprinkle pans with light coating of minted sugar.
2. Mix together brown sugar, flour, and baking powder.
3. Mix together oil, milk, and egg. Stir into sugar/flour mixture.
4. Stir in walnuts and peppermint. Stir until well blended.
5. Pour into loaf pans.
6. Bake at 350° for 50-60 minutes, or until toothpick in center of bread comes out clean.

Note: This bread freezes well and will last several months in the freezer.

*** Minted Sugar**: Layer 1 Tbsp. dried peppermint leaves and 2 Tbsp. sugar in a glass container. Mix well. Let stand for several days before using to allow flavors to blend.*

Lemon Tea Bread

Timothy L. Newcomer
The Herb Merchant
Carlisle, PA

Makes 1 loaf

¾ cup milk
1 Tbsp. finely chopped fresh lemon
   thyme
1 Tbsp. finely chopped fresh lemon balm
1 tsp. finely chopped fresh lemon
   verbena
6 Tbsp. butter, softened
1 cup sugar
2 eggs, beaten
1 Tbsp. grated lemon zest
2 cups flour
1½ tsp. baking powder
¼ tsp. salt

Glaze
juice of 2 lemons
1-2 cups powdered sugar, sifted

1. Heat milk until very warm. Add chopped herbs. Set aside to steep until cool.
2. Cream together butter and sugar until well blended. Beat at high speed until light and fluffy.
3. Beat in eggs until blended. Stir in lemon zest.
4. Mix together flour, baking powder, and salt. Add alternately with herbed milk to creamed mixture. Mix just until blended.
5. Pour into greased 9" x 5" pan.
6. Bake at 350 for 50 minutes, or until toothpick inserted in center comes out clean.
7. Remove cake from pan onto a wire rack. Cool.
8. Mix together lemon juice and powdered sugar, adding sugar until mixture becomes thick and smooth. Drizzle over cooled cake.

Heard's Easy Herb Bread

Mary Lou Heard
Heard's Gardens
Westminter, CA

Makes 1 loaf

1 lb. freshly made pizza dough*
2 Tbsp. olive oil
2 Tbsp. minced garlic
1 cup shredded Parmesan cheese
1 Tbsp. chopped fresh basil
1 Tbsp. chopped fresh rosemary
1 Tbsp. chopped fresh oregano
1 cup sliced black olives
1/2 Tbsp. butter or margarine, melted
1 Tbsp. cornmeal

1. Roll out pizza dough as if making a pizza.
2. Brush with olive oil and sprinkle with minced garlic.
3. Sprinkle with Parmesan cheese.
4. Sprinkle with herbs.
5. Sprinkle with black olives.
6. Roll up dough jelly-roll fashion. Brush top with butter. Place on greased cookie sheet which has been sprinkled with cornmeal.
7. Bake at 325° for 30-45 minutes, or until golden brown.
8. Slice and serve hot.

Pizza Dough

Lee A. Good
Lititz, PA

Makes 1 15" pizza crust

2 1/2 cups flour
1 pkg. dry yeast
1 tsp. sugar
1 tsp. garlic salt
3 Tbsp. chopped fresh oregano
   (1 Tbsp. dried)
3 Tbsp. chopped fresh basil
   (1 Tbsp. dried)
1 1/2 Tbsp. chopped fresh thyme
   (1 1/2 tsp. dried)
1 cup warm water
2 Tbsp. olive oil

1. Combine flour, yeast, sugar, salt, oregano, basil, and thyme. Mix well.
2. Stir in water and mix into a sticky ball.
3. Add oil and combine mixture with hands until all oil is mixed in.
4. Place in greased bowl, cover it with a towel, and allow to stand for 15 minutes in warm place.
5. Press dough into 15" pizza pan.
6. Bake at 375° for 10 minutes, or until lightly browned.
7. Remove from oven and cover with sauce and toppings.
8. Return to oven for another 10 minutes.

Note: This recipe makes an attractive and delicious pizza crust. The amount and types of herbs can be varied to include rosemary, sage, and parsley.

Variation 1: Add 1 tsp. chopped hot peppers to the crust.

Variation 2: Use 1 tsp. regular salt and 1-2 cloves minced garlic instead of garlic salt.

Variation 3: This recipe can be used to make stromboli. Follow the above instructions through Step 4. Then roll dough into a 15" x 12" rectangle. Layer the stromboli ingredients down the middle of the dough, covering the center third of its surface lengthwise. Gently lift up left and right sides and stretch them to cover the stromboli filling. Pinch together securely so the crust does not separate while baking. Bake at 375° for 20 minutes.

Variation 4: This recipe can be used for a quick Italian bread. Simply shape the dough into an oblong loaf and bake on a cookie sheet at 375° for 20 minutes.

Tip for Preserving Herbs

Ernestine Schrepfer
Herbal Scent-Sations
Trenton, MO

Susan Jenal
Rose Manor Bed and Breakfast
Manheim, PA

Fill an ice cube tray half full with fresh, minced herbs. Fill with water and freeze. When frozen, place cubes in plastic bag in the freezer. Add herb ice cubes to your winter soup broth.

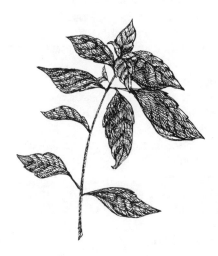

Breakfast Foods

Bruschetta

Sheryl Lozier
Summers Past Farms
El Cajon, CA

Makes 8 servings

12-15 fresh ripe plum tomatoes (1³/4 lbs.)
2 Tbsp. minced garlic
2 Tbsp. minced shallots
1 cup chopped fresh basil (¹/3 cup dried)
1 tsp. fresh lemon juice
salt to taste
coarsely ground black pepper to taste
¹/3 cup extra virgin olive oil
3 cloves garlic, slivered
¹/4 cup extra virgin olive oil
8 thick slices round peasant bread

1. Cut tomatoes into ¹/4" chunks and place in bowl. Add garlic and shallots and toss well.
2. Stir in basil, lemon juice, salt, pepper, and ¹/3 cup olive oil. Set aside.
3. Saute slivered garlic in ¹/4 cup olive oil until golden, about 2-3 minutes. Discard garlic and reserve oil.

4. Toast the bread. Cut each slice in half. Brush garlic-flavored oil over each slice. Spoon tomato mixture over bread and serve immediately.

Tomato Egg Bake with Basil

Judith M. Graves
Lambs & Thyme at Randallane
Richmond, NH

Makes 4 servings

4 large ripe firm tomatoes
4 Tbsp. dry bread crumbs, or more
1 heaping Tbsp. chopped basil
   (1 tsp. dried)
1 Tbsp. chopped chives (1 tsp. dried)
salt to taste
pepper to taste
4 eggs
4 slices hot buttered whole grain toast, crusts removed
fresh basil sprigs

1. Cut tops off tomatoes. Scoop out center with a teaspoon. Place pulp in bowl and mash with fork.
2. Stir bread crumbs, basil, chives, salt, and pepper into tomato pulp. Mix to a thick paste, adding more bread crumbs if needed to make the mixture hold together.
3. Break an egg into each tomato. Top each with one-fourth of the bread crumb/chopped tomato mixture.
4. Bake at 350° until eggs are cooked and tomatoes are soft but still able to hold their shape, approximately 45-55 minutes.
5. Place tomatoes on toast and garnish with sprigs of basil.

Feta-Herb Omelet

Anna L. Brown
Longfellow's Greenhouses
Manchester, ME

Makes 2 servings

4 large eggs
2 Tbsp. water
1 Tbsp. chopped fresh parsley
  (1 tsp. dried)
1 tsp. minced fresh rosemary
  (1/3 tsp. dried)
olive oil
1 small tomato, seeded, drained, and chopped
2 Tbsp. coarsely crumbled feta cheese
black pepper to taste

1. Whip together eggs, water, and herbs until thoroughly blended.
2. Preheat large, heavy skillet over medium heat until a drop of water dropped onto it "dances." Coat bottom and sides of pan with olive oil.

3. Pour in egg mixture. As bottom cooks, lift edges with spatula so that liquid egg runs under cooked egg.
4. Turn heat to low when most of egg is cooked, but top is still moist. Sprinkle with tomato, cheese, and pepper.
5. Gently fold omelet in half. Continue cooking until inside is well heated and outside is lightly browned.

Sunday Scrambled Eggs

Sheryl Lozier
Summers Past Farms
El Cajon, CA

Makes 2 servings

4 eggs, beaten
dash of Tabasco sauce
1 Tbsp. butter or margarine
1 medium tomato, cored and chopped
1 Tbsp. chopped fresh chives
  (1 tsp. dried)
1/4 cup cream cheese, cubed
salt to taste
pepper to taste

1. Add Tabasco to eggs.
2. Melt butter in pan. Lightly saute tomato. Stir in eggs and cook until lightly scrambled.
3. Fold in chives, cream cheese, salt, and pepper. Cook until eggs are set.
4. Serve with toasted English muffins.

Tomatoed Eggs and Pesto

Leslie Scott
Once Upon a Thyme
Troy, NY

Makes 2 servings

2-3 Tbsp. pesto (see page 57-60)
3 eggs, beaten with a little water
1 dozen or more cherry tomatoes,
    sliced in half
salt to taste
pepper to taste

1. Place pesto in skillet over medium heat.
   Pour eggs into pan. Toss in tomatoes.
2. Scramble mixture lightly. Season with
   salt and pepper.
2. Serve with toast.

Cheddar-Chives Scrambled Eggs

Nancy T. Dickman
Cascade Country Gardens
Marblemount, WA

Makes 2 servings

4 eggs
salt to taste
pepper to taste
1 Tbsp. chopped fresh chives
1 Tbsp. butter or margarine
1/4 cup grated cheddar cheese

1. Whip eggs with fork. Add salt, pepper,
   and chives.
2. Melt butter in skillet. Pour in egg
   mixture. Sprinkle with cheese. Scramble
   eggs until cooked.

Basiled Eggs

Jacoba Baker & Reenie Baker Sandsted
Baker's Acres
Groton, NY

Makes 4 servings

8 eggs
1/2 cup milk
1/2 cup chopped basil (3 Tbsp. dried)
1 Tbsp. butter or margarine
salt to taste
pepper to taste
1 cup freshly grated Parmesan cheese
paprika

1. Beat together eggs, milk, and basil.
2. Melt butter in pan. Scramble egg
   mixture until nearly set.
3. Sprinkle with salt, pepper, and cheese.
   Remove from heat.
4. Cover briefly until cheese melts.
5. Sprinkle with paprika. Toss gently and
   serve.

Individual Baked Eggs

Susan Jenal
Rose Manor Bed & Breakfast
Manheim, PA

Makes 1 serving

1 tsp. butter or margarine, softened
1 Tbsp. heavy cream
1 large egg
chopped fresh chives or dried chives
grated sharp cheddar cheese

1. Grease all sides of a 3$\frac{1}{2}$- 4 oz. ramekin with butter.
2. Pour in cream.
3. Gently crack egg into the ramekin.
4. Sprinkle with chives and cheese.
5. Bake at 425° for 11 minutes, until white is firm but yolk is soft.

Dilled Scrambled Eggs

Diane Tracey
Chestnut Herb Farm
North Ridgeville, OH

Makes 4 servings

6 eggs, beaten
$\frac{1}{2}$ cup cottage cheese
1 tsp. fresh dill ($\frac{1}{4}$-$\frac{1}{2}$ tsp. dried)

1. Beat eggs. Stir in cottage cheese and dill.
2. Cook on medium high, stirring frequently until eggs are set.

Tarragon Chive Omelet

Jacoba Baker & Reenie Baker Sandsted
Baker's Acres
Groton, NY

Makes 1 serving

$\frac{1}{2}$ tsp. chopped fresh tarragon
  ($\frac{1}{4}$ tsp. dried)
$\frac{1}{4}$ tsp. chopped fresh rosemary
  ($\frac{1}{8}$ tsp. dried)
1 Tbsp. chopped fresh chives
  (1 tsp. dried)
1$\frac{1}{2}$ Tbsp. crumbled feta cheese
2 eggs
1 Tbsp. water
1 tsp. butter or margarine

If using fresh herbs:
1. Combine tarragon, rosemary, chives, and feta cheese. Set aside.
2. Beat the eggs and water together with about 20 strokes of a fork.
3. Melt butter in pan. Add eggs and cook until set.
4. Sprinkle with herb and cheese filling. Fold omelet in half. Serve immediately.

If using dried herbs:
1. Beat the eggs and water together with about 20 strokes of a fork.
2. Stir in tarragon, rosemary, and chives.
3. Melt butter in pan. Add eggs and cook until set.
4. Sprinkle with cheese. Fold omelet in half. Serve immediately.

Eggs with Lovage and Marigolds

Stephen Lee
The Cookbook Cottage
Louisville, KY

Makes 1 serving

1 Tbsp. unsalted butter
2 eggs
1 Tbsp. heavy cream
black pepper to taste
1 tsp. finely chopped fresh lovage
finely chopped top of green onion
petals from marigold flower
1 pita bread, toasted
marigold flowers
fresh lovage sprigs

1. Melt butter over low heat.
2. In a separate bowl mix together eggs, cream, pepper, lovage, onion, and marigolds. Pour into butter and scramble over low heat.
3. Fill toasted pita with eggs and serve immediately. Garnish with marigolds and lovage sprigs.

Dressed-In-Sunday's-Best Scrambled Eggs

Kelly Wisner
Herbal Heaven
Wernersville, PA

Makes 1 serving (mutliply as often as you like!)

2 eggs, beaten
1/4 apple, peeled and grated
2 Tbsp. chopped fresh chives
   (1 tsp. dried)
2 Tbsp. bulk sausage, cooked

2 tsp. chopped fresh sage (2/3 tsp. dried)
2 tsp. chopped fresh rosemary
   (2/3 tsp. dried)

1. Mix together all ingredients.
2. Pour into greased pan and cook over medium heat until set.
3. Serve immediately.

Country Breakfast Eggs

Marilyn Jones
Jones Sheep Farm Bed & Breakfast
Peabody, KS

Makes 5 servings

3 Tbsp. butter or margarine
1/4 cup chopped mushrooms
3 Tbsp. flour
1 cup, plus 2 Tbsp. milk
1/2 cup salad dressing or mayonnaise
1/2 cup milk
6 hard-boiled eggs, chopped
1 Tbsp. chopped fresh chives
   (1 tsp. dried)
black olives
toast points or toasted English muffins
bacon bits
chive blossoms

1. Melt butter or margarine.
2. Saute mushrooms in butter until tender. Add flour and stir until smooth.
3. Gradually, over low heat, add milk and stir until thickened. Cool.
4. Combine mushroom sauce, salad dressing, and milk. Add chopped eggs and chives. Refrigerate mixture for at least 8 hours.
5. Pour into baking pan and bake at 350° for 20 minutes.
6. Spread toast points or English muffin halves on 5 plates. Spread egg mixture over top.

7. Garnish with black olives, crumbled bacon bits, and/or chive blossoms.

Breakfast Pizza

Sue Floyd
Herb Herbert's Herbs
Tahlequah, OK

Makes 6-8 servings

1 Tbsp. butter or margarine
1/2 cup chopped onion
6-oz. chipped ham, or 6-oz. mild sausage, cooked and drained
1 medium tomato, chopped
2 cups biscuit mix
1/2 cup cold water
1 cup shredded Swiss or cheddar cheese
1/4 cup milk
2 eggs
1/4 tsp. salt
1/4 tsp. pepper
3/4 tsp. fresh dill (1/4 tsp. dried)
2 Tbsp. chopped fresh chives

1. Saute onion in butter until onion is tender. Stir in meat and tomatoes.
2. Mix baking mix and water until soft dough forms. Pat dough into greased 12" pizza pan, pushing up at least 1/2" of dough around edge of pan.
3. Spread meat and vegetable mixture over dough. Sprinkle with cheese.
4. Beat together milk, eggs, salt, pepper, and dill until foamy. Pour over cheese. Sprinkle with chives.
5. Bake at 350° for 25-30 minutes, or until golden brown.
6. Delicious served with fresh fruit salad or freshly squeezed fruit juice.

Huevos Mexicajun

Barbara Corrales
Honeysuckle Farm Herbs
Lafayette, LA

Makes 2 servings

1 Tbsp. oil
1 medium onion, diced
1/2 sweet green pepper, diced
1-1 1/2 cups cooked and diced mixed vegetables: potatoes, broccoli, carrots, tomatoes
1 tsp. chopped fresh oregano (1/3 tsp. dried)
1 tsp. chopped fresh cilantro
1/4 tsp. cayenne or black pepper
pinch of salt
1/4 cup sliced chives or green onion tops
3 large eggs, slightly beaten
1/2 cup grated cheddar or Monterey Jack cheese (or combination)
Mexican salsa
tortillas

1. Saute onions and green pepper in oil until tender, about 5 minutes.
2. Stir in mixed vegetables, green pepper, oregano, cilantro, pepper, salt, and chives or green onions. Cover and heat thoroughly on low heat.
3. Pour eggs over vegetables, cover, and cook until eggs are set, about 3-5 minutes.
4. Sprinkle cheese over top. Remove from heat and let stand until cheese begins to melt.
5. Serve with a spoonful of Mexican salsa on top of cheese and with warm, buttered tortillas.

Quick Rice and Egg Stir-Fry

Nancy Raleigh
HBB
Belcamp, MD

Makes 2 servings

1/3 cup chopped red bell peppers
1/3 cup chopped mushrooms
1/3 cup chopped green onions
1 tsp. olive oil
1 clove garlic, minced
1 tsp. minced fresh ginger or
   1/2 tsp. ground ginger
1 cup cooked rice
1 Tbsp. soy sauce
3 eggs
1 Tbsp. water
1 1/2 Tbsp. fresh dill (1/2 Tbsp. dried), or
   1 1/2 Tbsp. fresh basil (1/2 Tbsp. dried)

1. Saute bell peppers, mushrooms, and onions in oil over medium high heat for 2 minutes.
2. Add garlic and ginger and stir-fry 1 minute more.
3. Add rice and stir-fry 2 minutes.
4. Blend soy sauce into rice/vegetable mixture.
5. Beat together eggs, water, and herbs until blended. Pour over rice mixture and stir-fry until eggs are firm.

Fried Peppered Grits with Sage

Stephen Lee
The Cookbook Cottage
Louisville, KY

Makes 6 servings

3 cups water
3/4 cup quick-cooking grits
1/4 tsp. salt
2 Tbsp. unsalted butter
1 Tbsp. freshly ground black pepper
1 Tbsp. chopped fresh sage
2 green onions, sliced thin
1/2 cup grated Gruyere cheese
2 Tbsp. olive oil
1 Tbsp. unsalted butter

1. Bring water to a boil. Slowly stir in grits and salt. Cover and reduce heat to medium-low. Cook for 5-7 minutes, or until thickened, stirring occasionally. Remove from heat.
2. Heat 2 Tbsp. butter over medium heat. Stir in pepper, sage, and green onions and cook for 3 minutes, stirring constantly.
3. Stir butter mixture and cheese into grits. Immediately spread grits in a greased 9" pie plate. Let cool to room temperature.
4. Heat oil and butter in large skillet over medium-high heat. Cut grits into 8 wedges. Fry wedges in hot fat for 3 minutes on each side, until golden and crisp on the outside. Drain on paper towel and serve hot.

Apple Delight with Herbs

Jacqui Savage and Norma Constien
Golden Creek Herbs
Perkins, OK

Makes 8 servings

1/2 cup milk
3 Tbsp. chopped fresh mint or lemon
   thyme (1 Tbsp. dried)
1 1/3 cups whole wheat flour, or
   2/3 cup white flour and
   2/3 cup whole wheat flour
1 rounded tsp. baking powder
3/4 tsp. ground cinnamon
1 2/3 cups peeled and chopped apples
1/4 cup chopped walnuts or pecans
1 egg
1/4 cup honey
3 Tbsp. butter or margarine

Crumb Topping:
2 Tbsp. butter or margarine
1/4 cup brown sugar
1/4 tsp. cinnamon
3 Tbsp. flour

1. In saucepan, mix together milk and herbs. Heat for 15 minutes. Do not boil.
2. Mix together flour, baking powder, and cinnamon.
3. Stir in apples and nuts until well coated with flour mixture.
4. Strain milk into measuring cup. If milk is less than 1/2 cup, add enough to fill a 1/2-cup measure. Pour into small bowl and add egg. Beat together.
5. Melt honey and 3 Tbsp. butter together over low heat. Pour into flour mixture.
6. Add milk and egg and stir just until dry ingredients are wet. Do not overmix.
7. Pour into greased 8" round cake pan.
8. Prepare Topping by mixing together butter, brown sugar, cinnamon, and flour until crumbly. Sprinkle over cake mixture.
9. Bake at 375° for 25-30 minutes.

Tip for Drying Herbs

Mary C. Wenger
Sassafras Hill Herbs
Kimmswick, MO

A good place to dry herbs is on a cake rack on top of the refrigerator. Place a paper towel on the rack, then one layer of herbs, and cover with another paper towel. The air currents around the refrigerator will dry the herbs, which are out of your way and take little of your time.

Soups and Stews

Easy Multi-Bean Soup

Davy Dabney
Dabney Herbs
Louisville, KY

Makes 16 servings

4 cups dry beans—a combination of
    Northern, navy, garbanzo, pinto, black,
    kidney, and/or lima, lentils and split
    peas, or use pkg. of bean soup mix
ham hock or 6-oz. can V8 juice
1/2 cup chopped onion
3 garlic cloves, minced
1/4 tsp. chopped fresh rosemary
    (1/8 tsp. dried)
15-oz. can tomato sauce
salt to taste
pepper to taste
crushed jalapeno pepper (optional)

1. Soak beans overnight in 4 quarts water.
   In the morning, add ham hock or V8
   juice to the beans and soaking water.
   Cover and simmer for 2-2 1/2 hours, or
   until beans and ham hock are tender.
3. Stir in onion, garlic, rosemary, and
   tomato sauce. Cover and simmer until
   onions are tender.
4. Season with salt, pepper, and jalapeno
   before serving.

White Bean Soup

Barbara Warren
Provincial Herbs
Folsom, PA

Makes 12 servings

1 lb. dry cannellini beans or
    48 oz. canned beans
3 oz. prosciutto or bacon
4 oz. carrots, diced
8 oz. red onion, diced
1 bay leaf
1 Tbsp. fresh rosemary
3 qts. chicken stock
salt to taste
pepper to taste
fresh sprig of rosemary

1. Soak dry beans overnight in water to soften. Use 4 cups water to 1 cup dry beans. Bring beans to boil in water in which they have soaked, cover soup pot, and simmer 2 to 3 hours, or until beans are tender but not mushy.
2. In large stockpot, saute prosciutto until fat is rendered. Stir in carrots, onions, bay leaf, and rosemary. Cook until soft.
3. Add beans and stock. Simmer until heated through.
4. Season with salt and pepper.
5. Garnish with a sprig of rosemary before serving.

Black Bean Soup

James O'Toole
O'Toole's Herb Farm
Madison, FL

Makes 8 servings

1 lb. dry black beans
10 cups water
1 large bell pepper, quartered, with seeds removed
1 large onion, chopped fine
1 large bell pepper, chopped fine
6 large garlic cloves, minced
2 Tbsp. extra virgin olive oil
3 tsp. salt
1 tsp. pepper
1$^{1}/_{2}$ tsp. chopped fresh oregano ($^{1}/_{2}$ tsp. dried)
$^{1}/_{2}$ cup green olives with pimento, cut in half
1 bay leaf
1$^{1}/_{2}$ tsp. sugar
4 Tbsp. juice from olive jar
2 Tbsp. red wine
half a large onion, chopped fine
half a bell pepper, chopped
fresh cilantro to taste
$^{1}/_{3}$ cup extra virgin olive oil, if desired

1. Wash beans. Cover beans with water and soak with one quartered bell pepper overnight.
2. Cook in soaking water for 1$^{1}/_{2}$ hours over medium heat, stirring occasionally, adding water if necessary, until beans are soft.
3. Saute onion, 1 chopped bell pepper, and garlic in 2 Tbsp. oil until soft. Add 1 cup softened beans and mash mixture.
4. Stir in salt, pepper, oregano, olives, bay leaf, and sugar. Allow to boil over low heat for 1 hour.
5. Add juice from olives and wine. Cook over low heat for an additional 20 minutes, or until soup has reached desired thickness.
6. Combine remaining finely chopped onion, bell pepper, and cilantro.
7. Remove soup from heat and remove bay leaf.
8. Pass the chopped onion, pepper, and cilantro to the diners to add to their individual soup bowls. Pass the olive oil so that each may drizzle oil over their soup, if they wish.

Tip for Growing Herbs

Linda Jani & Chris Aylesworth
Viewhurst Farm Herb & Garden Shop
Hebron, IN

Locating your kitchen garden close to your back door or close to the kitchen is essential. If you can't easily slip out and cut fresh herbs, you won't use them as much or as often.

Mexican Black Bean Soup

Carolee Snyder
Carolee's Herb Farm
Hartford City, IN

Makes 6 servings

1 cup diced onion
1 cup chopped carrots
1 cup diced celery
1 clove garlic, minced
1 Tbsp. oil
2 15-oz. cans black beans
3/4 cup water
2 Tbsp. mild taco sauce

Salsa:
4 plum tomatoes
6 tomatillos
1/4 cup chopped onion
juice of lime
dash of salt
1 jalopena pepper, finely chopped
1/2 cup chopped fresh cilantro

sour cream, optional

1. Saute onion, carrots, celery, and garlic in oil until tender.
2. Stir in beans, water, and taco sauce. Cover and simmer, stirring occasionally, for 30-45 minutes.
3. Place tomatoes, tomatillos, and onion in food processor. Chop coarsely. Add lime juice, salt, jalopena, and cilantro. Mix well. Chill.
4. Dip soup into bowls. Place a spoonful of salsa and a spoonful of sour cream on top of each bowl.

Tomato Basil Soup

Janet Melvin
Heritage Restaurant Gardens and Gifts
Cincinnati, OH

Makes 12 servings

2 Tbsp. butter or margarine
1/2 cup diced onion
1 Tbsp. minced garlic
2 cups chicken stock
2 28-oz. cans crushed tomatoes
2 cups heavy cream
1/4 cup chopped fresh basil
1 Tbsp. salt
1 1/2 tsp. white pepper
chopped fresh basil

1. Saute onions in butter until transparent.
2. Add garlic and saute for 1 minute.
3. Stir in remaining ingredients, and heat through. Make sure consistency of the soup is only a little thicker than heavy cream. If the soup is too thick, thin with half-and-half.
4. Serve hot with chopped fresh basil on top as garnish.

Basil-Tomato Soup

Sandie Shores
Herbs' Herbs and Such . . .
Rochester, MN

Makes 6 servings

3 Tbsp. butter
1 large carrot, shredded
1 large onion, chopped
4 large ripe tomatoes, peeled, seeded,
  and chopped
1/8 tsp. pepper
3/4 cup sugar
1/2 cup lightly packed fresh basil leaves,
  chopped
14 1/2-oz. can chicken broth
salt to taste
chopped parsley for garnish

1. Melt butter in 3-quart saucepan over
   medium heat. Stir in carrot and onion.
   Cook, stirring often, until onion is
   slightly soft.
2. Stir in tomatoes, pepper, sugar, and half
   of basil. Bring to boil, stirring to
   prevent sticking. Reduce heat. Cover
   and simmer for 15 minutes.
3. In blender or food processor, whirl the
   tomato mixture, a portion at a time,
   until smooth.
4. Return mixture to saucepan over
   medium heat. Stir in chicken broth,
   remaining basil, and salt. Heat.
5. Serve, garnished with parsley.

Tomato Soup with Lentils

Anne Walker
Sweet Annie Herbs
Centre Hall, PA

Makes 6 servings

1/2 cup dried lentils
1 clove garlic, minced
1/4 tsp. black pepper
2 Tbsp. extra virgin olive oil
4 medium tomatoes, cubed
1 medium green pepper, chopped
3 Tbsp. chopped fresh parsley
  (1 Tbsp. dried)
1 1/2 Tbsp. chopped fresh oregano
  (1/2 Tbsp. dried)
1 tsp. ground coriander
8 cups vegetable stock
1 Tbsp. tomato paste
1 tsp. brown sugar
pinch of cayenne pepper
salt to taste
1 Tbsp. burgundy

1. Cover lentils with water and simmer for
   45 minutes. Set aside.
2. Saute garlic and black pepper in oil for
   4-6 minutes. Stir in tomatoes and
   simmer for 20 minutes.
3. Stir in green pepper, parsley, oregano,
   coriander, and stock. Bring to boil.
   Lower heat and simmer until slightly
   reduced, about 30 minutes.
4. Drain lentils and add to soup.
5. Stir in remaining ingredients and
   continue to simmer for 20-30 minutes,
   stirring frequently.

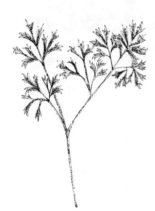

Quick Tomato Soup

Peggy Ritchie
Herbs and More
Ocala, FL

Makes 4-6 servings

2 Tbsp. butter or margarine
4 Tbsp. flour
3 cups chicken stock
3 cups home-canned tomato or V8 juice
3 large fresh tomatoes, peeled and diced
1 cup cooked rice
1/2 tsp. coriander
3 Tbsp. chopped fresh dill (1 Tbsp. dried)
1 Tbsp. raspberry vinegar, or vinegar of
   your choice
Parmesan cheese

1. Mix together butter and flour. Brown.
2. Add stock, stirring constantly.
3. Stir in juice and tomatoes. Bring to boil.
   Reduce heat and simmer for 5-10
   minutes.
4. Stir in rice, coriander, dill, and vinegar.
   Serve hot, sprinkled with Parmesan
   cheese.

Hearty Vegetable Soup

Sheryl Lozier
Summers Past Farms
El Cajon, CA

Makes 5-6 servings

1/2 cup diced onion
2 cloves garlic, minced
1/2 cup diced leek
1/2 cup diced celery
1/2 cup diced cabbage
1/2 cup diced carrot
8 Tbsp. butter
2 tsp. chopped fresh thyme (2/3 tsp. dried)
2 bay leaves
2 tsp. tomato paste
11/2 qts. vegetable stock
1/4 cup corn kernels
1/4 cup shredded spinach
1/4 cup sliced mushrooms
2 Tbsp. grated Asiago cheese
2 tomatoes, diced
12 oz. poached chicken breast, diced
2 tsp. chopped fresh parsley
   (2/3 tsp. dried)

1. In stockpot, mix together onion, garlic,
   leek, celery, cabbage, carrot, and butter.
   Cover with lid and cook for 2-3
   minutes, being careful not to brown
   vegetables while cooking.
2. Stir in thyme, bay leaves, tomato paste,
   and vegetable stock. Simmer for 20
   minutes.
3. Stir in corn, spinach, and mushrooms.
   Simmer for 3 minutes.
4. Remove soup from stove. Skim if
   necessary.
5. Ladle soup into warm soup bowls.
   Garnish with cheese, tomatoes, chicken,
   and parsley.

Minestrone Soup

Connie Johnson
Heartstone Herb Farm
Loudon, NH

Makes 6-8 servings

3 Tbsp. olive oil
2 large onions, chopped
4 garlic cloves, crushed
2 qts. chicken broth
1-lb. can tomatoes
1 cup shredded cabbage
2 large carrots, sliced
2 bay leaves
cayenne pepper to taste
3 tsp. chopped fresh basil (1/2 tsp. dried)
2 Tbsp. chopped fresh parsley
   (2 tsp. dried)
2 stalks fresh lovage
1-lb. can garbanzo beans
1-lb. can kidney beans
1 cup cooked pasta
grated cheese

1. In large saucepan, saute onions and garlic in oil. Cook until onions are transparent.
2. Add broth, tomatoes, cabbage, carrots, bay leaves, cayenne pepper, basil, and parsley. Cook until vegetables are tender.
3. Stir in lovage, garbanzo beans, kidney beans, and pasta. Simmer for 10 minutes.
4. Sprinkle with grated cheese and serve.

Hotch-Potch

Helen N. Lamb
Lavender Hill Herb Farm
Hockessin, DE

Makes 4-6 servings

2 cups young vegetables (carrots, turnips, cauliflower, or any combination you prefer), diced
2 quarts water or chicken broth
half a head of lettuce, shredded
1 cup fresh green peas
1 cup fresh lima beans
2-4 scallions, chopped
1/4 cup chopped fresh parsley
   (5 tsp. dried)
1 Tbsp. chopped fresh thyme
   (1 tsp. dried)
1 Tbsp. chopped fresh savory
   (1 tsp. dried)
1 tsp. salt
1/4 tsp. pepper
1 tsp. sugar

1. Place carrots, turnips, and cauliflower in water or broth. Simmer until tender.
2. Add lettuce, peas, lima beans, and scallions. Cook another 10 minutes.
3. Before serving, add parsley, thyme, savory, salt, pepper, and sugar. Heat to piping hot.

Tim's Stew

Tim Brown
Full Circle Farm
Rockford, TN

Makes 8-10 servings

3 cans whole kernel corn
5-6 large potatoes, diced
3 large yellow onions, chopped
4-5 cloves garlic, minced
2-3 dashes black pepper
2-3 dashes red pepper
2 cups water
8 oz. sliced or shredded sharp cheddar
   cheese
soy sauce to taste
3/4 tsp. chopped fresh thyme
   (1/4 tsp. dried)

1. Drain corn juice into large pot. Add
   potatoes, onions, garlic, and pepper.
   Add water. Simmer until potatoes are
   tender, 30-40 minutes.
2. Stir in corn, cheese, and soy sauce. Heat
   until cheese is melted.
3. Garnish with thyme and serve.

Tip for Using Herbs

Charles R. Fogleman
Ashcombe Farm and Greenhouses
Mechanicsburg, PA

For the person or family trying herbs
for the first time, start with only one
herb per dish and get your diners'
comments before adding more or
different herbs.

Vegetarian Chili

Nancy Ketner
Sweet Earth
West Reading, PA

Makes 8-10 servings

1/4 cup olive oil
1/3 cup tamari soy sauce
2 tsp. chili powder
1 Tbsp. cumin
1 lb. tofu, cut into 3/4" cubes
1 onion, diced
1 tsp. minced garlic
4 Tbsp. olive oil
1/2 tsp. mustard seeds
15-oz. can red kidney beans, drained,
   with liquid reserved
19-oz. can black beans, drained, with
   liquid reserved
20-oz. can crushed plum tomatoes
1/2 cup chopped fresh cilantro
2 Tbsp. chopped fresh basil
1 tsp. cayenne pepper

1. Mix together 1/4 cup olive oil, soy sauce,
   chili powder, and cumin. Pour over tofu
   and marinate for 30 minutes.
2. In skillet saute onion and garlic in 4
   Tbsp. olive oil. Stir in mustard seeds.
3. Remove tofu from marinade with slotted
   spoon. Add to skillet. Saute for 10
   minutes, until all sides are brown.
4. In a slow cooker, combine marinade,
   tofu-onion mixture, beans, tomatoes,
   cilantro, basil, cayenne, and enough
   bean liquid to just cover the
   ingredients.
5. Cook on low for at least 6 hours.
   Remove lid to thicken if desired.

Creamy Potato-Carrot Soup

Barbara Corrales
Honeysuckle Farm Herbs
Lafayette, LA

Makes 6-8 servings

1 large onion, chopped
1/2 cup chopped celery
3-5 cloves fresh garlic, minced
1 Tbsp. oil
6 carrots, chopped or sliced
2 medium potatoes, peeled and chopped
   or sliced
2 14 1/2-oz. cans chicken broth
1/3 cup fresh parsley (5 tsp. dried)
2 Tbsp. fresh lemon thyme (2 tsp. dried)
1 tsp. ground cumin
1/4-1/2 tsp. cayenne or black pepper, or
   combination
1/2-1 cup evaporated milk, skim or
   regular
salt to taste
finely sliced chives

1. In large kettle, saute onion, celery, and
   garlic in oil until onion wilts, about 5
   minutes.
2. Add chopped or sliced carrots and
   potatoes, chicken broth, parsley, lemon
   thyme, cumin, and pepper. Bring to boil.
   Reduce heat to medium-low. Cover and
   cook until vegetables are fork-tender,
   approximately 20 minutes. Remove from
   heat and cool enough to process
   vegetables in food processor or blender.
3. Puree soup in small batches. Return to
   kettle.
4. Add milk until desired consistency is
   reached. Season with salt. Heat to
   simmering on low heat.
5. Garnish with sliced chives just before
   serving.

Potato Soup

Marian E. Sebastiano
Salt Box Gallery Herbs
Hubbard, OH

Makes 8 servings

4 strips bacon, diced
2 cloves garlic
1/2 cup chopped onion
1 celery stalk chopped,
   or 1/4 tsp. celery salt
8 medium-sized potatoes, peeled and
   cubed
bay leaf
1 1/2" thick piece of Velveeta cheese
1 cup milk
salt to taste
pepper to taste
parsley leaves, or chopped fresh dill

1. Saute bacon until pan is coated with
   drippings.
2. Add garlic, onion, and celery. Saute until
   onion is transparent and bacon is still
   soft.
3. Add potatoes and bay leaf. Cover with
   water. Cook until potatoes test soft,
   about 15 minutes.
4. Mash potatoes or puree in a blender.
5. Stir in cheese, milk, salt, and pepper.
   Bring to boiling point.
6. Sprinkle with parsley or dill before
   serving.

French Onion Soup

Linda Kosa-Postl
Never Enough Thyme
Granite Fall, WA

Makes 4 servings

3 Tbsp. butter or margarine
1 Tbsp. olive oil
4-5 cups thinly sliced onions
1 tsp. salt
1/2 tsp. sugar
3 Tbsp. flour
6 cups beef bouillon
3 cups light red wine
1 bay leaf
1 1/2 tsp. chopped fresh thyme
  (1/2 tsp. dried)
salt to taste
pepper to taste

1. Cook onions in butter and olive oil over
   low heat for 15-20 minutes, covered,
   stirring occasionally.
2. Uncover and raise heat to medium. Stir
   in salt and sugar. Cook for 30 minutes,
   stirring frequently, until onions turn a
   golden brown.
3. Lower heat. Stir in flour to make a
   paste.
4. Add bouillon, wine, bay leaf, and thyme.
   Simmer for 20-30 minutes. Season with
   salt and pepper.

*Variation: Use white wine instead of red
wine for a more delicate taste.*

Essence of Mushroom Soup

Judy Kehs
Cricket Hill Herb Farm
Rowley, MA

Makes 6-8 servings

1/2 lb. fresh mushrooms, or 14-oz. canned
1 carrot, cut in small chunks
1 stalk celery, chopped, or 4 4"-sprigs of
  fresh lovage, chopped
2 Tbsp. chopped fresh parsley
  (2 tsp. dried)
2 tsp. chopped fresh tarragon
  (2/3 tsp. dried)
2 tsp. chopped fresh thyme (2/3 tsp dried)
1/2 cup water
10 oz. chicken broth
4 Tbsp. Madeira wine
sour cream for garnish

1. Cook mushrooms, carrot, celery, parsley,
   tarragon, and thyme in water until soft.
2. In blender, mix together vegetables and
   chicken broth. Blend until smooth.
   Return to pan and reheat.
3. Stir in Madeira. Serve garnished with
   dollop of sour cream

*Variation: Add slivers of fresh
mushrooms, freshly grated provolone
cheese, and a dash of white pepper as
garnishes.*

Fresh Minted Pea Soup

Ary Bruno
Koinonia Farm
Stevenson, MD

Makes 8 servings

3 cups fresh shelled peas
2 Tbsp. chopped fresh chives
1 tsp. chopped fresh mint
1 tsp. chopped fresh thyme leaves
4 Tbsp. chopped fresh Italian parsley
4 cups chicken stock
sea salt to taste

1. Process the peas, herbs, and 1 cup of stock in a blender until smooth.
2. Heat the rest of the stock to boiling. Stir in pea mixture.
3. Heat to simmer. Cook gently for 4-5 minutes. Salt and serve.

Variation: For a cream soup, substitute 1/2 cup heavy cream for 1 cup of stock. Add cream just before serving.

Yogurt Mint Soup

Gerry Janus
Vileniki—An Herb Farm
Montdale, PA

Makes 5 servings

2 cups plain yogurt
1 small cucumber, chopped
1/4 tsp. salt
dash of freshly ground pepper
2 Tbsp. chopped fresh mint leaves
3 Tbsp. chopped mint blossoms
mint blossoms

1. Place yogurt, cucumber, salt, and pepper in food processor or blender and process until smooth.
2. Stir in chopped mint and blossoms. Chill for at least 2 hours.
3. Garnish with additional mint blossoms just before serving.

Cool Cucumber Soup

Mark Silber
Hedgehog Hill Farm
Sumner, ME

Makes 4 servings

2 medium-sized cucumbers
1 cup buttermilk
1/4 cup chopped fresh parsley
2 tsp. chopped fresh chives
1 1/2 tsp. chopped fresh dill (1/2 tsp. dried)
6 fresh mint leaves (1/4 tsp. dried)
1/4 tsp. chopped fresh tarragon
   (1/8 tsp. dried)
2 tsp. lemon juice
1 1/2 cups yogurt
3 Tbsp. chopped fresh dill and mint leaves, combined

1. Peel cucumbers. Cut in half lengthwise and scoop out seeds. Cut flesh into chunks.
2. Place cucumbers, buttermilk, parsley, chives, dill, mint, tarragon, and lemon juice in blender. Blend until smooth and then transfer to a bowl.
3. Whisk in yogurt. Chill.
4. Sprinkle with dill and mint leaves before serving.

French Sorrel Soup

Janette Petersen
The Rose Herb Nursery
La Center, CO

Makes 4 servings

2 Tbsp. butter
1 medium onion, chopped
4 Tbsp. chopped fresh lovage leaves
   (4 tsp. dried)
4 Tbsp. chopped fresh French sorrel
   leaves (4 tsp. dried)
2 Tbsp. flour
2 cups chicken or vegetable stock
1 cup milk
salt to taste
pepper to taste

1. Saute onion in butter for 5 minutes,
   or until onions are soft.
2. Stir in lovage and French sorrel.
3. Stir in flour and cook for 1 minute,
   stirring constantly.
4. Gradually stir in stock. Cover and
   simmer gently for 15 minutes.
5. Stir in milk, salt, and pepper. Reheat
   slowly. Do not boil.

Cream of Zucchini Basil Soup

Debbie Tissot
Cottage Herbs
Albuquerque, NM

Makes 2 quarts

6-8 zucchini, chopped into 3/4" chunks
3-5 chicken bouillon cubes
1 large onion, chopped
3 Tbsp. butter or margarine
2 cloves garlic, minced
1/4-1/2 cup chopped fresh basil
   (11/2-3 Tbsp. dried)
1 Tbsp. chopped fresh tarragon
   (1 tsp. dried)
2 Tbsp. chopped fresh parsley
   (2 tsp. dried)
8 oz. cream cheese
freshly ground pepper to taste
salt to taste

1. In large kettle, mix together zucchini
   and bouillon cubes. Cover with water
   and bring to a boil.
2. Saute onion in butter until transparent.
   Add garlic and saute for several
   minutes. Stir into zucchini mixture.
3. Stir in basil, tarragon, and parsley.
   Reduce heat and simmer for 10
   minutes.
4. In blender or food processor, mix
   together a portion of soup and half the
   cream cheese. Blend until smooth. Add
   rest of cream cheese and blend until
   smooth. Return to pot and stir until
   cream cheese is dissolved.
5. Season with salt and pepper.

Crab and Sage Bisque

Martha Gummersall Paul
Martha's Herbary
Pomfret, CT

Makes 6 servings

6 scallions, finely chopped
4 Tbsp. unsalted butter
$1/3$ cup flour
3 cups milk
$1^1/2$ cups half-and-half
2 tsp. salt
$1/2$ tsp. ground mace
$1/2$ tsp. paprika
3 Tbsp. chopped fresh sage (3 tsp. dried)
Tabasco to taste
1 lb. crabmeat, picked over for shell and
    cartilage
paprika for garnish
chopped fresh sage for garnish

1. Saute scallions in butter until softened,
   3-4 minutes.
2. Blend in flour and cook over low heat
   for 5 minutes.
3. Stir in milk and half-and-half. Cook until
   just thickened.
4. Stir in spices, sage, and Tabasco. Mix
   well.
5. Fold in crabmeat. Heat gently, garnish
   with paprika and/or sage, and serve.

Fish Chowder

Linda E. Sampson Costa
Sampson's Herb Farm
East Bridgewater, MA

Makes 6 servings

1 large onion, chopped
1 Tbsp. butter
1 Tbsp. olive oil
2 cups water
1 large fresh or dried bay leaf
5 large potatoes, cut in small pieces
2 lbs. haddock or cod
10-12-oz. can evaporated milk
$1/2$ cup cream
2 Tbsp. flour
freshly ground black pepper
2 tsp. chopped fresh thyme
    ($2/3$ tsp. dried)
2 tsp. salt

1. In heavy stockpot saute onions in butter
   and oil until translucent, about 10
   minutes.
2. Stir in water, bay, and potatoes. Simmer
   10-15 minutes, until potatoes are
   almost soft.
3. Add fish to top of potatoes. Simmer for
   7-8 minutes until fish flakes easily.
4. Add milk.
5. Mix together cream, flour, pepper,
   thyme, and salt. Add to potato/fish
   mixture and stir gently. Heat through
   and serve.

New England Clam Chowder

Stephanie L. Distler
Sweet Posie Herbary
Johnsonburg, PA

Makes 18 servings

1 lb. bacon, diced
3 celery stalks, diced
2 medium onions, diced
1 large carrot, diced
1/2 tsp. lovage seeds
1/2 cup butter or margarine
1 cup flour
3 quarts water
2 cups chicken stock
2 6-oz cans minced clams, with juice
   reserved
1 Tbsp. chopped fresh thyme
   (1 tsp. dried)
1 Tbsp. chopped fresh parsley
   (1 tsp. dried)
3 fresh or dry bay leaves
4 medium potatoes, diced
2 cups milk
ground cayenne pepper (optional)

1. Saute bacon until almost crisp. Stir in celery, onions, carrots, and lovage seeds. Saute for 5 minutes.
2. Add butter. Stir until melted. Stir in flour.
3. Add water, chicken stock, clam juice (reserving clams), thyme, parsley, and bay leaves. Cover and simmer for 45-60 minutes.
4. Add potatoes. Simmer on medium heat for 10-15 minutes, or until potatoes are soft.
5. Add clams and simmer for 5 minutes.
6. Lower heat, pour in milk, and season with pepper.

Chicken Barley Soup

Candace Liccione
The Herbal Sanctuary
Royersford, PA

Makes 4 servings

de-boned chicken breast
2 quarts water
2 stalks celery, chopped
half a medium onion, chopped
2 carrots, chopped
1 leek, chopped
1/2 cup barley
coarse black pepper, to taste
1 Tbsp. chopped fresh thyme
   (1 tsp. dried)
1/4 cup chopped fresh parsley
   (5 tsp. dried)
2 Tbsp. chopped fresh sweet marjoram
   (2 tsp. dried)

1. Simmer chicken in water for 20 minutes. Remove meat and chop into bite-sized pieces.
2. Stir vegetables and barley into chicken broth and cook until barley is soft.
3. Add seasonings and herbs and bring to boiling point. Add chicken and serve.

Japanese Noodle Soup

Diane Tracey
Chestnut Herb Farm
North Ridgeville, OH

Makes 4 servings

6 cups vegetable broth
2 carrots, diced
2 celery stalks, diced
2 scallions, sliced
1 tsp. fresh dill or parsley
1¹/₂ tsp. fresh thyme (¹/₂ tsp. dried)
5 oz. Japanese bean noodles or
    soy noodles
sea salt to taste

1. Bring broth to boil. Add carrots and celery. Cover and bring to boil. Reduce heat and simmer about 10 minutes, or until vegetables are almost tender.
2. Turn up heat and add scallions, dill or parsley, thyme, and noodles. Stir to break noodles apart. Simmer, covered, until noodles are done (about 3 minutes). Serve immediately.

Tip for Storing Herbs

Barb Perry
Lizard Lick Organic Herbs
Huron, TN

Store herbs in glass, away from light and away from the oven. Keep them in a closet rather than displaying them on a shelf. They will maintain color and flavor longer under those conditions.

Autumn Bisque

Kathy Hertzler
Lancaster, PA

Makes 6 servings

1 lb. butternut squash
2 tart apples, peeled, cored, and cubed
1 medium onion, chopped
2 slices white or wheat bread, crusts
    removed and cubed
4 cups chicken broth
¹/₂ tsp. salt
¹/₄ tsp. pepper
1 tsp. fresh rosemary (¹/₄ tsp. dried)
1 tsp. fresh marjoram (¹/₄ tsp. dried)
2 egg yolks beaten with ³/₄ cup milk and
    ¹/₄ cup whipping cream
apple slices
fresh rosemary

1. Cut uncooked squash into quarters. Peel, seed, and cut into 1" cubes.
2. Combine squash, apples, onion, bread cubes, chicken broth, salt, pepper, rosemary, and marjoram in 4-quart saucepan. Bring to boil; then reduce heat and simmer uncovered for 35-40 minutes, or until squash and apples are tender. Remove from heat and cool slightly.
3. Spoon one-third of soup into blender container or food processor. Cover and blend or process until pureed. Repeat with remaining soup. Return to saucepan.
4. Reheat over low heat. Stir in milk mixture. Stir and heat just until it reaches the boiling point. Do not boil.
5. Garnish with apple slices and rosemary.

Harvest Stew

Jacqueline Swift
Rainbow's End Herbs
Perrysburg, NY

Makes 16 servings

1 1/2 lbs. venison or beef stewing meat
1 Tbsp. olive oil
10 medium-sized fresh tomatoes, peeled
   and chopped
2 medium onions, chopped
1 clove garlic, minced
2 cups water
1 tsp. salt (optional)
6 medium potatoes, quartered
4 carrots, cut in 2" chunks
2 cups fresh corn
2 cups fresh green beans, cut
3 celery stalks, sliced
1 cup small summer squash, sliced
1/4 cups snipped fresh parsley
freshly ground pepper

1. Brown meat in oil over medium-high
   heat.
2. Stir in tomatoes, onions, garlic, water,
   and salt. Bring to boil. Reduce heat,
   cover, and simmer for an hour.
3. Add potatoes, carrots, corn, green
   beans, and celery. Simmer 30 minutes
   more.
4. Stir in squash. Cook 10 more minutes.
5. Add parsley and fresh pepper.

Note: This soup freezes well.

Variation: In place of meat, substitute 1
lb. tofu mashed with soy sauce, oregano,
and rolled oats. Brown, then add
vegetables as directed above.

Rosemary Stew

Quailcrest Farm
Wooster, OH

Makes 4 servings

3 cups diced tomatoes
3/4 cup chopped celery
1/2 cup chopped fresh parsley
3/4 tsp. chopped fresh oregano
   (1/4 tsp. dried)
3/4 tsp. chopped fresh thyme
   (1/4 tsp. dried)
2 Tbsp. olive oil
salt to taste
pepper to taste
1 1/2 lbs. stewing beef cubes
2 Tbsp. butter or margarine
1 tsp. minced garlic
1/2 cup dry white wine
1 Tbsp. fresh rosemary (1 tsp. dried)

1. Mix together tomatoes, celery, parsley,
   oregano, thyme, oil, salt, and pepper.
   Bring to boil. Simmer 30 minutes. Put
   through food mill and set sauce aside.
2. Trim excess fat from meat. Heat butter
   in skillet and cook beef until it loses its
   red color. Stir in garlic. Pour into
   greased casserole.
3. Add wine to skillet. Cook over high heat
   until reduced by half. Pour wine,
   tomato sauce, and rosemary over beef
   in casserole. Cover and bake at 300° for
   2 hours, or until meat is tender.

Salads

Tomato Summer Salad

Kelly Stelzer
Elderflower Farm
Roseburg, OR

Makes 4 servings

4 large tomatoes
3 tsp. olive oil
1 1/2 Tbsp. fresh lemon juice
1 tsp. grated lemon peel
1/2 tsp. freshly ground black pepper
salt to taste (optional)
1/2 cup chopped fresh parsley
1/4 cup chopped green onions
1/2 cup chopped red or yellow bell
   peppers
1 cup cooked rice, mixed with
   1/4 tsp. saffron threads

1. Hollow out tomatoes and set shells aside. Save 1/4 cup of the pulp.
2. Mix together 1/4 cup tomato pulp, olive oil, lemon juice, lemon peel, pepper, and salt.
3. Mix together parsley, onions, peppers, and rice. Add tomato dressing and toss to coat vegetable/rice ingredients well.
4. Stuff tomatoes with rice mixture. Serve at room temperature.

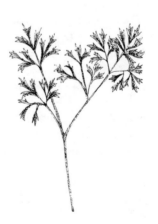

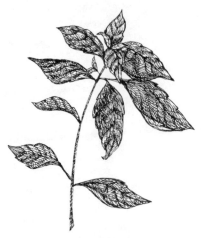

La Paix
Tomato/Basil Salad

Myra Bonhage-Hale
La Paix Farm Shop
Alum Bridge, WV

Makes 12 servings

3 large tomatoes (Pruden's Purple
   recommended)
18 leaves fresh Genovese basil
18 leaves fresh flat leaf parsley
1/4 lb. feta cheese, crumbled
1/2 cup wine vinegar
   (it's best with basil, Greek oregano,
   and garlic steeped in it)
4 Tbsp. olive oil
pinch of salt (optional)
1/2 tsp. cayenne pepper (optional)

1. Slice tomatoes and arrange on platter
   that has 4" deep bowl.
2. Place basil and parsley around outside
   edges and between tomatoes.
3. Sprinkle with cheese.
4. Mix together vinegar, oil, salt, and
   pepper. Drizzle over tomatoes.
5. Let stand for at least 3 hours before
   serving.

Italian Tomatoes
and Cheese

Elaine Seibel
Scents and Non-Scents
Hill, NH

Makes 4 servings

4 ripe fresh tomatoes, thinly sliced
1/2 lb. mozzarella cheese, thinly sliced
2 Tbsp. chopped fresh basil
1/2 cup Italian salad dressing

1. Alternately arrange slices of tomatoes
   and mozzaralla cheese on a plate,
   slightly overlapping slices.
2. Sprinkle basil over top. Chill.
3. Just before serving, pour salad dressing
   over tomatoes and cheese.

Tomato and
Mozzarella Salad

Jacoba Baker & Reenie Baker Sandsted
Baker's Acres
Groton, NY

Makes 4-6 servings

2 fresh ripe medium tomatoes, cored,
   and cut into 1/4" slices
1/2 cup packed fresh basil,
   washed and drained
2 Tbsp. olive oil
1 tsp. fresh lemon juice
1/4 tsp. salt
1/2 lb. mozzarella, cut into 1/4" slices

1. Arrange tomato slices in single layer
   on paper towel and let drain for
   15 minutes.

2. Place basil, oil, lemon juice, and salt in blender. Blend on low speed until basil is finely chopped.
3. Arrange tomato and mozzarella slices overlapping in alternate rows on large platter. Drizzle with basil sauce.
4. Cover loosely, and let stand at room temperature for 30 minutes before serving.

Marinated Tomatoes

Lewis J. Matt III
White Buck Farm
Holbrook, PA

Makes 4 servings

2 large tomatoes, sliced
2 thin slices from center of large sweet onion
clove of garlic, thinly sliced in julienne strips
1/4 cup chopped fresh basil (5 tsp. dried)
1/4 cup chopped fresh parsley (5 tsp. dried)
1/4 tsp. chopped fresh lemon thyme (pinch of dried)
1 cup balsamic vinegar
1/4 cup olive oil
1/2 tsp. freshly ground pepper

1. Arrange tomatoes and onion on a plate.
2. Mix together remaining ingredients. Pour over tomatoes.
3. Cover with plastic wrap and refrigerate overnight.

Herby Tomato and Cucumber Salad

Lorraine Hamilton
Lorraine's Herb Garden
Neelyton, PA

Makes 6-8 servings

2 medium-sized ripe tomatoes, cut in 3/4" chunks
1 medium-sized onion, cut in 1/4" chunks
1 medium-sized cucumber, cut in 1/2" chunks
8 oz. mozzarella cheese, shredded
3 Tbsp. olive oil
3 Tbsp. herb vinegar (chive, basil, or flower)
1/3 cup chopped fresh herb flowers— choose chive, basil, oregano, or a combination of any of those
herb flowers for garnish

1. Toss together tomatoes, onions, cucumbers, and cheese.
2. Drizzle oil and vinegar over vegetable mixture. Toss.
3. Add herb flowers and toss well.
4. Refrigerate for 1 hour. Garnish with additional fresh herb flowers and serve.

Tip for Using Herbs

Diane Tracey
Chestnut Herb Farm
North Ridgeville, OH

Replenish dried herbs for cooking yearly. Use old herbs in the bath as bath herbs. The heat from the water will release remaining oils in the herbs.

Sweet and Sour Cucumbers

Connie Butto
The Herb Shop
Lititz, PA

Makes 6 servings

3 medium cucumbers
$1/4$ cup sugar
$1/2$ cup cider vinegar
$1/4$ cup water
$1/2$ tsp. salt
$1/4$ tsp. coarsely ground black pepper
1 Tbsp. minced parsley

1. Peel cucumbers, and then score them lengthwise with fork. Slice very thin. Put on paper towels and blot dry.
2. Mix together sugar, vinegar, water, salt, pepper, and parsley. Add cucumbers and toss lightly.
3. Chill for several hours before serving.

Sudanese Cucumbers

Mary Peddie
The Herb Market
Washington, KY

Makes 6 servings

2 cups plain yogurt
1 cup finely chopped fresh mint
5 small cucumbers
salt
juice of lemon or lime

1. Mix together yogurt and mint. Cover and chill for several hours.
2. Slice cucumbers very thin. Salt lightly and place in refrigerator to chill. When cucumbers "wilt," rinse them in icy water and drain well.
3. Just before serving, add lemon to yogurt mixture. Pour over cucumbers. Toss gently to coat. Serve immediately.

Cucumbers with Dill

Barbara Steele & Marlene Lueriu
Alloway Gardens & Herb Farm
Littlestown, PA

Makes 6 servings

2 cups thinly sliced cucumbers
$1/2$ cup sour cream
2 tsp. vinegar
$1/2$ tsp. sugar
2 tsp. chopped fresh chives
2 tsp. chopped fresh dill

Mix together all ingredients. Chill several hours before serving.

Moroccan Cucumbers

Linda Jani and Chris Aylesworth
Viewhurst Farm Herb & Garden Shop
Hebron, IN

Makes 6 servings

2 large cucumbers
1/2 cup white wine vinegar, or white wine
    vinegar with mint and lemon balm
1/2 cup sugar
pinch of salt
1/4 cup chopped fresh mint leaves
    (5 tsp. dried)

1. Peel and slice cucumbers.
2. Mix together vinegar, sugar, and salt
   until sugar is dissolved.
3. Pour over sliced cucumbers. Mix well.
4. Chill for one hour before serving.
   Garnish with chopped mint.

Basic Salad with Vinaigrette Dressing

Jacqui Savage and Norma Constien
Golden Creek Herbs
Perkins, OK

1 garlic clove
assorted lettuce leaves, rinsed and dried
3-4 Tbsp. olive oil
1-2 Tbsp. chopped fresh herbs
    (basil, dill, tarragon, and/or thyme)
3-4 Tbsp. herbal vinegar, or white wine
    vinegar
cucumber, sliced
green onions, sliced
bell peppers, chopped
tomatoes, cut in wedges

1. Rub inside of serving bowl with garlic
   clove.
2. Break up lettuce into bite-sized pieces
   and place in bowl.
3. Sprinkle olive oil over lettuce. Toss.
4. Scatter minced herbs over lettuce. Toss.
5. Sprinkle herbal or white wine vinegar
   over salad.
6. Add cucumber, green onion, and
   peppers. Toss.
7. Garnish with tomatoes. Serve.

Mint Salad

Judith M. Graves
Lambs & Thyme at Randallano
Richmond, NH

Makes 4-6 servings

1 head lettuce, broken into bite-sized
    pieces
1/2 cup shredded carrots
1/2 cup lightly cooked peas
1/2 cup chopped fresh mint
1/2 cup vegetable oil
1/4 cup mint vinegar (see page 56)
1/4 cup chopped almonds or walnuts
1/4 cup raisins

1. Toss together lettuce, carrots, peas, and
   mint.
2. Whisk oil, vinegar, nuts, and raisins
   together. Pour over salad. Toss. Serve
   immediately.

Clarence's Basil Salad

Marty Mertens & Clarence Roush
Woodstock Herbs
New Goshen, IN

1 sweet onion, sliced in rings
salad greens, mixed in these proportions:
   1/3 fresh spinach, 1/3 fresh basil
   (green and opal mixed for color),
   1/3 red leaf lettuce
Italian dressing, or mixture of herbed or
   balsamic vinegar and olive oil

1. Toss together onion, spinach, basil, and
   lettuce.
2. Add desired amount of dressing and
   toss well.

Grapefruit Grandeur

Carol Turner
Turkey Trot Trunk
Mountain City, GA

Makes 4 servings

4 large handfuls seasonal greens
2 grapefruit, sectioned*
1 red or green bell pepper, cut in rings

Dressing:
1/4 cup olive oil
1/4 cup reserved grapefruit juice
1 tsp. balsamic vinegar
1 Tbsp. chopped fresh parsley
   (1 tsp. dried)
1 Tbsp. chopped fresh rosemary
   (1 tsp. dried)

1. Arrange a handful of salad greens on
   each plate. Top with grapefruit sections
   and rings of bell pepper.

2. Mix together dressing ingredients.
   Sprinkle over each salad before serving.

* To section a grapefruit easily, cut off its
top and bottom. Place on cutting board
and cut skin in strips, exposing fruit,
then insert knife in one side of dividing
membrane and flip out secions, one at a
time.

Tasty and Colorful Garden Salad

Diane T. Morris
The Morris Farm
Seaboard, NC

lettuce leaves
tomato, chopped
cucumber, sliced
onion, sliced
parsley in bite-sized pieces
basil leaves
chive blossoms
lovage leaves and stems
cilantro leaves and blooms
thyme leaves and blooms
dill leaves and blooms
1/3 cup opal basil vinegar
2/3 cup mayonnaise

1. Mix together lettuce, tomato, cucumber,
   onion, and other salad ingredients.
2. Add all or some herbs.
3. Mix together vinegar and mayonnaise
   (it will be pink) and serve with salad.

Greek Salad

Harriette Johnson &
Dianna Johnson-Fiergola
Mustard Seed Herbs & Everlastings
Spring Valley, WI

Makes 8 servings

1 lb. rotini, cooked
1 3/4-2 cups kidney beans, drained
1 3/4-2 cups garbanzo beans, drained
1 cup black olives, drained and sliced
1 pt. cherry tomatoes, cut in half
1 bunch green onions, sliced
2 cucumbers, diced
1 lb. feta cheese, crumbled
coarse black pepper to taste
salt to taste
1/4-1/2 cup herbal flavored vinegar,
   to taste

Gently toss together all ingredients.

Pasta Salad

Donna Treloar
Harmony
Gaston, IN

*Makes 12-20 servings, depending on the
number and amount of ingredients*

1 pkg. (12 or 16 oz.) angel-hair pasta,
   fettuccini, or thin vermicelli
1 cup Harmony Italian Dressing
   (see pg. 50)
Any or all of the following (to taste):
   green onions, sliced with tops
   diced red onion
   diced green, red, or gold peppers
   fresh ripe tomatoes, diced (or a can of
      drained, diced tomatoes, if
      preparing salad out of tomato
      season)
sliced black olives
diced water chestnuts
grated cheese (cheddar, Colby, or
   Parmesan)
frozen peas or small pea pods
chopped raw broccoli or cauliflower
grated or diced zucchini
chopped celery
sliced mushrooms
poppy or caraway seeds

1. Cook pasta according to package
   directions. Do not overcook! Drain and
   rinse with cold water.
2. Toss dressing with pasta. Cut through
   pasta several times with a sharp knife.
   Cover and refrigerate.
3. Mix together selection of remaining
   ingredients to your liking. Mix with
   pasta. Add more dressing as needed.
   Cover and refrigerate for at least
   8 hours.

*Note: This makes a large amount to take
to carry-ins and picnics. It keeps well in
the refrigerator and gets better with age.*

Variation 1: Add tuna or chicken.

*Variation 2: Add 3/4 cup mayonnaise to
Italian dressing.*

Dilled Potato Salad

Cynthia E. Palmer
Braeloch Farm
Richland, MI

Makes 6 servings

4 cups diced, cooked potatoes
1 cup diced celery
3 green onions, thinly sliced
3 Tbsp. cider vinegar
3 Tbsp. salad oil
1/4 tsp. seasoned salt
1/4 tsp. pepper
1 Tbsp. fresh dill (1 tsp. dried)
3/4 cup sour cream
1 green or red pepper, slivered

1. Mix together potatoes, celery, and onions.
2. Mix together vinegar, salad oil, seasoned salt, pepper, and dill. Pour over vegetables while potatoes are still warm and gently mix.
3. Refrigerate for several hours.
4. Mix in sour cream and pepper slices. Serve.

Dilly Potato Salad

Janet Melvin
Heritage Restaurant Gardens and Gifts
Cincinnati, OH

Makes 10 servings

5 Tbsp. tarragon vinegar
1 Tbsp. minced shallots
2 Tbsp. Dijon mustard
1/2 tsp. curry powder
3/4 cup olive oil
2 Tbsp. minced capers
1/2 cup minced carrots
1/2 cup minced celery
6 Tbsp. minced sweet gherkin pickles
1/2 cup minced green onions, including tops
1/2 cup minced green bell pepper
1/2 cup minced red bell pepper
1/4 cup minced fresh parsley (5 tsp. dried)
1/4 cup minced fresh dill (5 tsp. dried)
1 Tbsp. salt
1 tsp. black pepper
1 gallon cold water
1/4 cup salt
2 lb. new red potatoes, cut in 1" cubes

1. Mix together vinegar, shallots, mustard, and curry powder in food processor.
2. Slowly add olive oil to make a dressing.
3. Add capers, carrots, celery, pickles, onions, peppers, parsley, dill, salt, and pepper. Pulse quickly to combine. Add more oil and vinegar if needed until the mixture becomes a thick dressing.
4. Combine water and salt. Add potatoes, making sure there is enough water to cover them. Bring to boil. Turn down and cook just above a simmer until potatoes are barely fork-tender. Be careful not to overcook. Drain.
5. While potatoes are still warm, combine them with enough of the dressing to

lightly coat them. Cover and refrigerate. Refrigerate extra dressing for future use.

German Potato Salad

Kelly Stelzer
Elderflower Farm
Roseburg, OR

Makes 4-6 servings

1¹/2 lbs. small red potatoes
¹/4 cup rice or wine vinegar
1 Tbsp. sugar
1 Tbsp. prepared mustard
¹/2 cup plain yogurt
¹/2 cup mayonnaise
2 slices bacon, cooked, drained, and
   crumbled
³/4 cup green onions, chopped
¹/4 cup fresh parsley, chopped
¹/4 cup fresh dill (5 tsp. dried)
¹/8 tsp. freshly ground pepper

1. Steam potatoes until tender. Cool slightly and cut into quarters.
2. Mix together vinegar and sugar. Heat until sugar is melted and vinegar is clear. Remove from heat.
3. Whisk in mustard, yogurt, and mayonnaise. Pour over potatoes.
4. Add bacon, onions, pepper, parsley, dill, and pepper. Toss gently until well coated. Serve slightly warm.

Black Bean and Potato Salad

Harriette Johnson
and Dianna Johnson-Fiergola
Mustard Seed Herbs & Everlastings
Spring Valley, WI

Makes 6-8 servings

1 lb. tiny new red potatoes
15-oz. can black beans, drained
1 lb. smoked salmon, flaked
3 Tbsp. fresh dill, minced (3 tsp. dried)
¹/2 cup finely minced parsley
   (3 Tbsp. dried)
1 Tbsp. capers
1 large leek, chopped
4 Tbsp. herb vinegar
   (dill is especially good)
¹/4 cup olive oil
2 Tbsp. lemon juice
1 tsp. grainy mustard
1 tsp. Dijon mustard
salt to taste
freshly ground pepper to taste

1. Cook new potatoes in their skins. Cool and quarter.
2. To potatoes, add beans, salmon, dill, parsley, capers, and leek. Mix gently.
3. Mix together vinegar, oil, lemon juice, mustards, salt, and pepper. Add to salad and toss lightly.

Variations:
1. *Use smoked turkey and cilantro in place of salmon and dill.*
2. *Eliminate any meat and serve as a vegetable salad.*

Garbanzo Bean Herb Salad

Jacqui Savage and Norma Constien
Golden Creek Herbs
Perkins, OK

Makes 4 servings

1 clove garlic, minced
4¹/2 Tbsp. chopped fresh spearmint
  (1¹/2 Tbsp. dried)
2¹/2 Tbsp. fresh lime juice
1 Tbsp. white wine vinegar
3 Tbsp. olive oil
salt to taste
3 cups garbanzo beans, drained

1. Mix together all ingredients except beans. Whisk well.
2. Pour over beans and stir to coat. Let stand for 30 minutes or longer before serving.
3. Serve on a bed of lettuce.

Five Bean Salad

Jacoba Baker & Reenie Baker Sandsted
Baker's Acres
Groton, NY

Makes 8-10 servings

12 oz. frozen baby lima beans
12 oz. frozen green beans
12 oz. frozen yellow beans
14-oz. can kidney beans, drained and rinsed
1 can ceci beans, drained
1-2 red onions, cut in rings
³/4 cup sugar
³/4 cup oil
³/4 cup wine vinegar

1 Tbsp. chopped fresh parsley
  (1 tsp. dried)
1 Tbsp. chopped fresh oregano
  (1 tsp. dried)
1¹/2 tsp. chopped fresh basil
  (¹/2 tsp. dried)
1¹/2 tsp. chopped fresh thyme
  (¹/2 tsp. dried)
¹/2 tsp. salt

1. Cook lima beans, green beans, and yellow beans until tender. Cool.
2. Combine cooked beans with kidney beans, ceci beans, and onions.
3. Mix together sugar, oil, vinegar, parsley, oregano, basil, thyme, and salt. Toss with beans. Marinate overnight.

Italian Olive Salad

Donna Treloar
Harmony
Gaston, IN

Makes 25 servings

21-oz. jar green olives, drained
4 6-oz. cans ripe olives, drained
2 15-oz. cans garbanzo beans, drained
2¹/2 cups Harmony Italian Dressing
  (see page 50)
2 4-oz. jars pimentos, drained
2 large onions, cut in chunks, then separated
1 quart pepperoncini peppers, drained

1. Mix together all ingredients. Stir gently to coat with dressing.
2. Marinate in refrigerator for at least 8 hours. Stir occasionally.

Note: This works well as a carry-in dish for picnics. If you don't need a large amount, you can cut the recipe in half or in fourths.

Marinated Vegetable Salad

Gerry Janus
Vileniki—An Herb Farm
Montdale, PA

Makes 6 servings

pinch of salt
1/4 tsp. freshly ground pepper
dash of cayenne pepper
1 tsp. Dijon mustard
3 tsp. tarragon vinegar
1/2 cup olive oil
1 Tbsp. lemon juice
1 tsp. chopped fresh tarragon
1 tsp. chopped fresh lemon balm
4 tsp. chopped fresh chives
2 Tbsp. chopped fresh parsley
2 cloves garlic, minced
1 small head cauliflower
1 small bunch broccoli
2 carrots

1. Combine salt, peppers, mustard, vinegar, oil, and lemon juice in blender or food processor. Process until smooth. Stir in herbs and garlic.
2. Separate cauliflower and broccoli into serving-size pieces. Cut carrots into 3"-long, thin sticks. Steam vegetables lightly, until crisp tender.
3. Pour dressing over hot vegetables. Stir to coat well.
4. Refrigerate for several hours, turning vegetables occasionally.

Southwest Carrot Salad

Shari Jensen
Crestline Enterprises
Fountain, CO

Makes 4 servings

1 medium onion, peeled and diced
3 cups sliced carrots, cooked just until crisp-tender
1/3 cup white wine vinegar
2/3 cup olive oil
1 tsp. dry minced garlic
1 tsp. sugar
1 tsp. lemon juice
1 1/2 Tbsp. chopped fresh dill (1/2 Tbsp. dried)
1 1/2 Tbsp. chopped fresh cilantro
1 1/2 Tbsp. chopped Mexican oregano (1/2 Tbsp. dried)
salt to taste
pepper to taste

1. Mix together onion and carrots.
2. Mix together remaining ingredients. Pour over carrots and toss to mix. Cover.
3. Refrigerate for 24 hours before serving. Will keep in the refrigerator for up to 2 weeks.

Pea Salad with Fresh French Tarragon

Robin Giese
Riverview Farm
Fall City, WA

Makes 6-8 servings

4 cups frozen peas, thawed
1 cup sour cream
1 cup sliced almonds
1 medium-sized onion, chopped
3 Tbsp. fresh chopped tarragon
   (1 Tbsp. dried)
salt to taste
pepper to taste

Mix together all ingredients. Allow to stand
   for several hours before serving.

Freezer Slaw with Lovage

Jacqueline Swift
Rainbow's End Herbs
Perrysburg, NY

Makes 1¹/2 quarts

1 medium head green cabbage, shredded
   (about 10 cups)
1 carrot, shredded
1 red bell pepper, diced
1 tsp. salt
1 cup white wine vinegar
2 cups sugar or less, according to taste
1 tsp. celery seeds
1 tsp. mustard seeds
¹/2 cup fresh lovage leaves and
   tender stems

1. Combine cabbage, carrot, pepper, and
   salt. Let stand for one hour.
2. In saucepan, combine vinegar, sugar,
   celery seeds, and mustard seeds. Boil
   one minute. Cool.
3. Drain vegetables. Mix together
   vegetables, cooked dressing, and
   lovage. Stir gently. Chill.
4. Serve (the slaw will keep up to one
   week in the refrigerator), or freeze for
   later use.

*Note: This is a good way to use the
cabbage your garden produces beyond
what you are able to use immediately.*

Norm's Coleslaw

Kim Snyder
Kim's Kakes, Kuttings, and Kandles, too!
Ivesdale, IL

Makes 8 servings

large head of cabbage, chopped fine
2-3 carrots, grated
1 cup sugar
1/4 tsp. garlic salt
1/4 tsp. pepper
1/4 tsp. dill seeds or celery seeds
1/2 cup herbal vinegar
   (basil, rosemary, or tarragon)
1/3 cup oil

1. Mix together cabbage and carrots.
2. Sprinkle sugar, garlic salt, pepper, and dill seeds over cabbage.
3. Pour vinegar over mixture.
4. Stir in oil. Mix gently until sugar is dissolved.

Variation: Use one small head of red cabbage and one small head of green cabbage for a colorful slaw.

Barley, Corn, and Rosemary Salad

Brandon Brown
Brown's Edgewood Gardens
Orlando, FL

Makes 10 servings

6 cups water
1/4 tsp. salt
1 cup pearl barley
2 cups corn, steamed for 5 minutes
1/2 cup chopped fresh rosemary
1/2 cup minced green onion
1 red bell pepper, diced
1/4 tsp. chopped fresh parsley
1/4 cup olive oil
2 Tbsp. fresh lemon juice
2 Tbsp. vinegar
   (plum vinegar is especially good)

1. Bring water and salt to boil. Rinse barley and add to water. Simmer 40 minutes. Cool.
2. Stir in corn, rosemary, onion, bell pepper, and parsley.
3. Mix together oil, lemon juice, and vinegar. Pour over barley and vegetables and mix well.

Tabouli

Jacoba Baker & Reenie Baker Sandsted
Baker's Acres
Groton, NY

Makes 6-8 servings

1 cup dry bulgur
2 cups water
1/2 cup chopped scallions
2 large tomatoes, chopped
1/4 cup olive oil
1 tsp. salt
1 heaping tsp. crushed fresh garlic
1/2 cup chopped fresh mint
2 cups chopped fresh parsley
1/4 cup lemon or lime juice
freshly ground pepper to taste

1. Soak bulgur in water for 2 hours, or until all water is absorbed.
2. Stir in remaining ingredients, allow flavors to blend, and serve.

Wild Rice Salad with Mint

Dawn Ranck
Harrisonburg, VA

Makes 6-8 servings

1/2 cup uncooked white rice
1/2 cup raw wild rice
5 1/2 cups chicken broth
4 scallions, sliced thin
1/4 cup chopped fresh mint
grated rind of 1 orange
1 cup yellow raisins
1 cup chopped pecans
1/4 cup oil
1/3 cup orange juice
1 tsp. salt
1/4 tsp. pepper

1. Mix together white rice, wild rice, and chicken broth. Simmer uncovered for 40-50 minutes. Rice should not be too soft. Drain.
2. Mix together remaining ingredients. Gently stir into rice mixture.
3. Let stand at room temperature for 2 hours before serving, or refrigerate for at least 8 hours before serving.

Shatoiya's Tabouli

Shatoiya de la Tour
Dry Creek Herb Farm
Auburn, CA

Makes 8 servings

1 cup dry bulgur wheat (sometimes called cracked wheat)
1 1/2 cups boiling water
1 1/2 tsp. chopped fresh lemon balm (1/2 tsp. dried)
1 cup chopped fresh parsley (1/3 cup dried)
1/2 tsp. chopped fresh marjoram or oregano (1/4 tsp. dried)
4-7 garlic cloves, minced
half a medium-sized onion, finely chopped
1/4 cup lemon juice (more or less to taste, depending upon the amount of zing you like)
1/4 cup olive oil
2 tomatoes, chopped

1. If using dried herbs, blend with dry bulgur wheat. Pour boiling water over mixture. Cover and let stand for 30 minutes. Uncover and let cool. Mix in garlic, onions, lemon juice, and olive oil, blending well. Refrigerate 3-4 hours before serving.
2. If using fresh herbs, add them to the cooled soaked bulgur, along with garlic, onions, lemon juice, and olive oil. Mix all ingredients well. Refrigerate 3-4 hours before serving.
3. Add tomatoes just before serving.

Tuna Salad with Lovage

Judy Kehs
Cricket Hill Herb Farm
Rowley, MA

Makes 4 servings

9-oz. can white tuna, drained and flaked
1/2 cup cottage cheese
2 Tbsp. grated horseradish
2 Tbsp. chopped fresh lovage leaves
   (2 tsp. dried)
lettuce
sliced tomatoes
sliced cucumbers
bread
fresh parsley sprigs
lemon slices

1. Mix together tuna, cottage cheese, horseradish, and lovage.
2. Serve on lettuce, garnished with sliced tomatoes and cucumbers, or serve as open-faced sandwiches. Sprinkle with fresh parsley and serve with slices of lemon.

Herbed Tuna Salad

Lorraine Hamilton
Lorraine's Herb Garden
Neelyton, PA

Makes 4 servings

6 1/2-oz. can tuna, drained
1/2 cup chopped celery,
   or 1/4 cup minced fresh lovage
2 hard-boiled eggs, chopped
3 Tbsp. minced fresh herbs
   (1 Tbsp. dried)—choose dill, thyme,
   chives, parsley, or a combination of
   any of those

1-2 Tbsp. herb vinegar (chive, floral, dill
   and lemon balm, lemon thyme, or
   tarragon)
1/4 cup mayonnaise
herb flowers or nasturtium leaves

1. Mix together all ingredients.
2. Chill at least one hour.
3. Garnish with herbs or herb flowers or roll in nasturtium leaves and hold together with toothpicks.

Spring Tuna Salad

Carol Frank
Summer Kitchen Herbs
Allenton, WI

Makes 4 servings

6 1/2-oz. can tuna, drained
2 hard-boiled eggs, cut into small pieces
1 fresh French sorrel leaf, chopped
3 fresh lovage leaves, chopped
1 sprig tarragon leaves, chopped
8 chive stalks, chopped
1 cup cooked elbow macaroni
salt to taste
pepper to taste
1/2 to 3/4 cup mayonnaise or salad
   dressing
1/2 tsp. prepared mustard

Mix together all ingredients. Serve on lettuce leaves.

Fusilli with Tomatoes and Tuna

**Harriette Johnson &
Dianna Johnson Fiergola
Mustard Seed Herbs**
Spring Valley, WI

Makes 6-8 servings

1 lb. fusilli
2 cups diced red & yellow tomatoes
2 6$^{1}/_2$ -oz. cans tuna
$^3/_4$ cup chopped fresh basil
1 Tbsp. capers
$^1/_2$ tsp. salt
$^1/_2$ tsp. freshly ground pepper
$^1/_3$ cup basil vinegar
$^1/_4$ cup olive oil

1. Cook, drain, and chill fusilli.
2. Stir in tomatoes, tuna, basil, capers, salt, and pepper.
3. Stir together vinegar and oil. Toss with salad.
4. Refrigerate 30 minutes before serving.

Shrimp Salad

**Harriette Johnson &
Dianna Johnson-Fiergola
Mustard Seed Herbs & Everlastings**
Spring Valley, WI

Makes 12-14 servings

8 oz. cooked shrimp
3 tomatoes, diced
2 cucumbers, diced
1 red onion, sliced
6-oz. can black olives, sliced
2 tsp. chopped fresh dill
2 tsp. chopped fresh parsley
$^3/_4$ cup Italian dressing or $^1/_3$ cup herbal
   vinegar mixed with $^1/_4$ cup olive oil
freshly ground black pepper to taste
salt to taste
4-6 oz. feta cheese, crumbled

Mix together all ingredients in order listed
   and then serve immediately.

Curried Seafood Rice Salad

**Toni Anderson
Cedarbrook Herb Farm**
Sequim, WA

Makes 10-12 servings

Dressing:
$^1/_2$ cup mayonnaise
$^1/_2$ cup plain yogurt
3 Tbsp. chopped fresh spearmint
   (1 tsp. dried)
1 Tbsp. lemon juice
1 tsp. curry powder
$^1/_2$ tsp. salt
1$^1/_2$ tsp. fresh basil ($^1/_2$ tsp. dried)
dash of cayenne

3 cups cooked brown rice
8 oz. smoked salmon, flaked
1 cup sliced celery
10-oz. pkg. petite frozen peas, thawed
1/2 cup sliced green onion, including
  some tops
1/4 cup diced red bell pepper
1 pint cherry tomatoes, cut in half
3 hard-boiled eggs, chopped
1/4 lb. small salad shrimp
fresh spearmint sprigs

1. Mix together all dressing ingredients.
   Chill for 3 hours.
2. Combine rice, salmon, celery, peas,
   onions, pepper, and tomatoes. Mix well.
   Stir in eggs. Mix together lightly.
3. Chill for 3 hours.
4. Pour dressing over salad and gently mix.
   Garnish with shrimp and fresh
   spearmint sprigs.

Jill's Dill-icious Chicken Salad

Betty Leonard
Hampton Herbs
New Carlisle, OH

Makes 6-8 servings

1 lb. lettuce, shredded
1 1/2 lbs. (about 2 cups) cooked chicken
  breast, cubed
2 cups dry three-color pasta, prepared
  according to package directions
1 medium cucumber, sliced
1 medium red onion, sliced thin
10 oz. frozen peas, thawed
2 cups salad dressing
2-3 Tbsp. fresh dill
1 cup shredded cheddar cheese

1. Layer ingredients, except cheese, in
   order given.
2. Refrigerate for several hours until ready
   to serve.
3. Toss well. Sprinkle cheese over top.

Cold Ham and Chicken Potato Salad

Judy Kehs
Cricket Hill Herb Farm
Rowley, MA

Makes 4 servings

2 lbs. potatoes
1 cup chicken broth
2 cups chopped cooked chicken
2 cups chopped cooked ham
4 oz. sour cream
5 Tbsp. chopped fresh dill
  (1 1/2 Tbsp. dried)
1 cup mayonnaise
2 Tbsp. dark mustard
2 green onions, chopped
1 green pepper, chopped
cucumber slices
2 hard-boiled eggs, sliced

1. Cook potatoes in chicken broth until
   tender. Cool, peel, and cut in small
   cubes.
2. Combine chicken, ham, sour cream, dill,
   mayonnaise, mustard, onions, and
   pepper. Mix well.
3. Add potatoes and toss. Chill.
4. Serve garnished with sliced cucumbers
   and hard-boiled egg slices.

Tarragon Chicken Salad

Harriette Johnson &
Dianna Johnson-Fiergola
Mustard Seed Herbs and Everlastings
Spring Valley, WI

Makes 4-6 servings

1 lb. diced chicken or turkey breast
1 cup red grapes
1 cup green grapes
2 cups pea pods, cut in pieces
1 cup fresh tarragon leaves
  (5 Tbsp. dried)
1 cup mayonnaise
1 cup plain yogurt
3 Tbsp. lemon juice
3 Tbsp. tarragon vinegar
1 tsp. salt
freshly ground pepper to taste
salad greens
1 cup broken cashews

1. Mix together chicken, grapes, pea pods, and tarragon.
2. Mix together mayonnaise, yogurt, lemon juice, vinegar, salt, and pepper. Pour over chicken mixture and gently toss until well coated.
3. Serve on salad greens and top with cashews.

Strawberry Chicken Salad

Jan Mast
The Herb Shop
Lititz, PA

Makes 4-6 servings

1 lb. fresh spinach, torn into pieces
half head romaine lettuce
half head red leaf lettuce
3 chicken breasts, cooked and cubed
1 quart strawberries, sliced
1 honeydew melon, balled

Dressing:
1/3 cup oil
1/2 cup strawberry vinegar
1 Tbsp. sugar
1 tsp. poppy seeds
2 Tbsp. orange juice
1/2 tsp. grated onion
1 tsp. dry mustard
freshly grated lemon rind
1 tsp. fresh parsley

1. Toss spinach and lettuces together. Toss in chicken, strawberries, and melon balls.
2. Mix together all dressing ingredients. Pour dressing over salad just before serving.

Tip for Growing Herbs

Carol Frank
Summer Kitchen Herbs
Allenton, WI

Cover perennial herbs with straw or evergreen boughs after the first hard frost. Remove after the last spring frost. This will winter-ize herbs that might otherwise be lost.

Vegetables

Green Beans with Parsley and Mint

Diane Clement
Clement Herb Farm
Rogers, AR

Makes 6 servings

1½ lbs. fresh green beans
¼ cup extra virgin olive oil
3 Tbps. chopped fresh mint (3 tsp. dried)
3 Tbsp. chopped fresh parsley
   (3 tsp. dried)
salt to taste
freshly ground black pepper to taste
2 Tbsp. fresh lemon juice
4 tsp. grated lemon peel

1. Cook beans in salt water until tender. Drain. Refresh in bowl of ice water. Drain well.
2. Mix together oil, mint, parsley, salt, and pepper. Pour over beans. Toss.
3. Just before serving, mix in lemon juice and lemon peel. Serve at room temperature.

Great Green Beans

Carol Frank
Summer Kitchen Herbs
Allenton, WI

Makes 4 servings

1 quart fresh green beans
3 6" branches summer savory
3 sprigs parsley
1 clove garlic, minced
2 Tbsp. butter or olive oil

1. Cook beans in salt water until crisp-tender.
2. Strip leaves off stems of savory. Cut leaves off parsley. Chop herbs as fine as possible.
3. Drain beans. Toss with herbs, garlic, and butter or oil. Serve immediately.

Lima Beans Catalance

Judy Keas
Cricket Hill Herb Farm
Rowley, MA

Makes 4 servings

4 Tbsp. butter
1 cup bacon bits
16-oz. pkg. frozen lima beans or
   1 lb. parboiled fresh limas
1/4 cup onion, chopped
1 clove garlic, minced
1 bay leaf
1 tsp. chopped fresh mint (1/3 tsp. dried)
2 tsp. chopped fresh parsley
   (2/3 tsp. dried)
1/4 cup cooking sherry
1 cup chunks of cooked sausage

1. Saute bacon bits in butter. Remove
   bacon bits and add lima beans. Cover
   and cook on low heat for 10 minutes.
2. Add onion, garlic, bay leaf, mint, and
   parsley. Cover and cook on low heat for
   5 minutes.
3. Stir in sherry. Cover and cook for 10
   minutes.
4. Add sausage, mixing well. Cook
   uncovered for several minutes until
   beans are tender.
5. Serve garnished with bacon bits.

White Bean Casserole

Jennifer Lommen
Passion Flower Nursery
Christiansburg, VA

Makes 6-8 servings

2 cups dried white beans
4 medium onions, chopped or sliced thin
2 Tbsp. fresh basil, chopped
   (1 Tbsp. dried)
2 Tbsp. fresh parsley, chopped
   (1 Tbsp. dried)
1 Tbsp. fresh thyme (1 tsp. dried)
1 tsp. olive oil
salt and pepper to taste
4 slices toasted bread
1 Tbsp. olive oil
2 Tbsp. butter or margarine

1. Soak beans overnight in 8 cups water;
   then cook until soft, approximately
   2 to 3 hours.
2. Saute onions and herbs in 1 tsp. olive
   oil.
3. Mix together tender beans and sauteed
   onions and herbs. Place in greased
   casserole.
4. Blend bread and 1 Tbsp. olive oil in
   food processor. Sprinkle bread crumbs
   over vegetables.
5. Place chunks of butter or margarine
   over top.
6. Bake at 350° for 20-30 minutes.

Basil Refried Beans

Jacqueline Swift
Rainbow's End Herbs
Perrysburg, NY

Makes 6-8 servings

1 Tbsp. vegetable oil
1 Tbsp. butter or margarine
1½ cups diced onion
2 cloves garlic, minced
3 cups cooked pinto beans (any brown or
    red bean will do)
1 tsp. cumin
2 Tbsp. chopped fresh basil (2 tsp. dried)
1½ tsp. chopped fresh rosemary
    (½ tsp. dried)
pinch cayenne pepper
salt to taste
½ cup cheddar cheese

1. Saute onion and garlic in oil and butter
   for 10 minutes.
2. Add beans, cumin, basil, rosemary,
   pepper, and salt. Cook for 15 minutes.
3. Remove half of beans and mash or chop
   in blender. Stir in cheese until melted.
4. Mix together both bean mixtures and
   serve.

Rosemary Kabobs

Kathy Mathews
Heavenly Scent Herb Farm
Fenton, MI

Take a 12" sprig of rosemary. Strip off
¾ of foliage. Thread onto sprig slices of
zucchini, onions, cherry tomatoes,
mushrooms, and red or green peppers.
Marinate in low fat Italian dressing for
4 hours in refrigerator. Grill.

Harvard Beets with Dill

Dorothy Weaver & Pat Dyer
Village Herb Shop
Blue Ball, PA

Makes 4-6 servings

2 16-oz. cans beets, drained
⅓ cup sugar
2 Tbsp. flour
¼ cup water
¼ cup dill vinegar (see pg. 55)
1½ Tbsp. chopped fresh dill
    (½ Tbsp. dried)

1. Place beets in crockpot.
2. Mix together sugar and flour. Stir in
   water and vinegar, blending until
   smooth. Pour over beets.
3. Cover and cook on high for 3-4 hours,
   stirring once each hour.
4. Sprinkle with dill leaves before serving.

Broccoli with Capers

Mary Clair Wenger
Sassafras Hill Herbs
Kimmswick, MO

Makes 6 servings

1 large head of broccoli,
    or 24-oz. frozen broccoli
¼ cup butter
⅛ tsp. ground black pepper
2 tsp. capers
1½ tsp. chopped fresh oregano
    (½ tsp. dried)

1. Steam broccoli. Keep warm.
2. Melt butter in saucepan. Stir in pepper,
   capers, and oregano. Mix well.
3. Pour over broccoli. Serve.

Broccoli Corn Casserole

Gerry Bauman
The Farmhouse
Grimes, IA

Makes 6 servings

10 oz. frozen chopped broccoli, thawed
2 cups cream-style corn
1/2 cup cracker crumbs
1 egg, beaten
1/2 tsp. salt
1 1/2 tsp. chopped fresh rosemary
   (1/2 tsp. dried)
1 1/2 tsp. chopped fresh thyme
   (1/2 tsp. dried)
1/2 cup cracker crumbs
1 Tbsp. minced onion
dash of pepper
2 Tbsp. butter
4 slices chopped, cooked bacon

1. Combine broccoli, corn, 1/2 cup cracker crumbs, egg, salt, rosemary, and thyme in greased casserole dish.
2. Mix together 1/2 cup cracker crumbs, onion, pepper, and butter. Spread over casserole. Top with bacon.
3. Bake at 350° for 45 minutes.

Minted Carrots

Sandie Shores
Herb's Herbs and such . . .
Rochester, MN

Makes 4-6 servings

1 1/2 lbs. young carrots
1/4 cup butter
1 heaping Tbsp. sugar
2 Tbsp. chopped fresh spearmint
   (2 tsp. dried)

1. Cut carrots into quarters, slices, or julienne strips. Steam until tender. Drain.
2. Slowly melt butter in saucepan. Stir in sugar. Stir over low heat for 3-4 minutes until the mixture is faintly caramelized. Cover and let stand for 2 minutes.
3. Stir in chopped mint.
4. Add carrots and coat well.

Note: If using dried mint, add after butter is melted in Step 2.

Rosemary Glazed Carrots

Nancy Ketner
Sweet Earth
West Reading, PA

Makes 3-4 servings

12 carrots, peeled and sliced
1/4-1/3 cup rosemary honey *
3 Tbsp. butter
1 tsp. fresh rosemary (1/3 tsp. dried)

1. Cook carrots until tender but firm.
2. Mix together honey and butter until butter is melted.
3. Drain carrots. Toss in honey mixture. Sprinkle with rosemary.

* Rosemary Honey
Steep several sprigs of fresh rosemary in a light flavored honey for a week or more.

Carrots Tarragon

Irene L. Weidenbacher
Herbs in the Woods
Hollidaysburg, PA

Makes 4 servings

6 large carrots, peeled and cut into
   3"-long strips
2 Tbsp. butter
1/4 tsp. white pepper
3 Tbsp. chopped fresh tarragon
   (1 tsp. dried)

1. Steam carrots until tender.
2. While carrots are cooking, melt butter in saucepan. Add tarragon and white pepper and simmer at low temperature.
3. Drain carrots. Add butter and tarragon. Toss and serve.

Grilled Eggplant

Linda E. Sampson Costa
Sampson's Herb Farm
East Bridgewater, MA

Makes 2 servings

large sprig fresh rosemary
1/2 cup extra virgin olive oil
2 small, homegrown eggplants

1. Mix together rosemary and olive oil. Let stand for 15 minutes.
2. Cut eggplant into 1/4" slices.
3. Brush each slice with oil and grill for 3-5 minutes on each side, until nicely browned.

Herb Mushrooms on the Grill

Irene L. Weidenbacher
Herbs in the Woods
Hollidaysburg, PA

Makes 4 servings

8 large mushrooms, whole or sliced
2 Tbsp. butter
3 tsp. chopped fresh oregano
   (1 tsp. dried)
3 tsp. chopped fresh thyme (1 tsp. dried)
3 tsp. chopped fresh summer savory
   (1 tsp. dried) (optional)

1. Make a pocket out of aluminum foil.
2. Place mushrooms, butter, and herbs in foil. Fold tightly to seal.
3. Place mushrooms on grill. Shake every 5 minutes to avoid burning. Grill for approximately 20 minutes.

Mediterranean Onions

Barbara Warren
Provincial Herbs
Folsom, PA

Makes 4-6 servings

4 medium onions
1/2 tsp. pepper
dash of saffron or turmeric
1 Tbsp. chopped fresh parsley
   (1 tsp. dried)
1 Tbsp. chopped fresh chives
   (1 tsp. dried)
1 Tbsp. chopped fresh thyme
   (1 tsp. dried)
1 tsp. butter
1 tsp. olive oil

1. Cut onions into 1/4" thick slices.
   Separate into rings.
2. Combine onions, pepper, saffron,
   parsley, chives, and thyme.
3. Melt butter in large skillet. Add olive oil
   and onions. Cook for 25 minutes, or
   until onions are tender and brown.

Herb Peas

Betty Summers
Herbs 'n Things
Muskogee, OK

Makes 4-6 servings

1 lb. small peas
1 Tbsp. chopped fresh chives
   (1 tsp. dried)
1 Tbsp. chopped fresh sweet marjoram
   (1 tsp. dried)
dash of white wine
sprinkle of nutmeg

In saucepan, mix together all
ingredients. Bring to a boil and simmer
for about 1 minute.

Braised Peas with Mint

Anna L. Brown
Longfellow's Greenhouses
Manchester, ME

Makes 4 servings

2 tsp. vegetable oil
1 tsp. finely minced ginger (optional)
2 scallions, white part only, finely
   chopped
1 Tbsp. chopped fresh mint leaves
   (1 tsp. dried)
2 cups fresh or frozen peas

1. Heat oil in medium saucepan. Add
   ginger, scallions, and mint. Stir-fry
   briefly.
2. Add peas (if using fresh peas, add
   2 Tbsp. water).
3. Cover and simmer just till tender.

Mint-Liscious Peas

Carol Lacko-Beem
Herbs-Liscious
Marshalltown, IA

Makes 4 servings

16-oz. pkg. frozen peas
2 tsp. chopped onion
1 small garlic clove, minced
3 Tbsp. thinly sliced or diced sweet red
　pepper (optional)
1 1/2 tsp. chopped fresh mint
　(1/2 tsp. cut and sifted dried)
1 Tbsp. butter
3 Tbsp. chicken broth
pinch of Hungarian paprika

1. Cook peas, onion, garlic, and sweet
　pepper in small amount of water until
　just tender.
2. Stir in remaining ingredients. Mix well.
　Return to heat until butter is melted.
3. Serve immediately.

Herb Roasted Potatoes

Nancy Raleigh
HBB
Belcamp, MD

Makes 6-8 servings

3 lbs. new potatoes, cut in half
3 Tbsp. olive oil
1 Tbsp. chopped fresh thyme
　(1 tsp. dried)
1 Tbsp. chopped fresh rosemary
　(1 tsp. dried)
1 tsp. coarse salt
1/2 tsp. black crushed peppercorns
minced fresh herbs for garnish

1. Combine all ingredients except herbs
　for garnish. Toss well.

2. Arrange in single layer in baking pan.
3. Roast at 400° for 20 minutes. Turn and
　roast for 15-20 minutes, or until tender
　and golden.
4. Top with fresh herbs and serve.

Garlic-Thyme Oven Roasted Potatoes

Linda Hangren
LinHaven Gardens
Omaha, NE

Makes 6 servings

3 Tbsp. olive oil
6 large potatoes, peeled and cut in
　1" pieces
3 cloves garlic
1 1/2 Tbsp. chopped fresh thyme, lemon
　thyme, or dill (1 1/2 tsp. dried)

1. Pour olive oil in bottom of 9" x 13" pan.
2. Stir in potatoes and garlic. Stir to coat
　with oil.
3. Bake at 400° for 25 minutes. Remove
　from oven. Sprinkle with thyme and stir
　well.
4. Bake at 350° for 30-40 minutes, or until
　potatoes are tender.

Tip for Harvesting Herbs

Tim Brown
Full Circle Farm
Rockford, TN

Harvest herbs after the dew has
dried but before the heat of the day.

Herbed Potatoes

Kelly Wisner
Herbal Heaven
Wernersville, PA

Makes 3-4 servings

4 new red potatoes,
  cut in bite-sized pieces
2 tsp. oil
1¹/₂ tsp. chopped fresh sage
  (¹/₂ tsp. dried)
1¹/₂ tsp. chopped fresh rosemary
  (¹/₂ tsp. dried)
4 tsp. chopped fresh parsley
  (1¹/₃ tsp. dried)

1. Mix together potatoes and oil. Stir to coat. Place in baking pan.
2. Bake at 350° for 30 minutes.
3. Sprinkle with sage, rosemary, and parsley. Serve.

Polish Potatoes

Mary "Auntie M" Mizio Embler
Auntie M's Enchanted Garden
Clayton, NC

Makes 4-6 servings

¹/₂ cup butter
2 Tbsp. chopped fresh chives
  (2 tsp. dried)
2 Tbsp. chopped fresh parsley
  (2 tsp. dried)
3 Tbsp. chopped fresh dill (1 Tbsp. dried)
1 lb. potatoes,
  boiled and cut into bite-sized pieces
salt to taste
pepper to taste

1. In saucepan, mix together butter, chives, parsley, and dill.

2. Add potatoes and saute until heated through.
3. Salt and pepper to taste.

Fabulous Fingerlings

Carol Turner
Turkey Trot Trunk
Mountain City, GA

Makes 6 servings

1 lb. potatoes (fingerlings are preferred)
1 tsp. salt
4 Tbsp. butter
1 Tbsp. olive oil
6 Tbsp. chopped fresh parsley
  (2 Tbsp. dried)
6 Tbsp. chopped fresh chives
  (2 Tbsp. dried)

1. Cook potatoes and salt in large pot for 20-25 minutes, until tender. Drain.
2. Mix together butter, oil, parsley, and chives. Pour over potatoes. Toss until well coated. Serve immediately.

Variations: Use any of these herb combinations, in place of the parsley and chives: lovage and sage, rosemary and parsley, tarragon and chives, oregano and paprika.

Herbed Sliced Baked Potatoes

Louise Hyde
Well-Sweep Herb Farm
Port Murray, NJ

Makes 4 servings

4 medium potatoes
2 Tbsp. butter, melted
3 Tbsp. chopped fresh herbs: savory, thyme, chives, and/or rosemary (or use 3 tsp. assorted dried)
4 Tbsp. grated cheddar cheese
2 Tbsp. Parmesan cheese

1. Cut potatoes into thin even slices from top to bottom, being careful not to cut all the way through the bottom of the potatoes. Put potatoes in baking dish, fanning the slices slightly.
2. Drizzle with butter. Sprinkle with herbs, making sure to get them between the slices.
3. Bake at 425° for 45 minutes, or until done. Remove from oven.
4. Sprinkle with cheese. Return to oven until cheese is melted.

Dill Potatoes

Jane D. Look
Pineapple Hill Herbs & More
Mapleton, IL

Makes 6 servings

6-8 potatoes, cut in half
1 tsp. salt
4 sprigs fresh dill (2 tsp. dried)
3 Tbsp. butter
3 Tbsp. chopped fresh dill (3 tsp. dried)

1. Place potatoes in pan. Cover with water.
2. Add salt and sprigs of dill. Bring to boil. Reduce heat and simmer for 20-30 minutes, or until potatoes are soft. Drain water and discard dill sprigs.
3. Mix together butter and chopped dill. Pour over potatoes and serve.

Lemon Oregano Potatoes

Mary Ellen Warchol
Stockbridge Herbs & Stitches
South Deerfield, MA

Makes 6 servings

2 Tbsp. butter
4 lbs. Idaho potatoes, peeled and cut into 1½" chunks
⅓ cup chopped fresh oregano (5 tsp. dried)
salt to taste
pepper to taste
½ cup lemon juice
½ cup olive or vegetable oil

1. Melt butter in bottom of 9" x 13" baking pan.
2. In large mixing bowl, toss together potatoes, oregano, salt, pepper, lemon juice, and oil. Return to baking pan and spread in single layer.
3. Add water to cover the potatoes about ⅓ of the way up.
4. Bake at 400° for about 45 minutes, or until potatoes are golden brown and soft.

Rosemary Roast Potatoes

Doris Delatte
Homestead Horticulture
Elk, WA

Makes 4 servings

1/4 cup olive oil
2 cloves garlic, minced
1 Tbsp. chopped fresh rosemary
   (1 tsp. dried)
salt to taste
2 lbs. potatoes, cut in large chunks
chives or garlic chives for garnish

1. Mix together oil, garlic, rosemary, and salt.
2. Roll potatoes in herb oil until coated. Transfer to shallow baking dish. Pour any remaining oil over potatoes.
3. Bake at 400° for 45 minutes, or until potatoes are tender and brown. Garnish with finely chopped chives.

Rosemary Potatoes

Madeline Wajda
Willow Pond Farm
Fairfield, PA

Makes 8 servings

8 large potatoes
1/2 cup olive oil
4 large garlic cloves, minced
salt to taste
pepper to taste
3 Tbsp. chopped fresh rosemary
   (1 Tbsp. dried)

1. Cut each potato into 8 spears.
2. Toss together potatoes, oil, garlic, salt, and pepper. Marinate at room temperature for 30 minutes.

3. Spread potatoes on baking sheet.
4. Bake at 350° for 45 minutes, tossing occasionally.
5. Sprinkle with rosemary and continue roasting until potatoes are crusty brown, about 15-20 minutes.

Rosemary Pan-Fried Potatoes

Linda Jani and Chris Aylesworth
Viewhurst Farm Herb and Garden Shop
Hebron, IN

Makes 6 servings

4 medium red potatoes, unpeeled but cubed
2 Tbsp. olive oil
2 Tbsp. chopped fresh rosemary
   (2 tsp. dried)
salt to taste

1. In non-stick pan, saute potatoes in oil until tender.
2. Add rosemary and salt during last 2-3 minutes of cooking.

Rosemary Baked Potatoes

Elizabeth O'Toole
O'Toole's Herb Farm
Madison, FL

Bake potatoes 3/4 of cooking time. Remove from oven. Pierce each potato 3-4 times with a sharp knife. Insert a sprig of rosemary in each gash. Wrap each potato in aluminum foil and return to oven until tender.

Oven-Fried Rosemary Potatoes

Connie Slagle
Rustic Garden Herbs
Roann, IN
Jim O'Toole
Madison FL

Makes 4 servings

2 lbs. russet potatoes, cut in 1/4" slices
1/2 cup olive oil
1 1/2 tsp. salt
freshly ground coarse black pepper
handful of fresh rosemary sprigs,
    1 1/2-2" long
3-4 cloves of garlic

1. Dredge both sides of potato slices in oil.
2. Place in slightly oiled 9" x 13" baking dish and sprinkle with salt and pepper.
3. Lay 1 or 2 rosemary sprigs on each potato slice. Fill in all the empty spaces between potato slices with sliced garlic cloves.
3. Cover and bake at 400° for 20-25 minutes. Remove cover, and turn potatoes over with a metal turner. Bake for an additional 20 minutes, or until potatoes are tender and golden brown.
4. Drain any excess oil and move potatoes onto serving platter, turning potatoes so their rosemary sides are up.

Potato Slices with Rosemary and Cheese

Mary Ellen Wilcox
SouthRidge Treasures Herb Shop
Scotia, NY

Makes 4 servings

4 medium-sized potatoes, unpeeled and
    sliced
2 tsp. vegetable oil
1 Tbsp. chopped fresh rosemary
    (1 tsp. dried)
1/4 tsp. paprika
3/4 cup shredded cheddar cheese with
    jalapeno peppers, or
    Monterey Jack cheese with jalapeno
    peppers

1. Place potatoes in shallow microwave-safe baking dish. Brush with oil.
2. Sprinkle with rosemary and paprika. Stir to coat potatoes. Cover with waxed paper.
3. Microwave on High for 10-12 minutes, stirring twice, until potatoes are almost tender.
4. Sprinkle with cheese. Cover and let stand for 5 minutes, until cheese is melted and potatoes are tender.

Hot Potato Salad

Elaine Seibel
Scents and Non Scents
Hill, NH

Makes 4 servings

1¹/₂ lbs. small new potatoes, cut in
   chunks
1 Tbsp. vegetable oil
4 cloves garlic, minced
4 sprigs fresh rosemary
1 Tbsp. herbal vinegar
2 Tbsp. Dijon-style mustard
¹/₄ tsp. black pepper
2 green onions, sliced

1. Combine potatoes with oil. Place in
   roasting pan. Top with garlic and sprigs
   of rosemary.
2. Bake at 400° for 30 minutes, stirring
   often.
3. Whisk together vinegar, mustard,
   pepper, and onions.
4. Pour over hot potoates. Stir and serve
   warm.

Sage Potatoes

Linda E. Sampson Costa
Sampson's Herb Farm
East Bridgewater, MA

Makes 4 servings

4-6 Red Bliss or new potatoes, cut in bite-
   sized pieces
2 Tbsp. butter
1 tsp. finely chopped fresh sage
salt to taste
freshly ground pepper to taste

1. Simmer potatoes in salt water until
   tender. Drain.
2. Add butter, sage, salt, and pepper. Toss
   well and serve.

Creamy Potatoes

Karen Ashworth
The Herb Shoppe
Duenweg, MO

Makes 8 servings

8 medium-sized potatoes, sliced thin
²/₃ cup chopped bell pepper
¹/₂ cup chopped fresh parsley
   (2¹/₂ Tbsp. dried)
6 Tbsp. minced scallions
2 Tbsp. grated fresh Parmesan cheese
4 Tbsp. cornstarch
3 Tbsp. margarine
dash of pepper
3 cups milk

1. Put thin layer of potatoes on bottom of
   greased baking dish.
2. Mix together pepper, parsley, scallions,
   cheese, and cornstarch. Pour half of
   mixture over potatoes. Dot with
   margarine. Repeat layers.

3. Season with pepper, and pour milk over top. Cover.
4. Bake at 350° for 90 minutes, or until done.

Herbed Potato Pie

Georgia Pomphrey
Full Circle Farm
Rockford, TN

Makes 8 servings

6-8 medium-sized potatoes
1 cup cottage cheese
1¹/₂ cups shredded sharp cheddar cheese
7 eggs
2 small green onions, chopped
   (include stems)
4 drops hot sauce
³/₄ tsp. salt
dash of pepper
³/₄ tsp. chopped fresh oregano
   (¹/₄ tsp. dried)
³/₄ tsp. chopped fresh thyme
   (¹/₄ tsp. dried)
³/₄ tsp. chopped fresh marjoram
   (¹/₄ tsp. dried)
³/₄ tsp. chopped fresh chives
   (¹/₄ tsp. dried)

1. Cook potatoes until soft. Cool, peel, and grate.
2. Add remaining ingredients to grated potatoes. Stir well.
3. Pour into greased 9" x 13" casserole dish. Refrigerate for at least 8 hours.
4. Bake at 350° for 30 minutes, or until firm. Cut into squares and serve.

Baked Stuffed Potatoes

Elaine Seibel
Scents and Non-Scents
Hill, NH

Makes 4 servings

4 baking potatoes
²/₃ cup sour cream
3 Tbsp. chopped fresh parsley
   (1 Tbsp. dried)
2 Tbsp. chopped fresh dill
   (2 tsp. dried)
1 Tbsp. chopped fresh chives
   (1 tsp. dried)
paprika to taste

1. Bake potatoes at 400° for 45-60 minutes, or until soft. Remove from oven. Cut in half lengthwise.
2. With spoon, scoop out potato, leaving shell intact.
3. Mix together hot potatoes, sour cream, and herbs. Mash until smooth and creamy. Spoon mixture back into potato skins. Sprinkle with paprika.
4. Place on baking sheet. Bake at 400° for 25 minutes, or until piping hot.

Note: These freeze well. After stuffing potato skins, place on cookie sheet or in a flat container, cover, and freeze. Before serving, bake at 400° for 30 minutes, or until heated through.

Potato Herb Stuffing

Lewis J. Matt III
White Buck Farm
Holbrook, PA

Makes 8 servings

4 celery stalks with leaves, chopped
1 large onion, chopped
1 clove garlic, minced
4 large potatoes, cooked and diced
1/4 lb. butter or margarine
1 quart vegetable or meat broth
6 eggs
10 slices whole wheat bread, diced
1/2 cup chopped fresh parsley
   (2 1/2 Tbsp. dried)
1 Tbsp. chopped fresh basil (1 tsp. dried)
1 1/2 tsp. chopped fresh thyme (1/2 tsp.
   dried)
1 1/2 tsp. chopped fresh lemon thyme
   (1/2 tsp. dried)
1 tsp. freshly ground pepper
3/4 tsp. salt
water

1. Saute celery, onion, garlic, and potatoes
   in butter. Cover with lid and steam until
   tender.
2. Beat together broth and eggs. Add
   bread, herbs, pepper, and salt. Mix
   completely.
3. Stir in celery mixture. If not moist, add
   water and stir in gently.
4. Press mixture into greased casserole
   dish.
5. Cover and bake at 350° for 1 hour.
   Uncover and bake until top begins to
   brown.
6. Serve with any gravy, or allow to cool
   and slice and serve cold. Excellent with
   currant or cranberry jelly, chutney, or
   relish.

Bean and Potato Thyme

Lucy Scanlon
Merrymount Herbs
Norris, TN

Makes 4 servings

3 cups water
3 tsp. instant bouillon
8 onions, 1" in diameter*
12 small new potatoes, 1" in diameter *
1 1/2 tsp. chopped fresh rosemary
   (1/2 tsp. dried)
3 cups snap beans, cut in 1" pieces
8 medium mushrooms, sliced
1 1/2 Tbsp. chopped fresh thyme
   (1/2 Tbsp. dried)
melted butter or margarine
freshly ground black pepper to taste

1. Boil together water and bouillon.
   Reduce heat slightly. Add onions and
   simmer for 4 minutes.
2. Stir in potatoes and rosemary. Simmer
   about 10 minutes more, or until onions
   and potatoes are almost soft.
3. Stir in green beans, mushrooms, and
   thyme. Continue gentle simmer until
   beans are crisp-tender.
4. Drain liquid. Stir butter or margarine
   into vegetables. Grind pepper over top.

** Or use large-sized potatoes and onions
and cut them in 1" cubes.*

Pan Roasted Vegetables with Rosemary & Garlic Chives

Ary Bruno
Koinonia Farm
Stevenson, MD

Makes 6-8 servings

1¹/₂ lbs. small, new potatoes, cut in half
3-4 Tbsp. olive oil
¹/₄ cup water
1 lb. small zucchini or other green
    summer squash, 4"-6" long
1 sweet red bell pepper, cored and cut in
    ¹/₄"-wide strips
1 lb. eggplant, peeled and sliced thin*
4 Tbsp. chopped fresh garlic chives
    (4 tsp. dried), or
    3 Tbsp. fresh chives (1 Tbsp. dried),
    plus 1 garlic clove, minced
1 Tbsp. minced fresh rosemary
    (1 tsp. dried)
16-oz. can chickpeas, drained and rinsed
pinch of sugar
sea salt to taste
black pepper to taste
¹/₄ cup water
¹/₂ cup grated fresh Parmesan cheese

1. Saute potates in oil for 2-3 minutes. Add
   ¹/₄ cup water and cover. Cook until
   water is mostly evaporated, about 8-10
   minutes.
2. Cut zucchini in matchstick-sized strips.
   Add to potatoes, along with pepper,
   eggplant, and garlic. Saute until brown.
3. Stir in rosemary, chickpeas, sugar, salt,
   and pepper. Add ¹/₄ cup water. Cook
   about 4 minutes, or until vegetables are
   tender, stirring occasionally.
4. Serve with Parmesan cheese.

If using regular, dark purple or Japanese eggplant, slice it 30 minutes before cooking time and soak it in salt water to remove its bitterness. Squeeze gently to remove excess water before sauteeing.

Roasted Vegetables

Nancy Raleigh
HBB
Belcamp, MD

Makes 8 servings

4 large potatoes, unpeeled, cut in chunks
1 medium-sized onion, cut in wedges
3 Tbsp. vegetable oil
¹/₂ tsp. salt
bunch of baby carrots
pattypan or yellow neck squash, cut into
    chunks
¹/₂ lb. green beans
2 large red peppers, cut into chunks
2 large yellow peppers, cut into chunks
1 Tbsp. chopped fresh thyme
    (1 tsp. dried)
1¹/₂ tsp. chopped fresh basil
    (¹/₂ tsp. dried)
¹/₂ tsp. ground pepper
1 large lemon, thinly sliced

1. In large roasting pan, toss potatoes,
   onion, oil, and salt.
2. Roast at 425° for 15 minutes.
3. Add carrots, squash, beans, peppers,
   thyme, basil, black pepper, and half the
   lemon slices.
4. Return to oven and roast for 45
   minutes, turning occasionally.
5. Arrange vegetables on platter and
   garnish with remaining lemon slices.

Note: Use any mix of vegetables. Sweet potatoes are also good.

Summer Veggie Bake

Eone Riales
Fogg Road Herb Farm
Nesbit, MS

Makes 8-10 servings

6 Tbsp. butter
3 medium-sized yellow squash, trimmed
  and sliced thin
10 oz. fresh spinach, washed and
  trimmed
3 medium-sized tomatoes, sliced
1 cup cream-style cottage cheese
1¹/₂ cups saltine cracker crumbs
3 tsp. chopped fresh lemon thyme
  (1 tsp. dried)
3 slices cheese, cut into strips

1. Saute squash in 2 Tbsp. butter. Set
   aside.
2. Saute spinach lightly in 2 Tbsp. butter.
   Set aside.
3. Saute tomatoes lightly in 2 Tbsp. butter.
   Set aside.
4. Mix together cottage cheese, cracker
   crumbs, and thyme in small bowl.
5. Place squash in shallow baking dish.
   Cover with half of cottage cheese
   mixture. Place spinach on top. Cover
   with remaining cottage cheese mixture.
   Top with sliced tomatoes. Arrange
   cheese strips over tomatoes in crisscross
   fashion.
6. Bake at 350° for 30 minutes.

Vegetable Stir-Fry

Karen Ashworth
The Herb Shoppe
Duenweg, MO

Makes 4 servings

1 cup red onions, chopped
1 cup carrots, cut in pieces
1 cup broccoli, cut in pieces
1 cup cauliflower, cut in pieces
2 garlic cloves, minced
1¹/₂ tsp. fresh basil (¹/₂ tsp. dried)
¹/₄ tsp. cumin
2 Tbsp. margarine
¹/₂ cup almonds, blanched and chopped
¹/₄ cup sunflower seeds
2 Tbsp. soy sauce

1. Saute vegetables, garlic, basil, and
   cumin in margarine for 5 minutes.
2. Stir in almonds. Cover and cook
   3 minutes.
3. Add sunflower seeds and soy sauce. Stir.
   Cover. Cook 2 minutes.
4. Serve over rice or any other cooked
   grains.

Spaghetti Squash Primavera

Shari Jensen
Naturalicious Products
Fountain, CO

Makes 4 servings

1 medium spaghetti squash
2 medium carrots, diced
2 cups broccoli florets
2 cups quartered mushrooms
1 medium zucchini, diced
1/2 cup chopped green onion
1 Tbsp. olive oil
2 cups peeled, seeded, and diced Roma
    or beefsteak tomatoes
1/2 cup chopped fresh basil leaves
    (3 Tbsp. dried)
1/2 cup chopped fresh parsley
    (3 Tbsp. dried)
4 Tbsp. grated fresh Parmesan cheese
1 clove garlic, minced
1 tsp. salt
pepper to taste

1. Prick skin of squash about 8 times. Place on cookie sheet.
2. Bake at 350° for 90 minutes, or until tender when pierced with fork. Let cool for 20 minutes.
3. Halve lengthwise. Remove seeds. With fork, scrape spaghetti-like strands of squash into a large pan. Set aside.
4. While squash is baking, cook carrots and broccoli until tender. Put in ice water to cool quickly.
5. Saute mushrooms, zucchini, and green onions in 1 Tbsp. olive oil until tender, about 6 minutes.
6. Add squash, carrots, and broccoli. Heat until hot.
7. Combine tomatoes, basil, parsley, Parmesan cheese, garlic, salt, and

pepper. Pour over squash mixture. Heat through and serve.

Baked Lentils with Cheese

Jan Mast
The Herb Shop
Lititz, PA

Makes 6 servings

13/4 cups lentils, rinsed
2 cups water
1 bay leaf
2 tsp. salt
1/4 tsp. pepper
1/2 tsp. chopped fresh marjoram
    (1/8 tsp. dried)
1/2 tsp. chopped fresh sage
    (1/8 tsp. dried)
1/2 tsp. chopped fresh thyme
    (1/8 tsp. dried)
2 large onions, chopped
2 garlic cloves, minced
2 cups canned tomatoes
2 large carrots, sliced 1/8" thick
1/2 cup thinly sliced celery
1 green pepper, chopped
2 Tbsp. parsley
3 cups shredded cheddar cheese

1. Combine lentils, water, bay leaf, salt, pepper, marjoram, sage, thyme, onions, cloves, and tomatoes in 9" x 13" baking dish. Cover tightly.
2. Bake at 375° for 30 minutes.
3. Uncover and stir in carrots and celery. Cover and bake for 40 minutes.
4. Stir in green pepper and parsley. Sprinkle cheese on top. Bake, uncovered, for 5 minutes, or until cheese melts.

Herbed Tomato Bake

Leslie Scott
Once Upon a Thyme
Troy, NY

Makes 6 servings

3 medium-sized tomatoes
margarine or butter
1¹/₂ tsp. chopped fresh basil
1¹/₂ tsp. chopped fresh oregano
1¹/₂ tsp. chopped fresh parsley
1¹/₄ cups grated Parmesan cheese
³/₄ cup fine-crumb bread crumbs
salt to taste
pepper to taste

1. Cut tomatoes in half around the middle. Place in baking dish, skin side down. Cut small slits across the top of each tomato, without cutting through the skin, to allow ingredients to bake in.
2. Place a chunk of margarine on each half.
3. Mix together herbs, Parmesan cheese, and bread crumbs. Sprinkle herb mix, salt, and pepper on each tomato.
4. Bake at 325° for 20-25 minutes.

Sauteed Green Tomatoes

Jacoba Baker & Reenie Baker Sandsted
Baker's Acres
Groton, NY

Makes 4 servings

6 medium-sized green tomatoes
¹/₂ cup flour
salt to taste
pepper to taste
3 Tbsp. butter or bacon drippings
2¹/₂ Tbsp. flour
1 cup milk
2 tsp. chopped fresh basil (²/₃ tsp. dried)

1. Slice tomatoes in ¹/₄" slices. Dredge slices in flour and season with salt and pepper.
2. In skillet, saute tomatoes in butter until browned. Remove to platter and keep warm while making sauce.
3. To make sauce, add flour to skillet and mix well. Cook briefly. Blend in milk, stirring until thickened. Add basil.
4. Pour sauce over tomatoes and serve hot.

Royal Spinach

Jennifer Shadle
The Spice Hunter, Inc.
San Luis Obispo, CA

Makes 3-4 servings

2 Tbsp. butter
4 oz. mushrooms, cleaned and sliced
1 lb. fresh spinach, cleaned and drained
1 Tbsp. fresh dill (1 tsp. dried)
1 Tbsp. sour cream
salt to taste
pepper to taste

1. Saute mushrooms in butter for 3 minutes.
2. Add spinach and stir for 2 minutes.
3. Stir in dill and continue heating for another minute, until spinach is soft and water has evaporated.
4. Remove pan from heat. Fold in sour cream. Mix well. Stir in salt and pepper.

Baked Herb Spinach

Jane D. Look
Pineapple Hill Herbs & More
Mapleton, IL

Makes 4 servings

1 lb. fresh spinach,
　or 10-oz. pkg. frozen spinach
2 eggs, beaten
1/2 cup milk
1 cup grated cheddar cheese
1 cup cooked rice
1/4 cup chopped onion
2 Tbsp. butter or margarine
1/2 tsp. Worcestershire sauce
1 tsp. salt
1 1/2 tsp. chopped fresh thyme
　(1/2 tsp. dried)

1. Cook and drain spinach. Set aside.
2. Combine remaining ingredients. Stir in spinach. Pour into greased casserole dish.
3. Bake at 350° for 20-25 minutes, or until set.

Herbed Rice

Maria Price-Nowakowski
Willow Oak Flower and Herb Farm
Severn, MD

Makes 4 servings

1 1/3 cups dry rice
1 Tbsp. olive oil
1 Tbsp. butter or margarine, melted
1 quart hot chicken stock
salt to taste
pepper to taste
3 Tbsp. chopped fresh lemon balm
　(1 Tbsp. dried)
1 Tbsp. chopped fresh fennel or dill
　(1 tsp. dried)

1 Tbsp. chopped fresh lemon thyme
　(1 tsp. dried)
1/2 tsp. cinnamon
3 Tbsp. chopped fresh parsley
　(1 tsp. dried)
1/2 tsp. cumin

1. Saute rice in olive oil and butter over medium heat for 5 minutes, stirring constantly. Reduce heat to low and add 1 cup chicken stock. Stir well. Season to taste with salt and pepper.
2. Cook rice, uncovered, over low heat for 18-20 minutes, adding 1/2 cup stock every 5 minutes and stirring well at each addition. Continue cooking until rice is al dente and slightly creamy. (It may not be necessary to use all the stock.)
3. Remove from heat and stir in herbs and seasonings. Serve immediately.

Rice Pilaf

Connie Slagle
Rustic Garden Herbs
Roann, IN

Makes 4 servings

1 Tbsp. chopped fresh sage (1 tsp. dried)
1 Tbsp. chopped fresh rosemary
　(1 tsp. dried)
2 Tbsp. chopped fresh parsley
　(2 tsp. dried)
1/2 tsp. garlic powder
1 cup dry rice
2 1/2 cups water
1 Tbsp. butter or margarine

1. Mix together herbs, garlic powder, and dry rice.
2. Add water and butter or margarine. Cover and microwave on High for 5 minutes. Microwave on Power 5 for 15 minutes. Stir and serve.

Main Dishes
Grains, Meats, Poultry, and Fish

Herb Rice Pilaf

Ernestine Schrepfer
Herbal Scent-sations
Trenton, MO

Makes 6 servings

1/2 tsp. dried rosemary
1/2 tsp. dried thyme
1/2 tsp. dried marjoram
1/2 tsp. dried celery
1/2 tsp. dried garlic
2 tsp. chicken or beef bouillon granules
scant tsp. seasoned salt
1 Tbsp. chopped dry onion
2 Tbsp. parsley flakes
dry rice

1. Mix together all ingredients except rice. Store in sealed container.
2. To use, mix 1 cup dry rice with 3 Tbsp. seasoning. Cook as directed on rice package.

Variation: Lightly steam 1/4 cup chopped broccoli, 1/4 cup chopped red bell pepper, and 1/4 cup sliced scallions. Toss with cooked herb rice and serve.

Wild Rice with Herbs

Kathy Little Star
Indian River Herb Co.
Millsboro, DE

Makes 4 servings

1 cup dry wild rice
4 cups water
1/2 tsp. sea salt
2 Tbsp. butter or margarine
1 cup thinly sliced mushrooms
2 whole wild onions, minced
2 tsp. chopped fresh parsley
   (2/3 tsp. dried)
2 tsp. chopped fresh sage (2/3 tsp. dried)
2 tsp. chopped fresh basil (2/3 tsp. dried)
2 tsp. chopped fresh marjoram
   (2/3 tsp. dried)
2 tsp. chopped fresh thyme
   (2/3 tsp. dried)
1/2 cup diced tomatoes
salt to taste
pepper to taste

1. In large saucepan, combine rice and water. Bring to boil. Reduce heat to

medium-low. Cover and cook until rice is tender and water is absorbed, about 45-60 minutes. Remove from heat and let sit 5 minutes.

2. Saute mushrooms in butter over medium-low heat until tender. Stir in onions, herbs, tomatoes, salt, and pepper. Continue cooking for 3-5 minutes. Remove from heat.

3. Pour over rice and mix well. Serve hot.

Herb Lover's Risotto ✓

Nichol Sheridan
Sweet Annie Herbs, Inc.
Centre Hall, PA

Makes 4 servings

3 pints chicken stock
2 shallots, chopped
2 Tbsp. butter
1³/4 cups dry arborio rice
2 Tbsp. butter
10-12 Tbsp. chopped mixed fresh herbs
 (choose from basil, chervil, chives,
 marjoram, mint, parsley, small amount
 of sage, tarragon, and/or thyme)
salt to taste
freshly ground black pepper to taste
1 cup grated Parmesan cheese

1. Bring stock to simmer.
2. In a separate saucepan, saute shallots in butter. Add rice and stir. Add one cup hot broth. Simmer until rice is sticky.
3. Continue adding stock, ¹/2 cup at a time, until risotto becomes creamy.
4. Stir in 2 Tbsp. butter and the mixed herbs. Season with salt and pepper. Add a few tablespoons Parmesan cheese. Cover and let simmer for a few minutes.
5. Serve immediately. Top with remaining Parmesan.

Zucchini Torte

Mary Clair Wenger
Sassafras Hill Herbs
Kimmswick, MO

Makes 8 servings

1 cup grated carrots
5 cups peeled, diced zucchini
1¹/2 cups biscuit mix
¹/2 cup grated Parmesan cheese
1 small onion, grated
4 eggs, beaten
¹/2 cup olive oil
salt to taste
pepper to taste
2 tsp. chopped fresh parsley or marjoram
 (²/3 tsp. dried)

1. Mix together all ingredients. Pour into greased 9" x 13" baking dish.
2. Bake at 350° for 45-50 minutes until lightly browned.
3. Cut into squares and serve either hot or cold.

Pasta with Fresh Tomatoes

Flo Stanley
Mililani Herbs
Mililani, HI

Makes 4 servings

4-5 medium, very ripe, red tomatoes, cut
   into 1/2" pieces
1/4-1/2 tsp. crushed red pepper (optional)
1 tsp. sugar
1 whole head garlic, peeled, sliced
   1/4" thick
1-2 Tbsp. extra virgin olive oil
salt to taste
pepper to taste
1/2 cup basil mint pesto
   (see recipe on page 57)
1/2 cup freshly grated Parmesan or
   Romano cheese (optional)
1 lb. dry spaghetti, linguine, or penne,
   cooked

1. Mix together tomatoes, red pepper,
   and sugar in large serving bowl. Cover
   and let stand at room temperature for
   1-2 hours.
2. Saute garlic in oil until golden, stirring
   constantly. Remove garlic and stir into
   tomatoes. Allow oil to cool.
3. Stir salt, pepper, and pesto into tomato
   mixture.
4. Add drained, hot pasta to tomatoes. Add
   garlic oil and cheese. Toss well. Serve
   warm or at room temperature.

*Variation: Instead of basil mint pesto,
add 1/2 cup chopped fresh basil and 1/2
cup chopped fresh mint to tomato mixture
before tossing with pasta.*

Fresh Basil and Tomato Sauce

Robin Giese
Riverview Farm
Fall City, WA

*Makes about 3 cups sauce,
or 3-4 servings*

5 large tomatoes, peeled, seeded, and
   chopped
1 cup chopped fresh basil
2 Tbsp. fresh lemon juice
1/2 cup olive oil
1 clove garlic, minced
salt to taste
pepper to taste
8 oz. dry spaghetti or linguini, cooked
grated Parmesan or Romano cheese

1. Mix together tomatoes, basil, lemon
   juice, olive oil, garlic, salt, and pepper.
2. Toss with hot pasta. Serve topped with
   grated cheese.

*Variation: To add more flavor, toss capers,
a chopped chili pepper, black olives, and a
few anchovies into tomato-basil mixture.*

Tip for Using Herbs

Dawn Ranck
Harrisonburg, VA

Before beginning to cook a meal, I
cut bunches of herbs from my herb
garden and arrange them in a vase on
my counter. I can then clip off the
herbs I need for cooking and for
decorating my food. The remaining
herbs make a nice bouquet to brighten
up the kitchen.

Fresh Garden Pasta

Susan Cameron
The Herb College
San Antonio, TX

Makes 4 servings

4 large tomatoes, chopped
1 bell pepper, chopped
1 large onion, chopped
10 cloves garlic, minced
1 Tbsp. oil
1/3 cup chopped fresh basil
1 tsp. chopped fresh rosemary
2 fresh bay leaves
12 oz. dry pasta, cooked

1. Saute tomatoes, pepper, onions, and
   garlic in oil. Cover and cook for 20
   minutes, or until vegetables are tender.
2. Stir in basil, rosemary, and bay. Cook for
   10 minutes. Pour over pasta and serve.

Fresh Tomato Spaghetti Sauce

Charles R. Fogleman
Ashcombe Farm and Greenhouses
Mechanicsburg, PA

Makes 2 quarts

3-4 Tbsp. olive oil
4 cloves garlic, minced
1 small onion, minced
6 lbs. fresh plum tomatoes, skinned and
   quartered, or 2 28-oz. cans tomatoes
salt to taste
pepper to taste
1 tsp. chopped fresh oregano
   (1/3 tsp. dried)
2 tsp. chopped fresh thyme
   (2/3 tsp. dried)
2 tsp. chopped fresh marjoram
   (2/3 tsp. dried)
4 fresh basil leaves, minced

1. Saute garlic and onion in olive oil.
2. Add tomatoes and their liquid to garlic
   and onion. Break up tomatoes.
3. Stir in salt, pepper, oregano, thyme, and
   marjoram. Bring mixture to a gentle
   simmer and cook uncovered for
   30 minutes, stirring occasionally.
4. Stir in basil leaves and simmer for
   5 more minutes.
5. Serve over spaghetti or other pasta.

*Note: This spaghetti sauce can be made
one or two days in advance of serving,
but stop with Step 3. Cool and store in
refrigerator. When ready to use, add basil
leaves, bring to a simmer for five minutes
and serve.*

*Variation: Add 1-2 lbs. browned ground
beef or turkey to sauteed garlic and
onion.*

Angel-Hair Pasta with Fresh Tomatoes and Basil

**Harriette Johnson and
Dianne Johnson-Fiergola
Mustard Seed Herbs and Everlastings**
Spring Valley, WI

Makes 4-6 servings

1 lb. dry angel-hair pasta
1 Tbsp. olive oil
3-4 garlic cloves, minced
5 cups diced fresh tomatoes
3-4 Tbsp. chopped fresh basil
   (3-4 tsp. dried)
3/4 cup chicken broth
1/2 cup grated fresh Parmesan cheese
salt to taste
freshly ground pepper to taste

1. Cook pasta according to directions on package. Drain.
2. Mix together remaining ingredients and toss with pasta.

Penne with Tomatoes, Olives, and Two Cheeses

**Diane Clement
Clement Herb Farm**
Rogers, AR

Makes 6-8 servings

3 Tbsp. olive oil
1 1/2 cups chopped onion
1 tsp. minced garlic
3 28-oz. cans Italian plum tomatoes,
   drained
2 tsp. dried basil
1 1/2 tsp. dried crushed red pepper
2 cups low-salt chicken broth

salt to taste
pepper to taste
1 lb. dry penne or rigatoni pasta
3 Tbsp. olive oil
2 1/2 cups grated Havarti cheese
1/3 cup sliced, pitted, brine-cured olives
   (such as Kalamata)
1/3 cup grated Parmesan cheese
1/4 cup finely chopped fresh basil

1. Saute onion and garlic over medium high heat in 3 Tbsp. olive oil until onion is translucent, about 5 minutes.
2. Stir in tomatoes, dried basil, and crushed red pepper. Bring to a boil, breaking up tomatoes with back of spoon.
3. Add chicken broth. Bring to a boil. Reduce heat to medium and simmer about 60-70 minutes, stirring occasionally, until mixture thickens to a chunky sauce and is reduced to 6 cups. Season with salt and pepper.
4. Boil pasta until tender, but still firm to bite. Drain well.
5. Toss pasta with 3 Tbsp. oil.
6. Pour sauce over pasta and toss to blend. Stir in Havarti cheese.
7. Transfer pasta to greased 9" x 13" baking dish. Sprinkle with olives and Parmesan cheese.
8. Bake at 350° for 30 minutes, until pasta is heated through.
9. Sprinkle with fresh basil.

Gardener's 10 Minute Fresh Tomato and Herb Sauce with Black Olives

Ary Bruno
Koinonia
Stevenson, MD

Makes 4-6 servings

2-2¹/2 lbs. vine- ripened tomatoes
1 Tbsp. fruity olive oil
1 lb. dry pasta
2 large cloves garlic, minced
1 large sweet onion, chopped
1 sweet red, yellow, or green bell pepper,
   cored and sliced in lengthwise strips
2 Tbsp. fruity olive oil
2 tsp. chopped fresh oregano
   (²/3 tsp. dried)
¹/2 tsp. chopped fresh rosemary
   (¹/4 tsp. dried)
1 Tbsp. chopped fresh parsley
   (1 tsp. dried)
¹/2 cup pitted, sliced black olives
sea salt to taste
¹/4 tsp. sugar
¹/4 cup chopped fresh basil (5 tsp. dried)
¹/2 cup freshly grated Parmesan cheese
1 Tbsp. fruity olive oil

1. In 6 quarts water parboil tomatoes for
   1-2 minutes, until skins start to split.
   Remove from water.
2. Add 1 Tbsp. olive oil and pasta to water.
   Cook according to package directions.
   Drain and keep warm.
3. Skin and coarsely chop tomatoes.
4. Saute garlic, onion, and peppers in
   2 Tbsp. oil for 3-4 minutes.
5. Add tomatoes, oregano, rosemary,
   parsley, olives, salt, and sugar. Cook
   until tomatoes are soft and sauce begins
   to develop, about 5 minutes. Turn off
   heat and add basil.

6. Pour sauce over pasta, sprinkle with
   Parmesan cheese and 1 Tbsp. olive oil,
   and serve.

Garlic Pasta

Sheryl Lozier
Summers Past Farms
El Cajon, CA

Makes 4-5 servings

¹/4 cup olive oil
2 Tbsp. minced garlic cloves
2 medium onions, chopped
1 large bell pepper, chopped
2 large fresh tomatoes, cored and
   chopped
1 quart canned whole, peeled tomatoes
¹/4 cup chopped fresh basil (5 tsp. dried)
2 Tbsp. chopped fresh oregano
   (2 tsp. dried)
1 bay leaf
2 tsp. sugar
salt to taste
pepper to taste
1 lb. dry fettucine, cooked al dente and
   drained under cold water
chopped fresh parsley for garnish
grated Parmesan cheese

1. Saute garlic in olive oil until lightly
   golden. Stir in onion and bell pepper.
   Saute for 5-7 minutes, until onion is
   translucent.
2. Stir in fresh tomatoes, canned tomatoes,
   basil, oregano, bay leaf, sugar, salt, and
   pepper.
3. Cook, uncovered, over medium heat for
   10-15 minutes, stirring frequently.
4. Add cooked pasta and toss. Serve with
   Parmesan cheese and garnish with
   parsley.

Tomato Sauce with Garlic and Basil

Anna L. Brown
Longfellow's Greenhouses
Manchester, ME

Makes 3-4 servings

1 Tbsp. olive oil
5 garlic cloves, minced
1 Tbsp. chopped fresh basil (1 tsp. dried)
2 8-oz. cans crushed tomatoes
salt to taste
pepper to taste

1. Simmer garlic in oil. Stir in remaining ingredients. Simmer for 20 minutes.
2. Serve over hot spaghetti, spaghetti squash, mashed winter squash, or sauteed sliced summer squash.

Marinara Sauce

Elaine Seibel
Scents and Non-Scents
Hill, NH

Makes 4-6 servings

1 small onion, chopped
1 clove garlic, minced
1 Tbsp. olive oil
2 8-oz. cans crushed tomatoes
3 Tbsp. chopped fresh parsley
    (1 Tbsp. dried)
1 Tbsp. chopped fresh oregano
    (1 tsp. dried)
1 Tbsp. chopped fresh basil (1 tsp. dried)
1 1/2 tsp. chopped fresh thyme
    (1/2 tsp. dried)
12 oz. dry linguine or spaghetti, cooked

1. Saute chopped onion and garlic in oil until transparent.
2. Add crushed tomatoes, half a tomato can of hot water, and herbs. Simmer for 30 minutes.
3. Serve over cooked linguine or spaghetti.

Variation 1: Add 1/2 cup sliced mushrooms during last 10 minutes of cooking sauce.

Variation 2: Add 1 can minced clams with juice during last 10 minutes of cooking sauce.

Rosemary Pasta

Maryland Massey
Maryland's Herb Basket
Millington, MD

Makes 4 servings

2-3 Tbsp. butter
3" fresh twig of rosemary (1 Tbsp. dried)
3/4 cup half-and-half
1/4 tsp. salt
1/4 tsp. paprika
2/3 cup grated Parmesan cheese
freshly ground pepper to taste
12 oz. dry angel-hair pasta, or your choice of pastas, cookd

1. Saute rosemary in butter for a few minutes.
2. Stir in remaining ingredients. Heat through.
3. Serve over favorite pasta.

Pasta with Basil and Mushroom Sauce

Jim O'Toole
O'Toole's Herb Farm
Madison, FL

Makes 6-8 servings

2-3 Tbsp. extra virgin olive oil
5-6 large garlic cloves, minced
1 tsp. anchovy paste
2 serrano peppers, finely chopped
2 16-oz. cans diced tomatoes
1 tsp. fennel seed
1 Tbsp. olive oil
6 medium shiitake mushrooms,
    coarsely chopped
1 tsp. water
1/4 cup red wine
2 pinches of sugar
1 1/2 cups chopped fresh basil
1 lb. dry linguine, cooked
1 Tbsp. olive oil
freshly grated Romano cheese

1. Saute garlic in 2-3 Tbsp. olive oil until garlic is clear and tender. Add anchovy paste. Stir until blended.
2. Stir in peppers. Cook, stirring for about 1 minute.
3. Add tomatoes and fennel seeds. Simmer.
4. In microwave-proof dish, stir together 1 Tbsp. olive oil, mushrooms, and water. Microwave on High for 1 1/2 minutes. Stir into tomato mixture.
5. Stir in wine and sugar. Add basil. Stir to blend.
6. Drain pasta. Drizzle with 1 Tbsp. olive oil. Pour sauce on top and mix. Serve with grated cheese.

Basil Pasta

Anna L. Brown
Longfellow's Greenhouses
Manchester, ME

Makes 4-6 servings

2-3 garlic cloves, minced
1/4-1/2 cup light olive oil
1 lb. dry noodles or spaghetti
1 cup chopped fresh basil leaves
    (5 Tbsp. dried)
1/2-3/4 cup grated Parmesan cheese
black pepper to taste
chopped tomatoes or black olives
    (optional)

1. Saute garlic in olive oil.
2. Cook noodles or spaghetti according to package directions.
3. Drain pasta, then gently stir in garlic and all remaining ingredients. Toss well and serve hot.

Spinach Pasta with Portabello Mushrooms

Janet Melvin
Heritage Restaurant Gardens and Gifts
Cincinnati, OH

Makes 6 servings

Sauce:
1/2 cup butter or margarine
4 cloves garlic, minced
4 Tbsp. minced shallots
2 cups port wine
2 cups beef stock
8 cups peeled, seeded, and
 diced fresh tomatoes
2 tsp. salt
1 tsp. black pepper
4 Tbsp. cornstarch
2 Tbsp. water
4 Tbsp. chopped fresh thyme
 (4 tsp. dried)

1/4 cup grilled and sliced portabello
 mushrooms
2 Tbsp. sliced green onions, cut on the
 diagonal
6 Tbsp. sauce (above)
1/4 cup heavy cream
1 lb. fresh spinach fettucine

1. To make sauce, saute garlic and shallots
 in butter until lightly golden.
2. Glaze pan with port wine. Stir in beef
 stock. Simmer until reduced by one-third.
3. Stir in tomatoes, salt, and pepper.
4. Make paste of cornstarch and 2 Tbsp.
 water. Stir into pan. Cook, stirring
 constantly, until thickened. Remove
 from heat.
5. Stir in thyme. Refrigerate until ready to
 serve.
6. Combine mushrooms, onions, 6 Tbsp.
 sauce, and heavy cream in pan. Cook

over high heat until thickened. Mix into
remaining tomato sauce.
7. Drop pasta into boiling water for about
 1 1/2 minutes. Toss with sauce and serve.

Mushroom and Cheese Ravioli Filling

Karen Ashworth
The Herb Shoppe
Duenweg, MO

Makes 4 servings

3/4 cup chopped onion
1/4 cup chopped red pepper
1/2 cup chopped fresh mushrooms
1 scant Tbsp. safflower oil
2 Tbsp. chopped fresh parsley
 (2 tsp. dried)
1 1/2 tsp. chopped fresh oregano
 (1/2 tsp. dried)
freshly ground pepper to taste
1/2 cup cottage cheese
2 tsp. freshly grated Parmesan cheese
1 Tbsp. dry bread crumbs
12 large ravioli

1. Saute onion, pepper, and mushrooms in
 oil for 5 minutes.
2. Stir in parsley, oregano, and pepper.
 Cook for a few minutes. Cool.
3. Add cottage cheese and Parmesan
 cheese. Add bread crumbs and mix
 well.
4. Follow directions on the box for
 cooking ravioli, stuffing and baking it.

*Variation: This filling mixture could be
stirred into hot, cooked spaghetti or
angel-hair pasta.*

Gorgonzola and Fresh Thyme Sauce

Martha Gummersall Paul
Martha's Herbary
Pomfret, CT

Makes 4 servings

1 cup half-and-half
1 cup heavy cream
8 oz. aged Gorgonzola cheese, crumbled
4 tsp. chopped fresh thyme
   (1¼ tsp. dried)
3 generous grates of fresh nutmeg
salt to taste
pepper to taste
1 lb. dry rotelli-type pasta, cooked
½ cup toasted walnuts
1 cup chopped Granny Smith apple

1. Combine half-and-half, cream, cheese, thyme, and nutmeg. Cook gently until reduced by one-fourth. Stir in salt and pepper to taste.
2. Toss with hot pasta, walnuts and apple.

Carrot-Thyme Pasta

Barbara Sausser
Barb's Country Herbs
Riverside, CA

Makes 4 servings

1 large garlic clove, minced
1 Tbsp. olive oil
2 cups shredded carrots
3/4 tsp. Herbs de Provence*
1 large onion, chopped
2 fresh tomatoes, chopped
1 pkg. Ramen-type noodles
freshly grated Romano cheese

1. Saute garlic in oil for 1 minute. Stir in carrots and Herbs de Provence.
2. Add onion and tomatoes. Cook until mixture bubbles.
3. Gradually break Ramen noodles into cooked mixture. Add a couple of tablespoons of water if needed. Stir to finish cooking the noodles.
3. Serve with cheese sprinkled over top.

* To make 1¹/2 cups Herbs de Provence, mix together ¹/4 cup dried marjoram, ¹/4 cup dried oregano, ¹/2 cup dried rosemary, ¹/2 cup dried thyme, and 2 Tbsp. dried lavender buds.

Tip for Storing Herbs

Linda Hangren
LinHaven Gardens
Omaha, NE

All herbs should be stored in glass containers and kept inside a cabinet, out of the light. Light, as well as plastic or metal containers, can distort the color and flavor of the herbs.

Pasta with Four Cheeses and Basil

Stephen Lee
The Cookbook Cottage
Louisville, KY

Makes 4 servings

1 lb. dry rigatoni pasta
1/2 stick butter, unsalted
1/2 lb. Gruyere cheese, grated
    (about 2 cups)
1/2 lb. mozzarella cheese, grated
    (about 2 cups)
1/2 lb. Gorgonzola cheese, crumbed
    (about 2 cups)
1/2 lb. Parmesan cheese, grated
    (about 2 cups)
1 2/3 cups heavy cream
2 Tbsp. chopped fresh basil
freshly ground black pepper to taste
grated Parmesan cheese

1. Cook pasta until tender but still firm to bite. Drain.
2. Melt butter in large saucepan over low heat. Add cheeses and stir until melted. Slowly stir in cream until incorporated.
3. Add cooked pasta to cheese mixture. Stir in basil and ground pepper. Toss until pasta is well coated.
4. Top with additional Parmesan cheese and serve immediately.

Variation: To prepare a low-fat version of this dish, reduce butter to 3 Tbsp. Use only 1/2 cup of each grated cheese. Substitute milk for cream. Increase the amount of fresh basil to 5 Tbsp.

Angel-Hair Pasta with Peanut Sauce

Cynthia E. Palmer
Braeloch Farm
Richland, MI

Makes 4 servings

3 Tbsp. creamy peanut butter
5 Tbsp. salad oil
4 Tbsp. soy sauce
4 Tbsp. sugar
1 Tbsp. white vinegar
1 tsp. sesame oil
1/4 tsp. cayenne pepper
2 Tbsp. minced onion
2 Tbsp. fresh cilantro, chopped
1 lb. dry angel-hair pasta
shredded lettuce

1. Stir together peanut butter and salad oil.
2. Add soy sauce, sugar, vinegar, sesame oil, pepper, onion, and cilantro. Mix well. Set aside to marinate.
3. Cook pasta.
4. Place pasta on plates. Top with shredded lettuce and drizzle with sauce. Serve extra sauce separately.

Note: This sauce is also good on hot or cold pasta.
    Shredded cooked pork or chicken can be added on top of lettuce and pasta.

Thai Noodle Stir-Fry

Martha Gummersall Paul
Martha's Herbary
Pomfret, CT

Makes 4 servings

3 garlic cloves, minced
2/3 cup creamy peanut butter
6 Tbsp. fresh lime juice
3 Tbsp. soy sauce
1/2 cup vegetable broth
12 oz. dry Japanese noodles or linguini
16 oz. snow peas, halved lengthwise
3 Tbsp. vegetable oil
2 red peppers, sliced thin
8-10 oz. firm tofu, cubed and drained on
    paper towels
2 green onions, sliced
5 Tbsp. chopped fresh cilantro

1. In food processor or blender, mix
   together garlic, peanut butter, lime
   juice, and soy sauce.
2. Slowly pour in vegetable broth. Process
   until smooth.
3. Cook noodles in large amount of water
   until tender. Add snow peas during last
   30 seconds of cooking. Drain.
4. Heat oil in wok or skillet over high heat.
   Stir-fry peppers until tender. Remove.
5. Add tofu to wok and stir-fry until brown,
   about 2 minutes. Return bell peppers to
   wok and stir until hot. Remove skillet
   from heat.
6. Add noodles, snow peas, and sauce. Mix
   to coat evenly. Garnish with green
   onions and cilantro.

Summer Herb Pasta

Connie Johnson
Heartstone Herb Farm
Loudon, NH

Makes 6 servings

1 lb. dry pasta of your choice
1/4 cup olive oil
1 small zucchini, cut in bite-size pieces
1 small yellow summer squash, cut in
    bite-size pieces
1 red bell pepper, cut in bite-size pieces
1 green bell pepper, cut in bite-size pieces
1 small carrot, shredded
1/4 lb. fresh pea pods
1 large onion, chopped fine
4 cloves garlic, chopped fine
1 tsp. grated lemon rind
1/2 cup chopped fresh parsley
salt to taste
pepper to taste

1. Cook pasta.
2. While pasta is cooking, stir-fry zucchini,
   squash, peppers, carrot, pea pods,
   onion, and garlic in oil over medium
   heat. Remove from heat.
3. Toss vegetables with pasta. Stir in lemon
   rind, parsley, salt, and pepper. Toss and
   serve.

*Variation 1: For an Italian flavor, use
3 Tbsp. chopped fresh basil (3 tsp. dried)
and 3 Tbsp. chopped fresh oregano
(3 tsp. dried) in place of lemon rind.
Serve with grated cheese.*

*Variation 2: Add 1/2 cup reconstituted sun-
dried tomatoes, julienned, and 1 1/2 cups
sliced mushrooms during last minute of stir-
frying.*

Tina's Fettucine

Karen Ashworth
The Herb Shoppe
Duenweg, MO

Makes 6-8 servings

1/4 cup chopped onion
1/2 clove garlic, minced
1 Tbsp. margarine
1 tomato, peeled and diced
2 Tbsp. tomato paste
1 Tbsp. fresh oregano
1 Tbsp. fresh basil
1 Tbsp. fresh thyme
salt to taste
4 oz. fresh vegetables, cut up and
    steamed (squash, zucchini, carrots,
    broccoli, cauliflower, etc.)
8 oz. dry fettucine, cooked
1 Tbsp. margarine

1. Saute onion and garlic in 1 Tbsp.
   margarine.
2. Stir in tomato, tomato paste, oregano,
   basil, thyme, and salt. Simmer sauce for
   10 minutes.
3. Toss together cooked fettucine, steamed
   vegetables, and margarine. Top with
   sauce.

Fresh Basil and Tomato Casserole

Jacoba Baker and Reenie Baker Sandsted
Baker's Acres
Groton, NY

Makes 6-8 servings

12 plum or 4 large ripe tomatoes,
    sliced thin
20 fresh basil leaves, torn
3-4 cloves garlic, minced
1/2 cup oil
1 tsp. salt
long, thin, sweet yellow pepper
    (optional)
1 lb. dry ziti or other large macaroni,
    cooked
8 oz. grated mozzarella cheese
1/2 cup grated Parmesan cheese
dash of pepper

1. Marinate tomatoes, basil, garlic, oil, salt,
   and pepper for 2 or more hours.
2. Mix together hot cooked macaroni and
   grated mozzarella cheese. Toss with
   tomato mixture.
3. Sprinkle with Parmesan cheese.

Herb Lasagna

Barb Perry
Lizard Lick Organic Herbs
Huron, TN

Makes 12-14 servings

1 lb. dry lasagna noodles
3 Tbsp. fresh basil (1 Tbsp. dried)
3 Tbsp. fresh oregano (1 Tbsp. dried)
3 Tbsp. fresh parsley (1 Tbsp. dried)
3 Tbsp. fresh sage (1 Tbsp. dried)
3 Tbsp. fresh rosemary (1 Tbsp. dried)

3 Tbsp. fresh winter savory (1 Tbsp. dried)
3 Tbsp. fresh bee balm or peppermint
   (1 Tbsp. dried)
2 qts. red sauce, warmed
1 lb. Ricotta cheese
1 lb. mozzarella cheese, sliced
1 lb. Monterey Jack cheese, sliced
1/4 lb. Parmesan cheese, grated
1/4 lb. Romano cheese, grated

1. Boil lasagna noodles in salted water
   until pliable but still firm. Drain and
   rinse.
2. Chop fresh herbs and mix together.
3. Pour thin layer of sauce in bottom of
   2 greased 9" x 13" baking dishes.
4. Make a layer of several noodles, topped
   with one-fourth of the Ricotta cheese,
   mozzarella cheese, and Monterey Jack
   cheese. Sprinkle with one-fourth of the
   herbs, Parmesan cheese, and Romano
   cheese. Cover with one-fourth of red
   sauce. Repeat layers in both pans until
   all ingredients are used.
5. Bake at 350° for 45 minutes, until
   cheeses melt and sauce is bubbly.

Potato Pizza with Bacon Rosemary

Kathy Hertzler
Lancaster, PA

Makes 4 servings

Quick Pizza Dough:
2-2 1/4 cups flour
2 1/2 tsp. fast-acting dry yeast
1/2 tsp. sugar
2/3 cup hot water (110°)
1 Tbsp. olive oil
1/2 tsp. salt
yellow cornmeal

Pizza Topping:
2 Tbsp. olive oil
3/4 lb. red potatoes
salt to taste
pepper to taste
1 small onion
1/4 lb. sliced lean bacon (about 4 slices),
   chopped
1 Tbsp. chopped fresh rosemary
   (1 tsp. dried)
3 Tbsp. freshly grated Parmesan cheese

1. To make the pizza dough, whisk
   together 3/4 cup flour, yeast, sugar, and
   hot water. Stir in 1 Tbsp. oil, 1 1/4 cups
   flour, and salt. Blend until mixture
   forms a dough.
2. Knead on lightly floured surface for 5-10
   minutes, incorporating as much of the
   remaining 1/4 cup flour as necessary to
   keep the dough from being sticky.
   Cover and let rise for 30 minutes.
3. Sprinkle an oiled 14" pizza pan or
   baking sheet with cornmeal.
4. Roll out dough. Place on the pan and
   brush with 1 Tbsp. olive oil.
5. Cut potatoes into paper-thin slices and
   arrange so that they overlap on dough.
   Sprinkle with salt and pepper.
6. Cut onion in very thin slices. Separate
   into rings and scatter over the potatoes.
7. In skillet, cook bacon until barely
   cooked but not crisp. Spread bacon
   over onions.
8. Sprinkle rosemary and Parmesan over
   bacon. Drizzle with remaining
   tablespoon of oil.
9. Bake at 475° for 10-15 minutes, or until
   crust is golden brown and potatoes are
   tender.

Pesto Pizza

Sheryl Lozier
Summers Past Farms
El Cajon, CA

Makes 4-6 servings

2 cups fresh basil
4 cloves garlic, peeled
1 cup pine nuts or walnuts
1 cup olive oil
1 cup grated fresh Parmesan cheese
1 cup grated fresh Romano cheese
salt to taste
pepper to taste
2 large sourdough bread rolls
4 ripe red tomatoes, sliced
2 Tbsp. olive oil
salt to taste
pepper to taste
16 oz. shredded mozzarella cheese
1 cup Parmesan or Asiago cheese, freshly
   grated
12 chopped fresh basil leaves

1. Combine 2 cups basil, garlic, and nuts
   in food processor. Chop. Slowly add
   1 cup olive oil. Mix well.
2. Add cheeses, salt, and pepper. Process
   briefly to combine. Pour into bowl and
   cover pesto with plastic wrap.
3. Slice rolls lengthwise and spread pesto
   sauce evenly over rolls.
4. Place tomato slices on top of pesto.
   Drizzle with 2 Tbsp. olive oil, salt, and
   pepper. Top with mozzarella and
   Parmesan cheeses.
5. Bake at 350° for 10 minutes, or until
   lightly golden. Remove from oven and
   sprinkle with chopped fresh basil.

Jane's Quiche

Jane Knaapen Cole
The Faded Rose
Green Bay, WI

Makes 6-8 servings

Crust:
1¼ cups flour
dash of salt
⅓ cup shortening, at room temperature
3 Tbsp. ice water
1 Tbsp. vinegar

Quiche Filling:
3 Tbsp. butter
3 Tbsp. flour
¼ tsp. salt
¼ tsp. pepper
⅛ tsp. ground nutmeg
1 Tbsp. chopped fresh basil (1 tsp. dried)
2 cups milk
4 beaten eggs
1 Tbsp. chopped onion
¼ cup chopped broccoli, parboiled
¼ cup sliced mushrooms
¾ cup shredded cheddar cheese
¾ cup shredded Swiss cheese

1. Stir salt into flour. Cut in shortening
   until crumbly.
2. Mix together water and vinegar. Sprinkle
   over flour, tossing to mix. Shape into
   ball. Roll dough on floured board to
   desired thickness.
3. Place in pie pan. Poke crust with fork.
4. Bake at 375° for 8 minutes.
5. Melt butter over medium heat. Stir in
   flour, salt, pepper, nutmeg, and basil.
6. Slowly add milk, stirring and cooking
   until bubbly and thickened.
7. Beat eggs. Pour milk mixture slowly into
   eggs, beating by hand or in mixer, on low.
8. Place onions, broccoli, and mushrooms
   in pie crust. Sprinkle with cheeses.
9. Pour milk/egg mixture over all.

10. Bake at 375° for 35 minutes. Let set for 5 minutes before slicing to serve.

Herbal Apple Cheese Casserole

Jane D. Look
Pineapple Hill Herbs & More
Mapleton, IL

Makes 4 servings

2 cups chopped tart apples
1/2 cup chopped onion
1/4 tsp. garlic powder
3/4 tsp. chopped fresh thyme
   (1/4 tsp. dried)
3/4 tsp. chopped fresh marjoram
   (1/4 tsp. dried)
1/4 cup butter
4 Tbsp. flour
1 tsp. salt
1 cup milk
1 cup grated cheese
1/4 cup chopped walnuts
2 strips fried bacon, crumbled
4 egg yolks
6 egg whites
1/4 tsp. cream of tartar

1. Saute apples, onion, garlic, thyme, and marjoram in butter for 3 minutes.
2. Gradually stir in flour, salt, and milk over low heat. Blend until thickened and creamy.
3. Stir in cheese, nuts, and bacon.
4. Beat egg yolks well and stir in.
5. Beat egg whites with cream of tartar until stiff. Fold into mixture.
6. Pour into greased and floured deep-dish casserole.
7. Bake at 350° for 45 minutes. Cover with foil during the last 15 minutes if dish becomes too brown.

Vegetarian Cutlet

Connie Johnson
Heartstone Herb Farm
Loudon, NH

Makes 4-6 servings

1 cup dry oatmeal
1/4 cup grated cheese
half an onion, grated
half a carrot, grated
1/8 cup mixed sweet red and green
   peppers, chopped fine
1 clove garlic, minced
3 Tbsp. chopped fresh basil
   (1 Tbsp. dried)
3 Tbsp. chopped fresh oregano
   (1 Tbsp. dried)
3 tsp. chopped fresh spearmint
   (1 tsp. dried)
1/2 tsp. cayenne pepper
1/4 cup soy sauce
1/2 cup hot water
1 egg, beaten
bread crumbs
4 Tbsp. olive oil

1. Mix together oatmeal, cheese, onion, carrot, peppers, garlic, basil, oregano, spearmint, cayenne pepper, and soy sauce. Pour hot water over all. Mix well and let stand for 10 minutes.
2. Stir in egg. Mix well.
3. Form into flat patties, about 1/4 inch thick. Pat into bread crumbs to cover.
4. Heat oil. Saute patties quickly, about 2 minutes on each side, until golden brown. Drain on paper towel.
5. Serve on roll with lettuce, tomato, and garlic mayonnaise, or with herbed tomato sauce and pasta.

Spanakopita

Maria Price-Nowakowski
Willow Oak Flower and Herb Farm
Severn, MD

Makes 12 servings

2 8-oz. pkgs. frozen spinach,
   or 1 lb. fresh spinach
1/2 lb. feta cheese, crumbled
1/2 lb. large curd cottage cheese,
   crumbled
1/4 cup grated Parmesan cheese
1/4 tsp. salt
1 bunch scallions, chopped
1 handful fresh dill (2 Tbsp. dried dill)
small handful fresh parsley
   (2 Tbsp. dried parsley)
6 eggs, well beaten
1/2 cup olive oil
1 stick butter
1 lb. phyllo

1. Thaw frozen spinach, or steam fresh
   spinach for 5 minutes. Press out water
   and chop coarsely.
2. Add feta cheese, cottage cheese,
   Parmesan cheese, salt, scallions, dill,
   and parsley to spinach. Mix well. Add
   eggs. Mix well.
3. Heat oil and butter in small pan. Using
   pastry brush, grease 9" x 13" pan with
   oil/butter mixture.
4. Unwrap phyllo. Keep covered with
   damp cloth. Lay one sheet of phyllo in
   pan, smooth it out, and brush it with oil
   and butter. Continue until half the
   phyllo is in the pan.
5. Spread spinach mixture evenly over
   phyllo. Continue procedure described
   in Step 4 with other half of phyllo.
6. Bake at 350° for 50 minutes. Let cool for
   10 minutes before cutting into serving-
   size squares.

Ary's Feta and Basil Stuffed Tortillas

Ary Bruno
Koinonia Farm
Stevenson, MD

Makes 4 servings

12 oz. feta cheese, drained
1/2 cup loosely packed fresh basil,
   chopped
4 Tbsp. chopped fresh chives
freshly ground pepper to taste
4 Tbsp. heavy cream
2 large sweet red peppers, roasted,
   seeded, and peeled
8 flour tortillas

1. Crumble cheese. Mix with herbs,
   pepper, and enough cream to make a
   smooth filling.
2. Cut peppers into 1/2"-wide strips.
3. Spoon one-eighth of cheese mixture
   down one side of each tortilla. Top with
   pepper strips. Roll up like an enchilada.
   Cut in half crosswise.
4. Place a non-stick skillet over medium-
   high heat. Place 2-3 tortillas, seam side
   down, in skillet for a few minutes. Turn
   over. Tortilla is ready to serve when
   both sides are lightly crisp and
   beginning to brown.

*Note: You can stop after Step 3, cover the
tortillas with plastic, and store them in
the refrigerator for 2-3 days before
proceeding to heat and brown them.*

Low Calorie Beef Burritos

Davy Dabney
Dabney Herbs
Louisville, KY

Makes 5 servings

1/2 cup chopped onion
2 cloves garlic, minced
1/2 lb. lean ground beef
1/2 lb. prepared soy meat substitute
3 oz. Neufchatel cheese
1/2 tsp. ground cumin
1 1/2 tsp. chopped fresh oregano
  (1/2 tsp. dried)
10 flour tortillas

Sauce:
16-oz. can whole tomatoes
4-oz. can chopped green chilies
1 tsp. cornstarch
1 tsp. sugar
1 tsp. coriander seeds

shredded lettuce
plain yogurt

1. Cook onion, garlic, and beef until browned. Drain.
2. Add soy meat substitute, Neufchatel cheese, cumin, and oregano.
3. Divide mixture evenly on tortillas. Roll and place seam side down in lightly greased 12" x 7" pan.
4. Bake at 350° for 20 minutes.
5. In blender combine tomatoes, chilies, cornstarch, sugar, and coriander. Process until smooth.
6. Pour into saucepan and heat.
7. Place hot burritos on shredded lettuce. Top each with sauce and 1/2 tsp. yogurt.

Enchilada Supper Treat

Deedra Bell
Hummingbird Farms
Nederland, TX

Makes 8 servings

2 large yellow onions, chopped
1 Tbsp. olive oil
2 lbs. ground round meat
2 12-oz. cans tomato sauce
10-oz. can enchilada sauce
1 tsp. salt
1 1/2 tsp. chopped fresh oregano
  (1/2 tsp. dried)
1 1/2 tsp. chopped fresh rosemary
  (1/2 tsp. dried)
1 1/2 tsp. chopped fresh marjoram
  (1/2 tsp. dried)
1 lb. cheddar cheese, shredded
1 package corn tortillas

1. Saute onions in oil. Add ground meat, breaking it up as it browns.
2. Mix together tomato sauce, enchilada sauce, salt, oregano, rosemary, and marjoram. Add half of this sauce to meat mixture. Simmer for 5-7 minutes.
3. Line bottom of greased 9" x 13" pan with 6 tortillas. Cover with meat mixture. Spread half of cheese over meat mixture.
4. Cover the cheese with 6 more tortillas. Pour remaining tomato sauce over top. Top casserole with rest of cheese.
5. Bake at 350° for 25-30 minutes.

Tacos

Candace Licceone
The Herbal Sanctuary
Royersford, PA

Makes 4 servings

1 lb. ground beef
1 Tbsp. oil
half a red pepper, chopped
1 large onion, chopped
1 tsp. dried cumin
2 Tbsp. chopped fresh cilantro
    (2 tsp. dried)
2 Tbsp. chopped fresh parsley
    (2 tsp. dried)
12 tortillas
oil
shredded lettuce
tomatoes
sliced black olives
1 cup cheddar cheese, shredded
guacamole (see adjoining recipe)
salsa
sour cream

1. Brown beef, pepper, onion, cumin, cilantro, and parsley in oil until meat is cooked. Drain.
2. Fry tortillas in oil. Remove from oil and quickly fold in half. Drain, dabbing off excess oil with paper towel.
3. Fill tortillas with meat mixture. Place lettuce, tomatoes, black olives, cheese, guacamole, and salsa in separate bowls. Invite all diners to add what they want. Garnish each taco with a dollop of sour cream.

Guacamole

1 or 2 ripe avocados, mashed
1 can green chile salsa
1 tsp. lemon juice
1 minced garlic clove
sprinkling of fresh cilantro
sprinkling of fresh parsley

Mix together until well blended.

Hamburger Spaghetti Sauce

Carol Ebbighausen-Smith
C&C Herb Farm
Spokane, WA

Makes 16 servings

1 lb. hamburger
1/2 lb. plain spaghetti sauce
    (not Italian or sweet)
1 onion, chopped
one-quarter of a green pepper, chopped
4 Tbsp. olive oil
2 tsp. onion powder
1 tsp. celery powder
2 tsp. garlic powder
1 1/2 tsp. black pepper
3 Tbsp. chopped fresh oregano
    (1 Tbsp. dried)
4 1/2 tsp. chopped fresh thyme
    (1 1/2 tsp. dried)
2 Tbsp. chopped fresh parsley
    (2 tsp. dried)
1 tsp. chopped fresh basil (1/4 tsp. dried)
2 14 1/2-oz. cans Italian stewed tomatoes
3 14 1/2-oz. cans regular stewed tomatoes
4 15-oz. cans tomato sauce
6-oz. can tomato paste
6 bay leaves

1. In large pot, brown together hamburger, spaghetti sauce, onion, green pepper, olive oil, onion powder, celery powder, garlic powder, pepper, oregano, thyme, parsley, and basil.
2. Stir in stewed tomatoes, tomato sauce, tomato paste, and bay leaves. Bring to boil. Reduce heat to simmer, stirring occasionally. Cover and cook for 2 hours, stirring from time to time.
3. Remove lid. Let sauce continue to simmer 2-3 hours, continuing to stir occasionally. Remove bay leaves before serving.

Note: This sauce freezes well.
The sauce can be used in lasagna.
Make this sauce on a weekend when you're working inside—or outside. Stir it whenever you come indoors!

Mushroom-Herb Spaghetti Sauce

Nancy T. Dickman
Cascade Country Gardens
Marblemount, WA

Makes 4 servings

oil
1 lb. ground beef
¹/₂ cup chopped onion or 5 chopped shallots
3 cloves of garlic, minced
¹/₈ tsp. ground black pepper
1¹/₂ Tbsp. butter or margarine
2 Tbsp. mushrooms, chopped
1¹/₂ Tbsp. flour
³/₄ cup milk
1 cup tomato sauce
¹/₄ tsp. chili powder
1 cup sliced mushrooms

¹/₂ cup finely chopped fresh parsley
(3 Tbsp. dried)
2 Tbsp. chopped fresh basil (2 tsp. dried)
1 Tbsp. chopped fresh oregano
(1 tsp. dried)
1 tsp. chopped fresh thyme
(¹/₃ tsp. dried)
¹/₂ tsp. chopped fresh rosemary
(scant ¹/₄ tsp. dried)
¹/₂ lb. dry spaghetti, cooked according to package directions
¹/₂ cup grated Parmesan cheese
fresh whole basil leaves

1. Lightly coat large skillet with oil. Cook ground beef, onions or shallots, garlic, and pepper over medium heat until beef is thoroughly browned.
2. In separate saucepan melt butter or margarine and lightly saute 2 Tbsp. mushrooms. Blend in flour. Stir in milk over low heat until smooth and thickened. Add to beef, along with tomato sauce and chili powder. Stir until well mixed.
3. Gently stir in sliced mushrooms, parsley, and basil. Add oregano, thyme, and rosemary.
4. Reduce heat to low and simmer for 20 minutes, stirring occasionally.
5. Pour over hot spaghetti noodles and sprinkle with grated Parmesan cheese.
6. Garnish with fresh whole basil leaves.

Variation: Increase amount of tomato sauce by 1 cup to create a juicier sauce.

Italian Style Red Sauce

Barb Perry
Lizard Lick Organic Herbs
Huron, TN

Makes 8 servings

4-6 cloves garlic, minced
1/2 lb. ground chuck
1/2 lb. pork sausage
1 Tbsp. salt
1 whole cayenne pepper, minced, or
    1 tsp. cayenne powder
1/4 cup olive oil
2 large green peppers, chopped
3 large onions, chopped
2 qts. tomato puree
1 qt. whole tomatoes with juice
3 Tbsp. fresh basil (1 Tbsp. dried)
3 Tbsp. fresh oregano (1 Tbsp. dried)
3 Tbsp. fresh sage (1 Tbsp. dried)
3 Tbsp. fresh parsley (1 Tbsp. dried)
6 fresh bay leaves (2 dried)
2 Tbsp. fresh rosemary (2 tsp. dried)
2 Tbsp. fresh winter savory (2 tsp. dried)
2 Tbsp. fresh thyme (2 tsp. dried)
2 Tbsp. fresh bee balm (2 tsp. dried)
1/2 cup Chianti, or other red wine,
    optional
1/4 cup honey (optional)

1. Saute garlic, meat, salt, and pepper in olive oil. Skim off half the fat.
2. Add peppers and onion and saute until onions are lightly browned, stirring frequently to prevent sticking and burning. Turn heat to low.
3. Stir in puree, tomatoes, and herbs. Cover and let simmer for 1-3 hours, stirring occasionally. If sauce is too thin, uncover to let some liquid evaporate.
4. Approximately 30-45 minutes before end of cooking time, add wine and honey.
5. Serve over pasta, or use as a sauce for pizza, lasagna, or baked ziti.

Note: Can be frozen for later use.

Variation 1: Eliminate meat for a hearty vegetarian sauce.

Variation 2: In place of the ground chuck and/or the pork sausage, use cubed chuck roast, fresh pork, venison, or Italian sausage.

Basil Hamburgers

Marty Mertens & Clarence Roush
Woodstock Herbs
New Goshen, IN

Form very thin hamburger patties. Place 2-3 fresh or frozen basil leaves on top of half of them. Cover with remaining patties and pinch edges together. Grill.

Saucy Meatballs

Timothy L. Newcomer
The Herb Merchant
Carlisle, PA

Makes 4-6 servings

1¹/₂ lbs. ground beef
¹/₄ cup chopped onion
¹/₄ tsp. dried oregano
1 egg
³/₄ cup dry oatmeal
1 tsp. salt
¹/₄ tsp. pepper
1 cup milk
¹/₂ cup chopped onion
¹/₃ cup chopped green pepper
1 Tbsp. oil
16-oz. can whole tomatoes
¹/₂ tsp. salt
¹/₄ tsp. garlic powder
1 cup tomato sauce
¹/₂ tsp. dried oregano
1 dried bay leaf

1. Combine beef, onion, oregano, egg, oatmeal, salt, pepper, and milk until just blended. Do not overmix. Shape into balls of desired size.
2. Place meatballs about 1¹/₂" apart on ungreased cookie sheet.
3. Bake at 350° for 20-25 minutes. Remove from cookie sheet and cool on paper towels.
4. Brown onion and green pepper in oil. Stir in remaining ingredients. Reduce heat and simmer for 15 minutes.
5. Place meatballs in large pan and coat with sauce. Simmer for 30 minutes.
6. Serve with buttered noodles or in a long sandwich roll with additional sauce and cheese.

Didn't Know I Liked Eggplant!

Tammy Bell
Hummingbird Farms
Nederland, TX

Makes 6 servings

1 large eggplant (1¹/₂ lbs.)
1¹/₂ cups water
1 large yellow onion, diced
1 large bell pepper, chopped
1 bunch onion chives, chopped
1 Tbsp. olive oil
1 lb. ground turkey or ground beef
2 cups tomato sauce
1 cup water
4 fresh bay leaves (2 dried)
3 Tbsp. chopped fresh parsley
    (3 tsp. dried)
salt to taste
pepper to taste
1 lb. dry fettuccine noodles, cooked
8 oz. cheddar cheese, grated

1. Peel eggplant, and cut into small bite-size pieces. Boil eggplant in 1¹/₂ cups water until tender. Drain. Mash eggplant.
2. Saute onion, bell pepper, and chives in oil until tender. Add ground meat and cook until brown.
3. Stir in eggplant, tomato sauce, 1 cup water, bay leaves, parsley, salt, and pepper. Simmer for 15 minutes. Remove from heat when sauce thickens like gravy. Remove bay leaves.
4. Serve sauce over noodles. Top with grated cheese.

Hamburger Stroganoff

Martha Moss
Moss' Florist and Greenhouses
Mt. Juliet, TN

Makes 6 servings

1/2 cup minced onion
2 Tbsp. butter
1 lb. ground beef
1 clove garlic, minced
1/2 tsp. salt
2 Tbsp. flour
1/4 tsp. pepper
1/4 tsp. paprika
3/4 tsp. chopped fresh basil (1/4 tsp. dried)
2 Tbsp. butter, melted
1 Tbsp. minced onion
1/4 cup chopped mushrooms
3 Tbsp. flour
11/4 cups milk
1/2 cup water
3/4 cup sour cream
noodles, rice, or toast
1/2 cup chopped fresh parsley, chives, or
    dill (3 Tbsp. dried)

1. Saute 1/2 cup onion in 2 Tbsp. butter
   until golden.
2. Stir in beef, garlic, salt, 2 Tbsp. flour,
   pepper, paprika, and basil. Cook until
   beef is browned. Set aside.
3. Saute 1 Tbsp. minced onion and
   chopped mushrooms in 2 Tbsp. butter.
   Add flour. Stir until smooth.
4. Gradually add milk and stir until
   thickened. Pour this white sauce into
   hamburger mixture. Stir in sour cream.
   Heat, but do not boil.
5. Serve over noodles, fluffy rice, or toast.
   Sprinkle with your choice of parsley,
   chives, or dill.

Flank Steak, Sweet Pepper, and Mint Stir-Fry

Flo Stanley
Mililani Herbs
Mililani, HI

Makes 6 servings

1 lb. flank steak, well trimmed
salt to taste
pepper to taste
2 tsp. oil
1 large yellow onion, cut into 1/2" slices
3-4 garlic cloves, minced
2 red, 2 green, and 2 yellow sweet
    peppers, cut into 1/2" strips
2" piece fresh ginger, peeled and grated
2 Tbsp. Thai fish sauce
10-12 4" sprigs fresh mint
salt to taste
pepper to taste
6 cups cooked rice

1. Salt and pepper steak. Saute in oil,
   cooking to medium rare. Set aside to
   cool. Slice across the grain into thin
   strips.
2. In same pan, stir-fry onion slices and
   minced garlic for 2 minutes.
3. Add pepper strips, ginger, Thai fish
   sauce, and mint sprigs. Cook another 2
   minutes.
4. Add steak slices and juices from steak.
   Stir-fry until beef is heated. Season with
   salt and pepper as needed.
5. Serve over hot steamed rice.

*Variation: Replace mint with Thai basil
or regular basil, or use half mint and half
basil.*

Spicy Beef and Black Bean Salsa

Harriette Johnson
Mustard Seed Herbs
Spring Valley, WI

Makes 4-6 servings

3-4 lb. beef roast
1 tsp. cayenne pepper
1 tsp. chili powder
1/2 tsp. crushed red pepper
1/2 tsp. cumin
1 can spicy black beans, undrained
1 cup chopped red onion
1/3 cup lemon juice
1/2-3/4 cup chopped fresh cilantro
salt to taste
pepper to taste
2 fresh tomatoes diced, or 8-10 tomatillos

1. Sprinkle beef with cayenne pepper, chili powder, red pepper, and cumin.
2. Bake at 350° until very tender, 2 1/2-3 hours.
3. Mix together beans, onion, and lemon juice. Mix well.
4. Stir in cilantro, salt, and pepper. Add tomatoes. Serve with beef.

Thyme for Pot Roast

Jane D. Look
Pineapple Hill Herbs and More
Mapleton, IL

Makes 8 servings

6 lbs. boneless chuck roast
2-3 Tbsp. vegetable oil
3 Tbsp. chopped fresh thyme
   (3 tsp. dried)
1 cup beef broth
8 large potatoes, peeled and quartered
8 onions, peeled and quartered
8 carrots, peeled and sliced in half
4 stalks celery, chopped

1. Trim excess fat from roast.
2. Heat oil in Dutch oven or roasting pan. Add roast and brown on both sides. Add broth.
3. Sprinkle roast with thyme, or slit roast and insert thyme for more flavor.
4. Simmer on low heat for 2 hours.
5. Add vegetables. Bake at 325° for an additional hour.

Tip for Storing Fresh Herbs

Lewis J. Matt III
White Buck Farm
Holbrook, PA

Fresh herb leaves can be stored for a long time if moistened and placed in an inflated plastic bag in the lower part of the refrigerator. Every day shake the bag, wipe out excess moisture, and reinflate the bag. The bag should never be more than half full of leaves and should be filled with as much air as possible.

Country Herbal Stew

Cassius L. Chapman
Mr. C's Cooking Castle
Tucker, GA

Makes 6 servings

1/2 cup flour
1 tsp. salt
1 lb. stewing beef chunks, well trimmed
2 Tbsp. oil
1/2-1 cup chopped onion
3-4 cloves garlic
2 14 1/2-oz. cans diced tomatoes
6-oz. can tomato paste
10 1/2-oz. can beef broth
3/4 cup sliced celery
1 lb. green beans
1 lb. whole-grain corn
1 cup fresh or frozen sliced okra
1 cup scraped and sliced raw carrots
1 cup peeled and sliced potatoes
1 Tbsp. chopped fresh thyme
   (1 tsp. dried)
1 Tbsp. chopped fresh rosemary
   (1 tsp. dried)
1 tsp. salt
1 cup water
1/4 cup chopped fresh parsley

1. Mix flour and salt in large bowl. Add meat and toss to coat. Shake off excess flour.
2. Heat oil in Dutch oven over medium heat. Add onion and garlic and cook for 5 minutes.
3. Add meat and cook, turning until brown on all sides.
4. Stir in tomatoes and tomato paste until well mixed. Stir in broth.
5. Add vegetables, thyme, rosemary, and salt. Add enough water to cover vegetables.
6. Bring to boil. Reduce heat. Simmer for 2 1/2 hours.
7. Serve with corn bread or corn muffins.

Variation: In place of salt, use 1 cube frozen basil. To make frozen basil cubes, put 8 cups chopped fresh basil and 1 Tbsp. olive oil in food processor and combine until well mixed and fine. Fill ice cube tray with mixture, pressing down so that each compartment is full. Freeze until solid, and then remove cubes from tray and store them in freezer bags. Add a cube to soups, stews, or sauces. (Note: The basil will stain the tray, so use one that you will not need to use again for regular ice cubes!)

Herbal Brisket

Judith Defrain
Eye of the Cat
Long Beach, CA

Makes 8-10 servings

5 lbs. brisket, well trimmed
5 cups water
1 1/2 cups blend of fresh rosemary, thyme, and oregano
5 cups cubed potatoes
3 cups carrot chunks
3 onions, diced
1 tsp. celery seeds

1. Place brisket in large roaster pan. Add water.
2. Place herb mixture in a paper coffee filter. Tie shut and place in roasting pan. Cover with foil or lid.
3. Bake at 350° for 1 hour.
4. Remove herb bag. Add vegetables and celery seeds to meat in pan.
5. Return to oven and bake at 250° for 3 hours.
6. Slice meat and serve with vegetables and broth over top.

Pot Roast

Charlotte Chandler
Honey of an Herb Farm
Walton, WV

Makes 6 servings

1¹/₂-2 lbs. beef chuck roast
salt to taste
pepper to taste
2 sprigs fresh rosemary
2 Tbsp. oil
3 Tbsp. butter or margarine
¹/₄ cup chopped mushrooms
1 Tbsp. chopped onion
3 Tbsp. flour
1¹/₃ cups milk
1¹/₃ cups water

1. Rub roast with salt, pepper, and rosemary.
2. Pour oil in saucepan. Add roast and quickly brown on both sides to seal in the juices.
3. Melt butter or margarine and saute mushrooms and onions in it. Stir in flour until smooth. Add milk gradually, stirring continually until lump-free and thickened. Then add 1 cup water, stir until smooth, and pour over roast.
4. Cover skillet and place in 350° oven for 3-4 hours, depending on the size of your roast.
5. Slice meat and serve with savory rosemary sauce.

Mustard-Crusted Pork Roast

Dawn Ranck
Harrisonburg, VA

Makes 8-10 servings

4-5 lb. pork roast
1 clove garlic
¹/₄ tsp. pepper
¹/₄ tsp. salt
¹/₄ cup prepared mustard
1 tsp. Worcestershire sauce
¹/₂ tsp. ground ginger
¹/₄ cup butter, melted
2 slices bread, crumbled
¹/₄ cup chopped fresh parsley
   (5 tsp. dried)
¹/₄ cup chopped fresh thyme
   (5 tsp. dried)
¹/₄ cup chopped fresh rosemary
   (5 tsp. dried)

1. Remove skin and excess fat from roast. Place on rack in roasting pan. Rub with garlic clove, pepper, and salt.
2. Roast at 325° until meat thermometer reads 170-180°, approximately 2-3 hours. Remove from oven.
3. Mix together mustard, Worcestershire sauce, and ginger. Remove 2 Tbsp. fat from pan drippings and add to mustard mixture. Mix well.
4. Combine butter, bread crumbs, parsley, thyme, and rosemary.
5. Using pastry brush, spread mustard mixture over pork roast. Gently pat bread crumbs onto pork. Return to oven. Bake an additional 15 minutes. Remove from pan and let stand for 15 minutes before slicing.

Rosemary Pork Roast

Jane D. Look
Pineapple Hill Herbs and More
Mapleton, IL

Makes 8-10 servings

4-5 lb. lean pork loin roast
2 cups apple cider
2 cloves garlic, minced
1 tsp. onion salt
3/4 tsp. chopped fresh oregano
   (1/4 tsp. dried)
1 Tbsp. fresh rosemary (1 tsp. dried)
1 bay leaf

1. Place roast in bowl.
2. Mix together remaining ingredients.
   Pour over roast. Refrigerate for at least 8
   hours.
3. Remove roast from bowl. Place on rack
   in roasting pan. Pour marinade mixture
   into pan.
4. Bake at 325° for 2-2½ hours. Baste
   frequently.
5. Slice and serve with marinade.

Oriental Pork Roast

Mary C. Wenger
Sassafras Hill Herbs
Kimmswick, MO

Makes 4-6 servings

1/4 cup soy sauce
1/2 cup ketchup
1/4 cup honey
2½-3 lb. pork loin
2-3 garlic cloves
freshly ground black pepper to taste
3 sprigs fresh rosemary (1 tsp. dried)
1 cup water

1. Mix together soy sauce, ketchup, and
   honey. Set aside.
2. Cut slits into pork loin. Insert slices of
   garlic in slits. Sprinkle pepper over
   pork. Lay rosemary sprigs on top of
   roast, or sprinkle with dry rosemary.
3. Place pork loin on shallow rack in
   roasting pan. Pour water in bottom of
   pan.
4. Brush pork with soy sauce mixture.
5. Roast at 350° until pork is well done,
   about 2-2½ hours. Continue basting
   with sauce every 15 minutes.
6. Serve with rice. The basting sauce
   makes an excellent gravy.

Pork and Apples

Bertha Reppert
The Rosemary House
Mechanicsburg, PA

Makes 6-8 servings

2 lbs. pork shoulder, cut into 1½" cubes
3 large onions, sliced
1 clove of garlic, minced
2 Tbsp. oil
1/2 cup flour
1 cup water
1 can consomme
1 Tbsp. chopped fresh rosemary
   (1 tsp. dried)
1 tsp. salt
3-4 sliced apples
1/4 tsp. cinnamon

1. Saute pork, onions, and garlic in oil.
   Pour into greased baking dish.
2. Add flour to oil in pan. Heat. Slowly add
   water and consomme. Stir in rosemary
   and salt. Stir constantly over medium
   heat until thickened. Pour over pork in
   casserole dish.
3. Bake at 350° for 1 hour.

4. Stir in apples and cinnamon. Bake 30-40 minutes longer, or until pork is tender.
5. Serve over rice.

Tomato-Glazed Pork with Grilled Corn Salsa

Janet Melvin
Heritage Restaurant Gardens and Gifts
Cincinnati, OH

Makes 8 servings

Tomato Glaze:
2 Tbsp. dry mustard
1 Tbsp. ground ginger
1 Tbsp. ground fennel
1 Tbsp. minced garlic
1/4 cup mayonnaise
1 cup tomato ketchup
1/4 cup honey
1 Tbsp. Worcestershire sauce
1/4 cup grated fresh horseradish
3 Tbsp. white wine mustard
2 Tbsp. minced capers
1 Tbsp. Tabasco sauce

Salsa:
3 ears sweet corn, husked and silked
1/2 cup olive oil
1/4 cup chopped sun-dried tomatoes
1 clove garlic, minced
1/2 cup wild mushrooms, sliced
2 Tbsp. chopped fresh cilantro
2 Tbsp. fresh lime juice
1 chipotle pepper in adobo sauce, finely chopped
1/2 tsp. salt

2 lb. pork tenderloin

1. To make glaze, mix together mustard, ginger, fennel, garlic, and mayonnaise.

2. When well blended, stir in remaining ingredients. Cover and refrigerate until ready to use.
3. Brush corn with olive oil. Wrap in foil. Bake at 350° for 15 minutes. Unwrap and grill or broil until evenly browned. Cool. Cut kernels from cob.
4. Combine corn with remaining ingredients. Cover and refrigerate until ready to use.
5. Place tenderloin in roasting pan and cover with glaze.
6. Bake at 350° for 1 1/2-2 hours, or until internal temperature is 140°.
7. Slice and serve on top of grilled corn salsa.

Herbed Pork Ribs with Sauerkraut

Karen Sanders
Your Flower Basket—
The Herbal Ingredient
Robinson, IL

Makes 4-6 servings

4-6 lean country pork ribs
1 Tbsp. olive oil
2 cups sauerkraut
6 medium potatoes, cut in half
1 onion, chopped
3 cloves garlic, minced
1 Tbsp. chopped fresh thyme (1 tsp. dried)
1 Tbsp. chopped fresh rosemary (1 tsp. dried)
freshly ground black pepper

1. Brown ribs in small amount of oil.
2. Add sauerkraut, potatoes, onion, garlic, thyme, rosemary, and pepper. .
3. Turn heat to low and simmer until potatoes are soft.
4. Serve from skillet or roaster.

Rosemary Pork Chops and Pasta

Michelle Mann
Mt. Joy, PA

Makes 4 servings

2 Tbsp. butter
3 Tbsp. olive oil, or rosemary-flavored oil
2 cloves garlic, minced
1/4 tsp. black pepper
1/4 tsp. ground red pepper
1 Tbsp. chopped fresh rosemary
    (1 tsp. dried)
4 pork chops
2 cups chopped tomatoes
3 Tbsp. chopped fresh parsley
    (1 Tbsp. dried)
1/2 tsp. salt
1 lb. dry spaghetti
4 Tbsp. butter
4 Tbsp. grated fresh Parmesan cheese

1. In skillet, saute garlic, black pepper, and red pepper in butter and oil.
2. Sprinkle rosemary on pork chops. Add to skillet. Slowly brown pork chops on both sides.
3. Add tomatoes, parsley, and salt. Cover and simmer for 20 minutes. Uncover and cook an additional 20 minutes, or until tender.
4. Cook spaghetti. Drain and toss with 4 Tbsp. butter and Parmesan cheese. Add 1/2 cup sauce from skillet.
5. Serve pork chops over spaghetti.

Lemon Sweet Pork Chops

Doris Slatten
Moss' Florist and Greenhouses
Mt. Juliet, TN

Makes 8 servings

8 1/2"-thick pork chops
salt to taste
pepper to taste
1 1/2 tsp. chopped fresh oregano
    (1/2 tsp. dried)
1 1/2 tsp. chopped fresh chives
    (1/2 tsp. dried)
1/2 tsp. chopped fresh dill
    (1/8 tsp. dried)
1/2 tsp. minced garlic
8 lemon slices
3 Tbsp. ketchup
3 Tbsp. brown sugar

1. Mix together salt, pepper, oregano, chives, dill, and garlic. Sprinkle over both sides of pork chops. Place in greased baking dish.
2. Place a slice of lemon on each pork chop.
3. Place 1 tsp. of ketchup and 1 tsp. brown sugar on top of each lemon slice.
4. Cover and bake at 350° for 40-60 minutes, or until chops are tender.

Basil Sage Pork Chops

Linda Hangren
LinHaven Gardens
Omaha, NE

Makes 4 servings

4 lean pork chops
1 Tbsp. olive oil
1/4 cup water
1 Tbsp. chopped fresh basil (1 tsp. dried)
1 Tbsp. chopped fresh sage (1 tsp. dried)

1. Brown pork chops in oil. Add water. Cover. Simmer on medium-low for 10 minutes.
2. Scatter basil and sage over chops. Add more water if pan is dry.
3. Cover and simmer for 10 minutes, or until chops are cooked through.

Portuguese Chili

Ralph Tissot
Cottage Herbs
Albuquerque, NM

Makes 5-6 servings

2 lbs. pork, cut in 1" chunks
2-3 cups dry sherry
7 cloves garlic
7 dried bay leaves
3 Tbsp. Spanish olive oil
1 large onion, sliced
1 lb. green chilies, frozen or fresh
6 cups chicken broth
2 oz. fresh jalapeno peppers, chopped
4 cups water
16-oz. can whole tomatoes,
  or 1 lb. fresh, peeled tomatoes
2 Tbsp. chopped fresh cilantro

1. Mix together pork, sherry, garlic, and bay leaves. Marinate for 5-7 days in the refrigerator. Stir daily.
2. Remove pork from marinade and saute in oil until well browned.
3. Reduce heat and add the onion and garlic from marinade. Stir in remaining ingredients, except the cilantro. Bring to a boil.
4. Reduce heat and simmer on low for several hours, or until meat is tender.
5. Stir in cilantro and serve stew with flour tortillas or French bread.

Hearty Tomato and Sausage Stew

Lee Good
Lititz, PA

Makes 2 servings

1/4 lb. sweet Italian sausage
1 Tbsp. butter
1/4 cup chopped onion
1 clove garlic, minced
1 1/2 cups crushed tomatoes in thick sauce
2 tsp. chopped fresh oregano
  (2/3 tsp. dried)
2 tsp. chopped fresh basil (2/3 tsp. dried)
1/2-1 cup water (optional)

1. Brown and drain sausage. Set aside.
2. Saute onion and garlic in butter until onion is translucent.
3. Stir in sausage. Heat briefly.
4. Add tomatoes, oregano, basil, and water. Heat through and serve.

Italian Sausage with Pasta

Karen Sanders
Your Flower Basket—
The Herbal Ingredient
Robinson, IL

Makes 4-6 servings

1 pound Italian or summer sausage
2 Tbsp. olive oil
1 qt. canned tomatoes
6 oz. tomato paste
pinch of salt, or 2 Tbsp. dried summer
  savory
2 Tbsp. honey
2 Tbsp. fresh basil (2 tsp. dried)
2 Tbsp. fresh oregano (2 tsp. dried)
2 Tbsp. fresh Italian parsley (2 tsp. dried)
2 Tbsp. fresh thyme (2 tsp. dried)
freshly ground pepper
1 lb. dry pasta, cooked

1. Brown sausage in olive oil.
2. Stir in tomatoes, tomato paste, salt or
   savory. Bring to boil. Reduce heat.
3. Add honey and simmer for 15 minutes.
4. Stir in basil, oregano, parsley, thyme,
   and pepper. Simmer an additional 5-10
   minutes.
5. Toss cooked pasta with sausage mixture
   and serve.

Lentil Casserole with Sausage

Kathy Hertzler
Lancaster, PA

Makes 4 servings

1 cup chopped onion
3/4 cup dry lentils, rinsed well and picked
  clean
3/4 cup uncooked brown rice
3/4 cup shredded cheddar cheese
2 cloves garlic, crushed
1/4 cup water
1 1/2 tsp. fresh thyme, chopped
  (1/2 tsp. dried)
1 1/2 tsp. fresh basil, chopped
  (1/2 tsp. dried)
1 1/2 tsp. fresh oregano, chopped
  (1/2 tsp. dried)
1/2 tsp. fresh sage, chopped
  (1/8 tsp. dried)
1/4 tsp. salt
freshly ground black pepper to taste
1-2 lbs. cooked hot or sweet Italian
  sausage, bratwurst, or your favorite
  sausage
2 14 1/2-oz. cans low-salt chicken broth

1. In a greased casserole, mix together all
   ingredients except broth.
2. Pour in broth and stir well.
3. Cover and bake at 350° for 1 1/2 hours.

*Note: If you prefer a moist casserole,
increase the amount of water or broth by
1/4 to 1/2 cup.*

Aromatic Spaghetti

Linda Kosa-Postl
Never Enough Thyme
Granite Falls, WA

Makes 6 servings

5 slices bacon, diced
1 large onion, diced
6 Tbsp. oil
2 Tbsp. flour
9 fresh rosemary leaves (¹/₂ tsp. dried)
3 fresh sage leaves (¹/₂ tsp. dried)
3 fresh bay leaves
3 whole cloves
2¹/₂ lbs. tomatoes, peeled and diced
salt to taste
pepper to taste
2 beef bouillon cubes dissolved in 1 cup
   hot water
2 small cloves garlic
3 fresh basil leaves (¹/₄ tsp. dried)
3 Tbsp. chopped fresh parsley
   (3 tsp. dried)
¹/₄ tsp. nutmeg
3 Tbsp. butter
1 cup grated Parmesan cheese
1 lb. dry spaghetti, cooked

1. Saute bacon and onion in oil. Stir in
   flour, rosemary, sage, bay, and cloves.
   Mix well.
2. Stir in tomatoes, salt, pepper, and
   bouillon broth. Simmer for 25 minutes.
3. Crush garlic, basil, parsley, and nutmeg
   together. Stir in butter and 1 Tbsp.
   grated Parmesan until a paste forms.
   Stir into sauce.
4. Pour sauce over cooked pasta. Sprinkle
   with remaining Parmesan.

Terrific Tenders

Carol Turner
Turkey Trot Trunk
Mountain City, GA

Makes 8 servings

2 lbs. boned whole pork tenderloin, or
   boneless, skinless chicken breasts, cut
   in strips
5-6 garlic cloves, halved or quartered
   lengthwise
salt to taste
pepper to taste
1¹/₂ cups opal basil, raspberry, or
   blackberry vinegar
1 Tbsp. butter
2 Tbsp. oil
2 tsp. shallots, chopped fine
1 Tbsp. fresh tarragon (1 tsp. dried)
1 tsp. Dijon mustard
fresh parsley sprigs

1. Pierce meat with knife about ¹/₂" deep at
   2" intervals. Insert piece of garlic in
   each slit. Place in covered container to
   marinate. Sprinkle with salt and pepper.
2. Pour in enough vinegar to come at least
   halfway up the sides of the meat. Cover
   and refrigerate for 8 hours, turning the
   meat every 2 hours.
3. Remove meat from marinade and sear
   on all sides in oil and butter over
   medium high heat. Place meat in
   roasting pan. Reserve marinade, and oil
   and butter.
4. Bake meat at 400° for 20-30 minutes.
5. Saute shallots in oil and butter in which
   meat was seared. Stir in tarragon and
   mustard. Mix well.
6. Stir in one cup marinade. Reduce heat
   and cook until slightly thickened and
   creamy. Pour over tenderloins on
   serving platter. Garnish with parsley
   sprigs.

Fruit Vinegar-Sauced Chicken Breast

Judy and Don Jensen
Fairlight Gardens
Auburn, WA

Makes 4 servings

4 boneless, skinless chicken breast halves
1 Tbsp. vegetable oil
1 Tbsp. butter or margarine
2 Tbsp. fruit or basil vinegar
1/2 cup whipping cream
salt to taste
pepper to taste
fresh chives, chopped

1. Saute chicken in oil and butter until cooked through, but not overcooked. Remove chicken to warm platter.
2. Stir vinegar into pan in which chicken was sauteed, scraping the bottom to loosen any bits of browned meat that cling to the pan. Slowly add the cream, and then simmer until the mixture thickens. Stir in salt and pepper to taste.
3. Spoon sauce over chicken breasts. Top with chopped chives.

Variation 1: Use evaporated skim milk instead of cream.

Variation 2: For a zestier dish, increase the vinegar to 3 Tbsp.

Variation 3: Garnish finished dish with raspberries.

Supreme Herb Chicken

Anna L. Brown
Longfellow's Greenhouses
Manchester, ME

Makes 4 servings

4 boneless, skinless chicken breast halves
2 Tbsp. chopped fresh herbs—marjoram, thyme, savory, sage, fennel, basil, rosemary, and/or lavender
1/2 tsp. salt
1/4 tsp. black pepper
4 Tbsp. butter or olive oil
1 Tbsp. lemon juice

1. Sprinkle chicken with herbs, salt, and pepper.
2. Place in oil in hot skillet and cook for 3 minutes on each side, or until done. Remove from pan.
3. Place on serving platter. Add lemon juice to pan drippings. Heat and pour over chicken. Serve.

Basil-Thyme Parmesan Chicken

Carol Lacko-Beem
Herbs-Liscious
Marshalltown, IA

Makes 4 servings

1/2 cup crisped rice cereal crumbs
1/2 cup grated Parmesan cheese
1 Tbsp. chopped fresh basil (1 tsp. dried)
1 1/2 tsp. chopped fresh thyme (1/2 tsp. dried)
1/4 tsp. onion granules
1/8 tsp. garlic granules
1/4 tsp. ground black pepper
2-3 Tbsp. oil

4 boneless, skinless chicken breast halves
1 egg, beaten
2-3 Tbsp. oil

1. Mix together cereal crumbs, Parmesan cheese, basil, thyme, onion granules, garlic granules, and pepper.
2. Pour oil into 9" x 13" baking pan.
3. Dip chicken into egg, then coat with crumb mixture. Place in baking pan.
4. Bake at 400° for 20-25 minutes, or until cooked through. Turn once, halfway through cooking time.

Basil Chicken with White Wine

Dawn Ranck
Harrisonburg, VA

Makes 4 servings

2 Tbsp. oil
4 boneless, skinless chicken breast halves
1/2 tsp. paprika
1/2 cup boiling water
1 chicken bouillon cube
1/3 cup white cooking wine
1 Tbsp. chopped fresh basil leaves
   (1 tsp. dried)

1. Add chicken to hot oil in skillet. Sprinkle with 1/4 tsp. paprika. Cook for 5 minutes. Turn chicken and sprinkle with remaining paprika. Cook for 5 more minutes.
2. Dissolve bouillon cube in water. Add bouillon, wine, and basil to chicken. Bring to boil. Cover and simmer for 10-15 minutes, or until juices run clear. Spoon sauce over chicken to serve.

Broiled Chicken Breast

Rachel Bell
Hummingbird Farms
Beaumont, TX

Makes 8 servings

4 Tbsp. butter or margarine, melted
1/2 cup freshly squeezed lemon juice
3 1/2 Tbsp. chopped fresh basil
   (3 1/2 tsp. dried)
1 medium onion, chopped
2 Tbsp. chopped fresh lemon basil
   (2 tsp. dried)
3 Tbsp. chopped fresh thyme
   (3 tsp. dried)
2 bunches fresh garlic chives, chopped, or 1 tsp. garlic powder
8 boneless, skinless chicken breast halves
thin lemon slices
sprigs of fresh herbs

1. Combine all ingredients except chicken breasts, lemon slices, and sprigs of herbs. Mix well.
2. Place chicken in greased baking dish. Pour mixture over chicken. Cover and marinate in refrigerator for at least 6 hours.
3. Cook chicken in hot broiler, 4-6 inches from flame for 10-15 minutes, basting often with sauce. Turn chicken over and continue broiling and basting for another 10-15 minutes.
4. Serve, topped with sprigs of fresh herbs and thin lemon slices.

Lemon Grass Chicken

Louise Hyde
Well-Sweep Herb Farm
Port Murray, NJ

Makes 4-6 servings

1 lb. boneless chicken breast, cut into
  strips
2 stalks lemongrass, chopped
1 tsp. sugar
1/2 tsp. salt
1/4 tsp. black pepper
3 green onions, diced
1 Tbsp. garlic, minced
2 red chile peppers, sliced
1/2 cup chopped fresh basil or mint

1. Mix together all ingredients. Marinate in
   refrigerator for at least 30 minutes.
2. Stir-fry chicken in hot skillet for 3-4
   minutes or until done.
3. Serve over rice.

*Variation: Add 2 Tbsp. apple vinegar to
the marinade.*

Herbed Chicken Breasts

Arlene Shannon
Greenfield Herb Garden
Shipshewana, IN

Makes 4 servings

4-6 boneless, skinless chicken breast
  halves
1/4 cup chopped fresh basil or cinnamon
  basil (2 Tbsp. dried)
1 cup Oriental bread crumbs
basil-flavored olive oil
lemon wedges or fresh tomato salsa

1. Flatten chicken breasts with mallet.
2. Mix together basil and crumbs. Dip
   chicken breasts into crumb mixture.
3. Saute in oil until cooked.
4. Serve with lemon wedges or fresh
   tomato salsa.

Raspberry Basil Chicken

Susan Jehal
Rose Manor Bed & Breakfast
Manheim, PA

Makes 4-6 servings

1 cup raspberry vinegar
2 Tbsp. soy sauce
2 Tbsp. minced fresh basil (2 tsp. dry)
2 Tbsp. Dijon mustard
2 Tbsp. honey
pinch of black pepper
1 lb. chicken cutlets

1. Combine vinegar, soy sauce, basil,
   mustard, honey, and pepper. Add
   chicken, turning to coat. Marinate in
   refrigerator for 15 minutes.
2. Remove chicken from marinade. Reserve
   marinade.
3. Broil chicken in oven or on charcoal
   grill until done, turning once to brown
   both sides.
4. Heat reserved marinade and simmer for
   5 minutes, or until reduced by half.
   Serve over chicken.

Chicken with Basil and Oregano

Gene Banks
Catnip Acres
Oxford, CT

Makes 4 servings

1 clove garlic, minced
1/4 tsp. salt
1 Tbsp. chopped fresh oregano
   (1 tsp. dry)
2 chicken breasts, split
1 Tbsp. olive oil
1 large onion, sliced into rings
1 large red or green pepper, sliced
2 very ripe tomatoes, chopped
1 Tbsp. chopped fresh basil (1 tsp. dried)
1 Tbsp. chopped fresh oregano
   (1 tsp. dried)
2 bay leaves

1. Mix together garlic, salt, and 1 Tbsp. fresh oregano. Rub onto chicken.
2. Pour olive oil into skillet. Add chicken.
3. Smother chicken with onions and peppers. Add tomatoes, basil, oregano, and bay.
4. Steam, covered, over low flame, just until tender.

Variation: Substitute chicken legs, or a small whole chicken, for the chicken breasts. Extend cooking time to about 1 hour, or until chicken is tender.

Italian Chicken Cutlets

Connie Johnson
Heartstone Herb Farm
Loudon, NH

Makes 6-8 servings

2 lbs. boneless, skinless chicken breasts
2 eggs
2 Tbsp. water
1 cup plain bread crumbs
1/2 cup grated Parmesan cheese
1/2 tsp. garlic powder
3 Tbsp. chopped fresh oregano
   (1 Tbsp. dried)
3 Tbsp. chopped fresh basil
   (1 Tbsp. dried)
1/2 tsp. cayenne pepper
1 1/2 Tbsp. chopped fresh parsley
   (1 tsp. dried)
1/4 cup olive or canola oil
2-3 cups tomato sauce
1 1/2 cups grated cheese

1. Wash and pat chicken dry. Pound into thin cutlets.
2. Beat together eggs and water. Set aside.
3. Mix together bread crumbs, Parmesan cheese, garlic powder, oregano, basil, pepper, and parsley.
4. Dip chicken in egg mixture; then into dry mixture. Coat well.
5. Heat oil in frying pan until a few bread crumbs dropped in turn brown immediately. Reduce heat to medium.
6. Cook chicken, turning when brown.
7. Serve on heated platter topped with tomato sauce and grated cheese.

Chicken with Basil Dressing

Cynthia E. Palmer
Braeloch Farm
Richland, MI

Makes 4 servings

2 whole chicken breasts, split
2 thin slices lemon
2 thin slices onion
1 slice fresh ginger
1 cup lightly packed fresh basil
1 clove garlic
1/4 cup white wine vinegar
1/2 cup salad oil
2 Tbsp. grated Parmesan cheese
freshly ground pepper to taste
3 tomatoes sliced
lettuce

1. Place chicken, lemon, onion, and ginger in covered pan. Cover with cold water. Bring to a boil. Turn off and let stand for 20-30 minutes. Check if chicken is done by slashing into thickest part of meat. If it is no longer pink, cool, skin, bone, and cut into chunks.
2. In food processor combine basil, garlic, vinegar, salad oil, Parmesan cheese, and pepper. Puree until smooth.
3. Line a platter with lettuce. Place chicken on top. Arrange sliced tomatoes around edges. Drizzle some dressing over top. Serve with remaining dressing.

Chicken Pesto

Gene Banks
Catnip Acres
Oxford, CT

Makes 3-4 servings

2 boneless chicken breasts,
   cut into small strips
1 tsp. Cajun seasoning, or more
1 Tbsp. olive oil
1 clove garlic
1/4 cup walnuts
2 cups fresh basil
1/2 cup olive oil
1/4 cup Parmesan cheese
1/4 cup chicken broth
1 small jar roasted peppers,
   cut into strips
1/2-1 lb. dry pasta, cooked

1. Sprinkle chicken with Cajun seasoning. Brown in 1 Tbsp. olive oil.
2. Chop garlic and walnuts in food processor. Add basil, olive oil, and Parmesan cheese. Blend well.
3. Add chicken broth and roasted peppers to basil mixture.
4. Pour basil mixture over chicken strips and warm. Serve over pasta.

Chicken or Fish Marinade

Gerry Janus
Vileniki—An Herb Farm
Montdale, PA

Add a handful of mixed herbs (chives, basil, thyme, oregano, or any favorite combination) to leftover white wine. Use as a marinade for chicken or fish.

Chicken Breasts Stuffed with Pesto

Janet Melvin
Heritage Restaurant Gardens and Gifts
Cincinnati, OH

Makes 8 servings

8$\frac{1}{2}$ lbs. boneless, skinless chicken
   breasts
$\frac{1}{2}$ cup chopped fresh basil
6 garlic cloves
$\frac{1}{3}$ cup extra virgin olive oil
$\frac{1}{2}$ cup Parmesan cheese
1 cup fresh bread crumbs
2 Tbsp. pine nuts
watercress (optional)

1. Flatten each chicken breast between two
   sheets of wax paper, until $\frac{1}{2}$" thick.
   Place each on a square buttered piece
   of aluminum foil, shiny side up.
2. In food processor, mix together basil,
   garlic, and olive oil. Pulse several times
   to chop and blend the ingredients.
3. Add cheese and bread crumbs. Process
   to a paste. Add small amount of hot
   water if needed to make the paste
   spreadable. Add pine nuts and pulse to
   chop.
4. Put a portion of basil mixture on the
   center of each breast. Roll the stuffed
   breast jelly-roll style. Wrap tightly in foil.
5. Bake at 350° for 30-35 minutes.
6. Remove each breast from foil. Slice into
   1" slices. Fan slices on serving plate.
   Pour cooking juices over top. Serve hot
   with a garnish of fresh watercress.

Lemon Thyme Chicken

Madeline Wajda
Willow Pond Farm
Fairfield, PA

Makes 4 servings

1-1$\frac{1}{2}$ lbs. boneless, skinless chicken
   breasts
12-15 sprigs of fresh thyme
   or lemon thyme
4 large garlic cloves, minced
2 Tbsp. olive oil
2 Tbsp. lemon juice
freshly ground black pepper
salt to taste

1. Place chicken in large dish.
2. Break thyme sprigs in half and bruise
   them. Layer over chicken.
3. Sprinkle garlic, olive oil, lemon juice,
   and black pepper over chicken. Toss
   until well coated.
4. Cover and marinate in refrigerator for 6-
   8 hours, turning 2-3 times. Brush
   marinade off chicken.
5. Grill over medium coals, or broil, for 10
   minutes, turning frequently. Sprinkle
   with a little salt when almost done.

Chicken Marinade

Robin Giese
Riverview Farm
Fall City, WA

Makes 5-6 servings

3 whole boneless, skinless chicken
  breasts, split and pounded to flatten
3 Tbsp. chopped fresh oregano
  (1 Tbsp. dried)
3 Tbsp. chopped fresh lemon thyme
  (1 Tbsp. dried)
1/2 cup olive oil
juice of one lemon
1 clove garlic, minced
salt to taste
pepper to taste

1. Mix together all ingredients. Pour over
   chicken and marinate for one hour.
2. Remove chicken from marinade and grill.

Thyme Marinade for Chicken

Connie Slagle
Rustic Garden Herbs
Roann, IN

Makes 4 servings

4 boneless, skinless chicken breast halves
2 Tbsp. virgin olive oil
2 cloves garlic, minced
3 Tbsp. chopped fresh lemon thyme
  (1 Tbsp. dried)
3 Tbsp. chopped fresh oregano
  (1 Tbsp. dried)
1/2 tsp. freshly ground pepper
1/2 cup water
1/2 cup white wine

1. Drizzle chicken with oil, and then
   sprinkle with garlic, lemon thyme,
   oregano, and pepper. Let stand for 2
   hours.
2. Place chicken and herbs in heavy skillet.
   Add water and wine. Cover and cook
   over low heat for 12 minutes, turning
   once, until chicken is browned on
   outside and no longer pink in center.
   Serve immediately.

Variation. Mix together all ingredients.
Place in plastic bag and refrigerate for
several hours. Grill.

Grilled Chicken with Honey Herbal Dipping Sauce

Donna Treloar
Harmony
Gaston, IN

Makes 4 servings

2 whole boneless, skinless chicken
  breasts, split
garlic clove, or 1/2 tsp. garlic powder
1/4 tsp. freshly ground pepper
1 1/2 tsp. chopped fresh thyme
  (1/2 tsp. dried)
3/4 cup honey
4 Tbsp. lemon juice
3 Tbsp. butter

1. Rub chicken breasts with garlic clove or
   sprinkle with garlic pepper. Sprinkle
   with pepper and thyme. Begin grilling
   chicken.
2. Mix together honey, lemon juice, butter,
   and any remaining garlic, thyme, and
   pepper. Heat in microwave and stir
   until well mixed.

3. Brush sauce on chicken as it is grilling, or serve as dip for grilled chicken breasts.

Baked Chicken Cutlets

Elaine Seibel
Scents and Non-Scents
Hill, NH

Makes 4 servings

4 boneless, skinless chicken breast halves
1 egg
1 Tbsp. water
1 cup plain bread crumbs
2 Tbsp. chopped fresh lemon thyme
   (2 tsp. dried)
3 Tbsp. chopped fresh parsley
   (1 Tbsp. dried)
1 Tbsp. chopped fresh chives
   (1 tsp. dried)

1. Pound chicken until thin. Set aside.
2. Beat together egg and water. Set aside.
3. Mix together bread crumbs, lemon thyme, parsley, and chives.
4. Dip chicken in egg mixture, and then in bread crumb mixture.
5. Place in single layer in greased pan.
6. Bake at 400° for 25-30 minutes.

Imperial Chicken

Anna L. Brown
Longfellow's Greenhouses
Manchester, ME

Makes 6 servings

1¹/₂ cups fine dried bread crumbs
¹/₂ cup grated Parmesan cheese
¹/₃ cup chopped fresh parsley
   (2 Tbsp. dried)

¹/₄ tsp. garlic powder
¹/₂ tsp. salt
¹/₈ tsp. pepper
6 boneless, skinless chicken breast halves
¹/₄ cup melted margarine

1. Mix together bread crumbs, Parmesan cheese, parsley, garlic powder, salt, and pepper.
2. Dip chicken into margarine; then into crumb mixture. Place in greased 9" x 13" pan. Drizzle with leftover margarine.
3. Bake at 350° for 40 minutes.

Lemon Rosemary Chicken

Sheryl Lozier
Summers Past Farms
El Cajon, CA

Makes 4 servings

¹/₂ cup olive oil
¹/₄ cup fresh lemon juice
1 clove garlic, minced
2 Tbsp. chopped fresh rosemary
   (2 tsp. dried)
2 Tbsp. chopped green scallions
2 tsp. grated lemon zest
¹/₂ tsp. salt
freshly ground pepper to taste
4 boneless, skinless chicken breast halves

1. Whisk together all ingredients except chicken.
2. Pour marinade over chicken. Cover and refrigerate for 4-5 hours.
3. Grill or broil chicken until tender, basting with marinade.
4. Serve marinade along with chicken.

Chicken with Tomatoes, Rosemary, and Wine

Gene Banks
Catnip Acres
Oxford, CT

Makes 4 servings

2 boneless, skinless chicken breasts, split
3 Tbsp. flour
4 Tbsp. olive oil
1 small onion, chopped
1 clove garlic, minced
2 cups chopped fresh or canned
   tomatoes
1/2 cup white wine
1 1/2 tsp. chopped fresh rosemary
   (1/2 tsp. dried)
salt to taste
pepper to taste

1. Dredge chicken with flour. Brown in oil in skillet.
2. Remove chicken. Saute onions and garlic until onions are translucent.
3. Add chicken, tomatoes, wine, rosemary, salt, and pepper. Cook over medium-low heat just until chicken is cooked through.
4. Serve topped with sauce.

Chicken Fillet O'Rose

Judi D. Fogleman
Ashcombe Farm and Greenhouses
Mechanicsburg, PA

Makes 4 servings

4 boneless, skinless chicken breast halves
1 cup flour
1 Tbsp. crushed fresh rosemary
   (1 tsp. dried)
2 tsp. paprika

1 tsp. freshly ground pepper
1/4 cup butter
2 Tbsp. Worcestershire sauce

1. Place chicken fillet on board and pat with flour. Pound with meat tenderizer and hammer until thin. Add flour and flip as needed.
2. Sprinkle with rosemary, paprika, and pepper.
3. Melt butter in 350° skillet or wok. Stir in Worcestershire sauce.
4. Saute chicken until golden brown.
5. Serve on a bed of sauteed vegetables.

Rosemary Garlic Stir-Fry

Sandie Shores
Herb's Herbs and Such . . .
Rochester, MN

Makes 4-6 servings

2 whole boneless, skinless chicken
   breasts, cut into bite-sized strips
1 Tbsp. olive oil
5 or more cloves garlic, minced
2 tsp. chopped fresh rosemary
   (2/3 tsp. dried)
3 cups chopped fresh vegetables
   (broccoli, cauliflower, zucchini,
   summer squash, onions, mushrooms,
   carrots, and/or green beans)
3/4 cup chicken broth
4-6 cups hot cooked rice
1/2 cup cashews
fresh rosemary sprig

1. In large skillet or wok, cook and stir half of the chicken in olive oil for 2 minutes, or until chicken is no longer pink. Remove from pan with slotted spoon. Repeat with remaining chicken. Remove from pan and keep warm.

2. In skillet or wok, cook and stir garlic and rosemary over medium heat for 1 minute. Stir in vegetables and broth. Bring to boil. Reduce heat. Cover and cook mixture for 3 minutes.
3. Return chicken to the skillet or wok. Toss to coat. Heat.
4. Serve over hot cooked rice. Sprinkle with cashews. Garnish with a sprig of fresh rosemary.

La Paix Rosemary Chicken

Myra Bonhage-Hale
La Paix Farm Shop
Alum Bridge, WV

Makes 4 servings

4 boneless, skinless chicken breast halves
5 garlic cloves, minced
3 Tbsp. butter or margarine
1 cup white or rose wine
1½ cups mushrooms (shiitake are preferred), sliced
4 sprigs fresh rosemary, chopped (2 Tbsp. dried)
1 green pepper, cut in strips
1 cup mozzarella cheese, grated
fresh rosemary sprigs

1. In iron skillet, saute chicken and garlic cloves in butter until breasts are golden brown.
2. Stir in wine, mushrooms, and rosemary.
3. Place skillet in oven and bake at 350° for 30 minutes. Check liquid. Add more wine if necessary. Spoon green pepper strips over chicken. Sprinkle mozzarella over chicken and vegetables.
4. Bake for 30 minutes more. Top with additional sprigs of rosemary and serve.

Variation: *Add 1 large onion cut in chunks to chicken before baking.*

Skewered Rosemary Chicken

Mary "Auntie M" Mizio Embler
Auntie M's Enchanted Garden
Clayton, NC

Makes 4-6 servings

1 cup white vinegar
1 cup olive oil
3 Tbsp. fresh rosemary (1 Tbsp. dried)
3 Tbsp. fresh chives (1 Tbsp. dried)
3 Tbsp. fresh parsley (1 Tbsp. dried)
1 clove garlic, minced
1½-2 lbs. chicken breasts, cut into 1" cubes
bamboo or rosemary skewers*

1. Mix together vinegar, olive oil, rosemary, chives, parsley, and garlic. Add chicken and marinate for 1 hour.
2. Thread meat onto bamboo or rosemary skewers that have soaked in water.
3. Bake at 400° for 20-30 minutes, basting 2-3 times with marinade.

* To make rosemary skewers, strip the leaves from stout, woody rosemary branches. Cut one end at an angle to form a sharp point.

To make skewering meat easier, first pierce the meat with an ice pick before threading onto skewers.

Skinny Tarragon Mustard Chicken

Maryanne Schwartz and Tina Sams
The Herb Basket
Landisville, PA

Makes 2 servings

2 boneless, skinless chicken breast halves
3/4 tsp. fresh tarragon (1/4 tsp. dried)
1/4 cup dry white wine
1 tsp. Dijon mustard

1. Spray a medium skillet with non-stick cooking spray. Cook chicken breasts for 3-5 minutes over medium-high heat. Turn chicken and cook a few minutes more until cooked through. Remove chicken from pan and set aside, keeping it warm.
2. Add tarragon, white wine, and mustard to skillet and cook over high heat until juices are syrupy, about 2 minutes.
3. Pour juices over chicken and serve.

Grilled Chicken Dijonnaise

Madeline Wajda
Willow Pond Farm
Fairfield, PA

Makes 4-6 servings

1/4 cup vegetable oil
1/4 cup lemon juice
1/2 tsp. ground pepper
6 boneless, skinless chicken breast halves
3 Tbsp. tarragon vinegar
2 Tbsp. dry white wine
1 Tbsp. chopped fresh tarragon
(1 tsp. dried)
4 Tbsp. butter or margarine
2 Tbsp. Dijon mustard

1. Combine oil, lemon juice, and pepper in shallow dish. Add chicken and turn to coat. Marinate for 30 minutes, stirring occasionally.
2. In saucepan, combine vinegar, wine, and tarragon. Boil until reduced to about 2 tablespoons. Reduce heat to low.
3. Add butter and mustard. Stir until butter melts. Set sauce aside, but keep warm.
4. Drain chicken. Grill or broil over medium heat, turning once. Baste frequently with mustard sauce until cooked through, about 5 minutes per side.
5. Top chicken with remaining sauce and serve.

Chicken-Nectarine-Tarragon Stir-Fry

Mark Silber
Hedgehog Hill Farm
Sumner, ME

Makes 5-6 servings

1/4 cup light oil
2 1/2 lbs. chicken breast, skinned,
    deboned, and cut into 3/4" pieces
1/2 cup slivered almonds
1/4 cup soy sauce, or 2 1/2 Tbsp. tamari
1/2 cup chopped fresh tarragon leaves
    (2 Tbsp. dried)
2 1/2 Tbsp. dry sherry
2 green peppers, chopped into 1" pieces
3 large nectarines, cut into wedges
    1/2" wide
1 1/2 Tbsp. cornstarch
2 1/2 Tbsp. sherry

1. Before cooking, cut up meat, vegetables,
   and fruit.
2. Heat oil in wok to 350°. In small
   handfuls, add chicken and stir until it is
   seared. Move cooked chicken up the
   side. When chicken is done, add slivered
   almonds, half the soy sauce, all of the
   tarragon, and 2 1/2 Tbsp. sherry. Reduce
   heat to 225°. Keep stirring mixture until
   smell of tarragon becomes intense.
2. Add rest of soy sauce and peppers. Stir
   until the peppers begin to turn a deep
   green.
3. Stir in nectarines.
4. Mix together cornstarch and a bit of sherry
   to make paste. When smooth, stir in
   remaining sherry. Add to mixture in wok.
5. Do not allow mixture to stick to the
   bottom of wok. You may need to add a
   bit of water or more sherry. As soon as
   nectarines are hot, remove wok from
   heat.

6. Serve chicken, vegetables, and fruit over
   rice.

Chicken Dijon

Elaine Seibel
Scents and Non-Scents
Hill, NH

Makes 4 servings

2 boneless, skinless chicken breasts,
    sliced into strips
1 Tbsp. oil
2 cloves garlic, minced
1/2 lb. mushrooms, sliced
1 Tbsp. chopped fresh tarragon
    (1 tsp. dried)
1 Tbsp. chopped fresh parsley
    (1 tsp. dried)
1 Tbsp. chopped fresh thyme
    (1 tsp. dried)
1 Tbsp. chopped fresh chives
    (1 tsp. dried)
1 Tbsp. Dijon-style mustard
1/4 cup water or white wine
1 1/4 cups medium white sauce*

1. Saute chicken strips in oil until lightly
   browned. Remove chicken from pan,
   reserving juices.
2. Stir-fry garlic, mushrooms, and herbs for
   1 minute, stirring constantly.
3. Add mustard, water or wine, and white
   sauce, stirring constantly.
4. Add chicken to the sauce and cook
   about 8 minutes more.
5. Serve over cooked rice or noodles.

*Use recipe for sauce on page 187, except
substitute milk for heavy cream, and
eliminate the tarragon.*

MAIN DISHES   185

Out-of-This-World Chicken and Rice

Doris Slatten
Moss' Florist and Greenhouses
Mt. Juliet, TN

Makes 8 servings

1/2 cup butter
1/2 cup olive oil
8-10 pieces of chicken
1 large onion, chopped
1 large green pepper, chopped
1 red pepper, chopped
1 large garlic clove, sliced
1 lb. fresh mushrooms, sliced
12 oz. sliced black olives
salt to taste
pepper to taste
1 1/2 tsp. chopped fresh oregano
    (1/2 tsp. dried)
1 1/2 tsp. chopped fresh rosemary
    (1/2 tsp. dried)
1 1/2 tsp. chopped fresh thyme
    (1/2 tsp. dried)
4 bay leaves
28-oz. can tomatoes, diced
8-oz. can tomato sauce
2 cups water
2 Tbsp. soy sauce
14-oz. box minute rice

1. In Dutch oven, saute chicken in oil and butter.
2. Remove chicken and set aside.
3. Saute onion, green pepper, red pepper, and garlic for 5 minutes. Add mushrooms and olives and saute for 1-2 minutes.
4. Stir in salt, pepper, oregano, rosemary, thyme, bay, tomatoes, tomato sauce, water, and soy sauce. When well mixed, lay chicken pieces on top, then push them down into the vegetables.

5. Bake for 30 minutes at 350°. Increase temperature to 375° and bake for 20 more minutes, or until chicken is tender.
6. Remove chicken from Dutch oven.
7. Add box of minute rice to pot. Cover and let stand for 10 minutes.
8. Place chicken back on top of rice and serve.

Chicken and Mushrooms

Barbara Steele and Marlene Lufriu
Alloway Gardens and Herb Farm
Littlestown, PA

Makes 6 servings

6 Tbsp. olive oil
2 tsp. fresh thyme (2/3 tsp. dried)
1 tsp. paprika
2 1/2-3 lb. chicken, cut in pieces
1/4 cup flour
1/2 cup white wine
2 cups sliced mushrooms
fresh parsley

1. Pour olive oil into 9" x 13" baking dish. Stir in thyme and paprika.
2. Roll chicken pieces in flour. Then roll in olive oil in pan until well coated. Arrange chicken in baking pan with skin side down.
3. Bake at 400° until browned, about 30 minutes.
4. Turn chicken pieces over. Add wine and mushrooms, and sprinkle with chopped parsley. Cover with foil and bake at 350° for 30 minutes.

Creamy Tarragon Chicken

Carol and Harry Miles
Herbs from the Heart
Sonora, CA

Makes 4 servings

1 small chicken
3 chopped shallots or green onions
1/2 lb. mushrooms, sliced
2 Tbsp. butter
1 Tbsp. chopped fresh tarragon
    (1 tsp. dried)
1 1/2 cups cream

1. Cut chicken into serving-sized pieces. Bake or steam until tender.
2. In saucepan, saute shallots and mushrooms in butter. Remove from heat.
3. Stir in tarragon, chicken pieces, and cream. Cook gently until heated through.

Herbal Roasted Chicken

Donna Treloar
Harmony
Gaston, IN

When making herbal roasted chicken in the summertime, I go out to the herb bed and pick a handful each of parsley, sage, thyme, and maybe a sprig or two of rosemary. I stuff all of the herbs into the chicken cavity and then roast it.

To enjoy this dish in the winter, I pick several sprigs of each herb and rubber-band them together to dry. I store the herbs in a dark area. When I'm ready to use them, I stuff the bundle into the cavity of the chicken.

Tarragon Chicken

Cassius L. Chapman
Mr. C's Cooking Castle
Tucker, GA

Makes 4 servings

3-lb. fryer, cut into serving pieces
salt to taste
pepper to taste
3 Tbsp. butter
1 Tbsp. chopped fresh tarragon
    (1 tsp. dried)
2 Tbsp. chopped onion
1/2 cup dry white wine

Sauce:
2 Tbsp. butter
2 Tbsp. flour
1/4 tsp. salt
1 cup heavy cream
1 Tbsp. chopped fresh tarragon

1. Sprinkle chicken with salt and pepper.
2. Melt butter in skillet over medium high heat. Place chicken skin side down in butter. Cook until golden brown.
3. Turn chicken. Sprinkle with tarragon and onions. Cover and cook over low heat for 15 minutes.
4. Lift cover and sprinkle with wine. Replace cover and cook another 15 minutes, or until tender.
5. Transfer chicken to warm bowl and keep warm while making sauce.
6. Add butter to skillet. Blend in flour and salt. Gradually add cream. Cook until sauce is thick.
7. Return chicken to skillet. Sprinkle with tarragon and serve immediately.

Variation: *For a lower calorie dish, use half-and-half instead of heavy cream in Sauce.*

Peggy's Crispy Oven-Baked Chicken

Peggy Ritchie
Herbs and More
Ocala, FL

Makes 4 servings

1/4 cup vinegar
1 tsp. crushed red pepper
1 tsp. coriander
1 tsp. lemon pepper
1 Tbsp. chopped fresh parsley
   (1 tsp. dried)
1 garlic clove, minced
1 Tbsp. chopped onion
1/4 tsp. pepper
1/4 tsp. paprika
1/4 tsp. oregano
dash of cumin
dash of cayenne pepper
3/4 cup olive oil
1 whole chicken, or 4 chicken legs and
   thighs, skinned
1 cup flour
1/4 cup olive oil

1. In blender, mix vinegar, red pepper, coriander, lemon pepper, parsley, garlic, onion, pepper, paprika, oregano, cumin, and cayenne. Mix well. Slowly add 3/4 cup oil and emulsify. Place in large zip-lock bag.
2. Place chicken pieces in bag. Marinate for 2-4 hours.
3. Remove chicken from bag and coat with flour. Let stand for 10 minutes.
4. In skillet, lightly brown chicken in 1/4 cup olive oil. Place in shallow roasting pan.
5. Bake at 425° for 30-40 minutes, or until brown and crispy.

Bar-B-Que Chicken

Dawn Ranck
Harrisonburg, VA

Makes 12 servings

1/2 cup vinegar
1/2 Tbsp. salt
1/4 cup butter, melted
12 pieces of chicken

Sauce:
1/4 cup lemon juice
1 Tbsp. brown sugar
1 Tbsp. Worcestershire sauce
1 tsp. salt
1/2 tsp. prepared mustard
6 Tbsp. butter or margarine, melted
1/2 cup ketchup
2 Tbsp. chopped fresh parsley
   (2 tsp. dried parsley)
2 Tbsp. chopped fresh lemon thyme
   (2 tsp. dried lemon thyme)
2 Tbsp. chopped fresh thyme
   (2 tsp. dried thyme)

1. Mix together vinegar, salt, and butter.
2. Grill chicken until cooked, basting with vinegar mixture every 5-7 minutes.
3. Mix together sauce ingredients. Brush on both sides of chicken. Grill an additional 5 minutes on each side, adding sauce as needed.

Note: If you parboil the chicken before grilling, it takes less time to grill, and the chicken stays very moist.

Rosemary Chicken

Barbara Zink
The Herb Shop
Lititz, PA

Makes 4 servings

3 Tbsp. butter
3-4 lb chicken
1/4 cup, or more, dried rosemary, crushed
salt to taste
pepper to taste
2 Tbsp. flour
fresh rosemary sprigs

1. Rub butter on inside and outside of chicken. Crush 1½ Tbsp. of rosemary on inside of chicken and scatter the remaining rosemary over the outside. Sprinkle with salt and pepper. Place on rack in roasting pan.
2. Bake at 350° for 1½ to 2 hours. Remove to warm platter.
3. Add ½ cup water to drippings and then stir in flour. Cook over low heat until mixture is smooth and bubbly.
4. Garnish chicken with fresh rosemary. Serve drippings over chicken and mashed potatoes.

Roasted Herbal Chicken

Donna Treloar
Harmony
Gaston, IN

Makes 4-6 servings

1 whole roasting chicken
1 onion, quartered
2 garlic cloves: 1 whole, 1 sliced
1 Tbsp. fresh parsley or several sprigs
   (1 tsp. dried)
1 Tbsp. fresh sage or several sprigs
   (1 tsp. dried)
1 Tbsp. fresh rosemary or several sprigs
   (1 tsp. dried)
1 Tbsp. fresh thyme or several sprigs
   (1 tsp. dried)
1 Tbsp. butter, softened
paprika to taste
salt to taste
pepper to taste

1. Clean and wash chicken. Pat dry.
2. In cavity of bird, place quartered onion and sliced garlic. Stuff parsley, sage, rosemary, and thyme in cavity.
3. Rub outside of chicken with garlic clove and then toss into cavity.
4. Rub outside of chicken with softened butter. Sprinkle with paprika, salt, and pepper.
5. Place chicken on rack in shallow baking pan.
6. Bake at 350° for 1¼-1½ hours, depending on size of bird, or until meat is tender, golden brown, drumstick moves freely, and juices run clear.

Note: Leftover chicken makes good sandwiches, or, added to fresh greens, makes a tasty salad.

Note: This chicken dish can also be made in a crockpot.

Variation: Replace chicken with a whole rabbit.

Pot Roast Chicken

Carol Ebbighausen-Smith
C&C Herb Farm
Spokane, WA

Makes 4-6 servings

3 medium onions, quartered
8 stalks celery, cut in thirds
8 medium carrots, cut in thirds
1¹/2 Tbsp. chopped fresh rosemary
  (1¹/2 tsp. dried)
1¹/2 Tbsp. chopped fresh thyme
  (1¹/2 tsp. dried)
1¹/2 Tbsp. chopped fresh parsley
  (1¹/2 tsp. dried)
1¹/2 Tbsp. chopped fresh sage
  (1¹/2 tsp. dried)
1¹/2 Tbsp. chopped fresh oregano
  (1¹/2 tsp. dried)
2 tsp. black pepper
1 tsp. salt
2 Tbsp. oil
3 lb. whole chicken
1 lb. small red potatoes
15-oz. can chicken broth
2 Tbsp. flour
³/4 cup water

1. In Dutch oven, brown together onions, celery, carrots, rosemary, thyme, parsley, sage, oregano, pepper, salt, and oil.
2. With slotted spoon, remove all ingredients to bowl, except drippings. Set aside.
3. Add chicken to Dutch oven. Brown on all sides; then place it on its back in the pan.
4. Return vegetable mixture to pan. Add potatoes and chicken broth. Cover.
5. Bake at 400° for 1¹/2 hours. When chicken is tender, remove to platter and cut into serving pieces. Surround with vegetables. Keep warm until gravy is finished.
6. Stir together flour and water until smooth. Slowly whisk into drippings and broth in Dutch oven. Bring to boil. Remove from heat. Place gravy in bowl and serve with chicken and vegetables.

Sage- & Thyme-Stuffed Roast Chicken

Ary Bruno
Koinonia
Stevenson, MD

Makes 4-6 servings

2¹/2-3 lb. whole frying chicken
1 cup chopped fresh sage (5 Tbsp. dried)
¹/2 cup chopped fresh thyme
  (3 Tbsp. dried)
half a fresh lemon
3 tsp. sea salt
1 tsp. ground black pepper

1. Rinse chicken in cold water.
2. Mix together sage and thyme. Place half in chicken. Put in lemon half and the remaining herbs.
3. Mix salt and pepper together. Rub or sprinkle over the chicken. Tuck in the legs and fold the wing tips under the breast. Place chicken on rack in shallow roasting pan. Loosely cover with aluminium foil.
4. Bake at 425° for 15 minutes. Reduce heat to 325° and roast for 45 minutes. Uncover chicken and cook 15 minutes more, or until chicken is browned and crispy and the juices run clear when it is pricked with a fok between the thigh and breast.
5. Remove "stuffing" and discard. Cut into serving pieces and serve.

Creamy Chicken with Herbs

Amy Hinman-Shade
Shady Side Herb Farm
Hungry Horse, MT

Makes 4 servings

3 cups cooked rice
1 large onion, sliced thin
6-8 mushrooms, sliced thin
2 Tbsp. butter
2 Tbsp. flour
1 cup cream or half-and-half
1 cup chicken broth
3 Tbsp. fresh parsley (1 Tbsp. dried)
1½ tsp. fresh thyme (½ tsp. dried)
2 cups cooked chicken or turkey, cubed
salt to taste
pepper to taste
¾ cup freshly greated Parmesan cheese

1. Spoon rice into bottom of 9" x 9" baking dish.
2. Saute onion and mushrooms in butter for 3-4 minutes. Add flour and whisk until it coats the vegetables.
3. Gradually add cream and chicken broth. Cook over low heat, stirring constantly for 5 minutes.
4. Add parsley, thyme, cubed chicken or turkey, salt, and pepper.
5. Pour mixture over rice. Sprinkle with Parmesan cheese.
6. Bake at 350° for 30-40 minutes, until hot and bubbly.

Note: This is a great way to use leftover chicken or turkey.

Hampton Herbs' Chicken Couscous

Betty Leonard
Hampton Herbs
New Carlisle, OH

Makes 4-6 servings

1 box couscous
salt to taste
veggie pepper to taste
10 oz. frozen peas, thawed
½ lb. boneless, skinless cooked chicken breast, cubed
1 Tbsp. chopped fresh dill (1 tsp. dried)
1 Tbsp. chopped fresh parsley (1 tsp. dried)
freshly grated Parmesan cheese

1. Cook couscous according to instructions on box. Add salt and veggie pepper.
2. Stir in peas, chicken, and herbs. Heat thoroughly.
3. Sprinkle with cheese. Serve immediately.

Tip for Using Herbs

Barb Perry
Lizard Lick Organic Herbs
Huron, TN

The primary rule for cooking with herbs is: let your taste buds be your guide. Using herbs is limited only by the imagination of the person who is cooking! When sprinkling herbs on a dish, if it looks like too much, it is probably just right!

Parsley, Sage, Ginger Turkey

Connie Butto
The Herb Shop
Lititz, PA

Makes 10 servings

15 lb. fresh turkey
10-15 sprigs fresh sage
10-15 sprigs fresh parsley
2 Tbsp. oil
1 Tbsp. ground ginger
3 cups chicken stock
1-2 cups white or rosemary wine
1 cup sweet onions, chopped

1. Rinse turkey and pat dry. Place sage and parsley sprigs in turkey. Place turkey on rack in roasting pan.
2. Rub outside of bird with oil and sprinkle with ginger.
3. Bake at 500° for 15 minutes. (If not using rack, slide turkey around to keep it from sticking.)
4. Add chicken stock, wine, and onions.
5. Cover with lid or foil and bake at 325° for 1½-2 hours, basting frequently. Remove lid or foil and bake another hour.
6. Slice and serve with broth.

Turkey Tenderloin au Poivre

Susie Scott
Little Farm Herb Shop
Allen, MI

Makes 4 servings

2 8-oz turkey tenderloins, butterflied
¼ cup balsamic vinegar
2 Tbsp. soy sauce
2 Tbsp. coriander seeds, cracked or ground
2 Tbsp. black peppercorns, cracked or ground
4 cloves garlic, minced
6 sprigs fresh thyme, chopped (½ tsp. dried)
4 tsp. olive oil
4 tart apples, cored and sliced thin
1 cup cider

1. Rinse and dry tenderloins.
2. Mix together vinegar, soy sauce, coriander, pepper, garlic, and thyme. Pour over turkey. Marinate in refrigerator for 2-5 hours. Remove from refrigerator 20 minutes before cooking.
3. Heat 2 tsp. oil in pan until it begins to smoke. Reduce heat. Add turkey. Cook for 5 minutes on each slide, basting with leftover marinade. Remove from pan and keep warm.
4. Heat 2 tsp. oil in pan over medium high heat. Add apples and cook for 5 minutes. Brown on both sides. Add cider. Reduce heat and cook 5 minutes more until apples are soft.
5. Cut each turkey cutlet in half. Top with apples and serve.

Hunters Duck Made Easy

Judith Defrain
Eye of the Cat
Long Beach, CA

Makes 4-6 servings

4 skinned duck breasts
16 fresh mint leaves
1/2 cup honey
2 Tbsp. butter, melted
1 1/2 tsp. fresh lemon thyme
1 1/2 tsp. fresh parsley
pinch of fresh rosemary
pinch of allspice
1 pkg. stuffing mix

1. Slice breasts on either side of breast
   bone. Place mint leaves in each slit.
2. Mix together honey, butter, thyme,
   parsley, rosemary, and allspice. Baste
   duck with sauce.
3. Make stuffing according to package
   directions. Place on bottom of baking
   dish.
4. Layer duck over stuffing. Cover.
5. Bake at 350° for 1 hour.

Shepherd's Chili

Marilyn Jones
Jones Sheep Farm Bed and Breakfast
Peabody, KS

Makes 5 servings

1 lb. ground lamb
1 large onion, chopped
1 Tbsp. oil
1 tsp. garlic salt
1 Tbsp. chopped fresh oregano
   (1 tsp. dried)
1 1/2 tsp. chopped fresh thyme
   (1/2 tsp. dried)
1/4 tsp. black pepper
14 1/2-oz. can Italian-style stewed
   tomatoes
14 1/2-oz. can diced canned tomatoes
2 cups garbanzo beans
1/2 cup sliced black olives
crumbled feta cheese

1. Saute lamb and onion in oil until meat
   loses pink color, stirring occasionally.
2. Add garlic salt, oregano, thyme, and
   pepper. Stir in tomatoes. Mix well.
3. Add beans and olives. Mix well. Simmer
   for 30 minutes.
4. Garnish with feta cheese and serve.

Lamb Shanks with Tomatoes and Rosemary

Janet Melvin
Heritage Restaurant Gardens and Gifts
Cincinnati, OH

Makes 6 servings

6 1-lb. lamb shanks
salt to taste
pepper to taste
2 Tbsp. olive oil
4 cups chopped onions
4 garlic cloves, minced
2 32-oz. cans tomatoes,
   chopped and drained
1¹/₂ cups dry white wine
1¹/₂ cups chicken stock
1¹/₂ Tbsp. chopped fresh rosemary
   (1¹/₂ tsp. dried)
³/₄ tsp. ground allspice
salt to taste
pepper to taste
1 Tbsp. chopped fresh parsley
   (1 tsp. dried)
1 Tbsp. chopped fresh rosemary
   (1 tsp. dried)

1. Season lamb with salt and pepper. Brown in olive oil. Transfer to roasting pan.
2. Saute onions in oil until soft. Stir in garlic and saute for 3 minutes.
3. Add tomatoes, wine, chicken stock, rosemary, allspice, salt, and pepper. Bring to boil.
4. Pour sauce over lamb. Cover tightly with foil.
5. Braise at 350° for 1¹/₂ hours, or until tender.
6. Remove lamb from sauce. Heat sauce over high heat until reduced to 4 cups. Stir in parsley and rosemary. Serve over lamb.

Fresh Dilled Fish

Maryanne Schwartz and Tina Sams
The Herb Basket
Landisville, PA

Makes 2 servings

12 oz. firm fresh fillets
   (orange roughy and salmon work well)
4 tsp. fresh lemon juice
2 tsp. chopped fresh dill (²/₃ tsp. dried),
   or more
dash of salt
dash of ground pepper
¹/₂ cup sour cream
2 thick slices red onion

1. Rinse and dry fillets. Place skin side down in an oiled baking dish.
2. Sprinkle with lemon juice, dill, salt, and pepper.
3. Spread sour cream evenly over fish. Break onion slices into rings and press into sour cream. Cover.
4. Bake at 375° until fish is no longer translucent and flakes easily with fork. Most fillets take 25-30 minutes, depending on their thickness.
5. Serve with rice or tabbouleh and garnish with a thin slice of lemon and sprig of dill.

Lemon-Thyme Fish

Doris Delatte
Homestead Horticulture
Elk, WA

Makes 2 servings

¹/₂ cup white cooking wine
6 5"-6" sprigs fresh lemon thyme
   (2 tsp. dried)
8 oz. white fish
¹/₂ tsp. chervil, parsley, or dill

1. Measure wine into skillet. Arrange lemon thyme on top of wine. Lay fish on top of lemon thyme.
2. Place lid on skillet and cook on medium high heat for 8 minutes, or until fish flakes easily with fork. Remove fish to serving plate. Garnish with chervil, parsley, or dill.

Variation: Use French tarragon in place of lemon thyme.

Lemon Thyme Fillets

Jennifer Shadle
The Spice Hunter, Inc
Centre Hall, PA

Makes 4 servings

2 Tbsp. butter
1 Tbsp. oil
1 cup fine bread crumbs made from a
   firm white bread
1 Tbsp. fresh lemon thyme
salt to taste
pepper to taste
4 thin, delicate fish fillets
   (sole or orange roughy are good
   choices)
1 egg, beaten

1. Melt butter in large shallow pan. Add oil.
2. Combine bread crumbs and lemon thyme in a bag. Add salt and pepper.
3. Dip fillets in egg, and then toss in bread crumb mixture. Lay in single layer in pan.
4. Bake at 450° for 10 minutes, until fish barely separates when tested with a fork.

Herb-Stuffed Fish

Evelyne Pepin
Ladybug Herbs of Vermont
Wolcott, VT

Makes 4 servings

1 medium onion, chopped
1 Tbsp. butter
2 Tbsp. chopped fresh parsley
   (2 tsp. dried)
2 Tbsp. chopped fresh lemon basil
   (2 tsp. dried)
2 Tbsp. chopped fresh lemon thyme
   (2 tsp. dried)
2 Tbsp. chopped fresh sage (2 tsp. dried)
3/4 cup bread crumbs
1/4 cup chopped walnuts
1 Tbsp. butter or margarine, melted
1 lb. flaky white fish
   (haddock, pollock, flounder, cod)
4-6 Tbsp. butter or margarine, melted
juice from half a lemon
2 fresh tomatoes

1. Saute onion in 1 Tbsp. butter over low heat, until onion is translucent.
2. Stir in parsley, lemon basil, lemon thyme, and sage. Cook for 3 minutes.
3. Add bread crumbs, walnuts, and 1 Tbsp. butter to moisten.
4. Spread mixture in bottom of greased baking dish.
5. Place fish over filling.
6. Mix together 4-6 Tbsp. butter and lemon juice and pour over fish.
7. Bake at 350° for 20 minutes or more, depending upon the thickness of the fish.
7. During the last 10 minutes of the baking time, slice tomatoes and place on top of fish. Continue baking until fish is flaky.

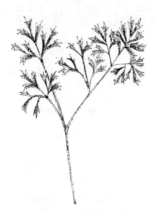

Roasted Fish on Bed of Vegetables

Nancy Raleigh
HBB
Belcamp, MD

Makes 4 servings

8-12 small new potatoes,
    cooked and sliced
2 Tbsp. olive oil
salt to taste
pepper to taste
1 large bunch leeks, trimmed
8-12 plum tomatoes, sliced in half
1/2 cup olive oil
1 Tbsp. chopped fresh parsley
2 garlic cloves, minced
1 Tbsp. chopped fresh basil
4 white fish steaks
1 sweet red onion, chopped

1. Toss together potatoes, 2 Tbsp. olive oil,
   salt, and pepper.
2. Arrange leeks, potatoes, and tomatoes
   in medium roasting pan.
3. Blend together 1/2 cup olive oil, parsley,
   garlic, and basil. Brush over fish.
4. Arrange fish over vegetables. Top with
   chopped onion.
5. Bake at 450° for 8-10 minutes.

Linguine with Clams and Herbs

Irene L. Weidenbacher
Herbs in the Woods
Hollidaysburg, PA

Makes 4 servings

4-5 large garlic cloves, minced
1 Tbsp. olive oil
2-3 Tbsp. butter
1 Tbsp. chopped fresh oregano
    (1 tsp. dried)
1 1/2 tsp. chopped fresh thyme
    (1/2 tsp. dried)
1 1/2 tsp. chopped fresh fennel
    (1/2 tsp. dried)
1 1/2 tsp. chopped fresh basil
    (1/2 tsp. dried)
10-oz. can baby clams with liquid
1/2 tsp. freshly ground pepper
2 Tbsp. chopped fresh parsley
1 lb. dry linguine, cooked
grated Romano cheese

1. Saute garlic for 2-3 minutes in oil and
   melted butter.
2. Add oregano, thyme, fennel, and basil.
   Stir in baby clams, reserving most of the
   liquid. Saute for 2-3 minutes. Add clam
   liquid if needed to create sauce.
3. Add pepper and parsley. Mix well.
4. Spoon clam mixture over drained
   linguine. Serve with grated cheese.

Pasta with Clam Sauce

Carolee Snyder
Carolee's Herb Farm
Hartford City, IN

Makes 4 servings

1/4 cup melted butter or margarine
1/4 cup olive oil
8 Tbsp. scallions, chopped
6 cloves garlic, minced
8-oz. can minced clams, drained,
   with juice reserved
10-oz. can baby clams, drained,
   with juice reserved
6 Tbsp. chopped fresh parsley
   (2 Tbsp. dried)
2 tsp. cornstarch
1/2 cup white wine
red pepper to taste
black pepper to taste
1/4 cup chopped fresh basil (5 tsp. dried)
1 lb. dry angel-hair pasta, cooked
grated Parmesan cheese

1. Melt butter and olive oil in large skillet.
   Add scallions and garlic. Cook just until
   transparent.
2. Stir in clams and parsley. In a separate
   bowl mix together cornstarch and clam
   juice, stirring until cornstarch dissolves.
   Add clam juice, wine, red pepper, and
   black pepper to skillet. Cook for 5
   minutes.
3. Add half the basil to sauce. Stir. Pour
   over pasta. Sprinkle with grated
   Parmesan and remaining basil.

Linguine with White Clam Sauce

Diane Tracey
Chestnut Herb Farm
North Ridgeville, OH

Makes 4 servings

4 Tbsp. virgin olive oil
4 cloves garlic, minced
3 cans chopped clams, drained, but with
   liquid reserved
3/4 tsp. chopped fresh oregano
   (1/4 tsp. dried)
3 Tbsp. chopped fresh parsley
   (1 Tbsp. dried)
4 Tbsp. freshly squeezed lemon juice
2 Tbsp. plain yogurt
1 lb. dry linguine, cooked
2 Tbsp. butter
grated Parmesan cheese

1. Saute garlic in oil for 1 minute. Stir in
   clams, oregano, and parsley. Saute for 1
   minute.
2. Add lemon juice and juice from clams.
   Simmer for 1-2 minutes.
3. Stir in yogurt. Remove from heat.
4. Toss linguine with butter over low heat.
   Serve topped with clam sauce and
   Parmesan cheese.

Stuffed Potatoes and Crab with Basil Butter

Donna Weeks
Old Sage Farm
Laytonsville, MD

Makes 4 servings

4 large baking potatoes
1 lb. crabmeat
4 Tbsp. butter or margarine, softened
1¹/₂ Tbsp. chopped fresh basil
  (1¹/₂ tsp. dried basil)
1 clove garlic, minced
2 Tbsp. chopped fresh dill (2 tsp. dried)
5 green onions, chopped
salt to taste
pepper to taste
4 Tbsp. grated Parmesan cheese

1. Bake potatoes and cut in half. Remove potato, being careful to leave small amount in the shell. Keep the shell for restuffing. Mash potatoes.
2. Stir basil into softened butter until well mixed.
3. Saute crab in 2 Tbsp. basil butter. Stir in remaining butter, garlic, dill, onion, salt, and pepper. Cook over low heat for 5 minutes. Remove from heat.
4. Stir crab mixture into mashed potatoes. Blend well. Put mixture back into potato skins.
5. Top with Parmesan cheese and broil for 5 minutes.

Fennel-Stuffed Flounder Fillets

Davy Dabney
Dabney Herbs
Louisville, KY

Makes 4 servings

2 cups fresh fennel leaves and stalks,
  or 2 Tbsp. fennel seeds
2 cups bread crumbs
¹/₂ cup chopped fresh lovage
  (3 Tbsp. dried)
2 Tbsp. shallots or green onions,
  chopped
¹/₂ cup stock (vegetable, fish, or chicken)
2 Tbsp. oil
4 flounder fillets
4 1" sprigs fresh lemon thyme
  (¹/₄ tsp. dried)

1. Mix together fennel leaves or seeds, bread crumbs, lovage, and shallots. Blend in stock and oil. Set aside.
2. Lay fish in greased baking dish. Divide the stuffing equally on tops of fillets. Top with lemon thyme.
3. Bake at 350° for 25 minutes, or until fish is flaky.

Note: This fish can also be done on the grill.

Herbed Halibut

Rita Holder
Holder's Herbs and Gifts
Choctaw, OK

Makes 4 servings

1/4 cup dry bread crumbs
1/4 cup grated Parmesan cheese
1 Tbsp. chopped fresh basil (1 tsp. dried)
1/4 cup chopped fresh chives
   (5 tsp. dried)
1/4 cup chopped fresh parsley
   (5 tsp. dried)
1/2 tsp. powdered cloves
1/8 tsp. salt
1/8 tsp. pepper
6 Tbsp. melted butter or margarine
4 halibut steaks, each about 3/4" thick
4 tsp. olive oil
lemon slices

1. Mix together crumbs, cheese, basil, chives, parsley, cloves, salt, pepper, and butter.
2. Tear foil into 4 12"-squares. Spray lightly with vegetable oil. Put a steak on each square of foil. Drizzle each with 1 tsp. olive oil. Spread one-fourth of herb mixture on top of each. Seal well.
3. Bake at 450° for 8 minutes.
4. Serve with lemon slices as garnish.

Herb Baked Orange Roughy

Carol Ebbighausen-Smith
C&C Herb Farm
Spokane, WA

Makes 4 servings

2 Tbsp. butter
2 lbs. orange roughy fillets
2 Tbsp. chopped fresh chives
   (2 tsp. dried)
2 Tbsp. chopped fresh dill (2 tsp. dried)
2 Tbsp. chopped fresh lemon thyme
   (2 tsp. dried)
2 Tbsp. chopped fresh tarragon
   (2 tsp. dried)
1 tsp. black pepper

1. Place fillets in one layer in center of large piece of foil. Lay chunks of butter evenly over fish.
2. Mix together chives, dill, lemon thyme, tarragon, and black pepper. Sprinkle herb mixture over fillets. Seal foil tightly. Place on cookie sheet.
3. Bake at 400° for 30 minutes.

Variation: Use your favorite fish fillet instead of orange roughy.

Tip for Using Herbs

Shari Jensen
Crestline Enterprises
Fountain, CO

Always crush dry herb leaves just before adding them to your recipes. This action releases their oils.

Baked Herb Parmesan Roughy

Kathy Mathews
Heavenly Scent Herb Farm
Fenton, MI

Makes 2 servings

10 club crackers, crushed
1 Tbsp. chopped fresh oregano
  (1 tsp. dried)
3/4 tsp. chopped fresh dill (1/4 tsp. dried)
1/4 tsp. garlic powder
2 Tbsp. grated Parmesan cheese
8 oz. orange roughy
2 Tbsp. butter or margarine, melted

1. Mix together cracker crumbs, oregano, dill, garlic powder, and Parmesan cheese.
2. Dip fish in butter and then coat with cracker mixture. Place on cookie sheet.
3. Bake at 450° for 10 minutes per inch of thickness.

Variation: Substitute sole or Boston blue fish for orange roughy.

Orange-Tarragon Salmon

Janet Piepel
The Herb Pantry
East Wenatchee, WA

Makes 8 servings

2 Tbsp. olive oil
1/4 cup orange juice
finely grated zest of one orange
2 tsp. minced garlic
2 Tbsp. fresh tarragon (2 tsp. dried)
salt to taste
pepper to taste
4 8-oz. salmon fillets
2 tsp. freshly snipped chives

1. Mix together olive oil, orange juice, zest, garlic, tarragon, salt, and pepper.
2. Add salmon, turning it over several times until it is well coated. Marinade for 1 hour at room temperature.
3. Place fillets in greased baking dish. Pour marinade over top.
4. Bake at 475° for 7-8 minutes, or until salmon is cooked through.
5. Garnish with chives to serve.

Summer Salmon

Toni Anderson
Cedarsbrook Herb Farm
Sequim, WA

Makes 4 servings

Tarragon Mayonnaise:
1 cup mayonnaise
2 Tbsp. tarragon vinegar
1 Tbsp. chopped fresh tarragon
  (1 tsp. dried)

1 quart water
1/2 cup sherry

4 shallots, cut in half
8 whole cloves (stick one in each shallot)
2 Tbsp. chopped fresh French tarragon
   (2 tsp. dried)
2 whole bay leaves, broken in half
2 salmon fillets
1 lemon, sliced thinly
2 sprigs fresh parsley

1. Mix together mayonnaise, tarragon vinegar, and fresh tarragon. Let stand for a few hours.
2. Combine water, sherry, shallots with cloves, tarragon, and bay. Boil for 5 minutes.
3. Place salmon fillets, skin side down, in broth mixture. Cook at slow boil for up to half an hour, or until salmon is done. Baste salmon with broth while cooking.
4. Place fillets in dish. Pour broth over salmon. Cool. Refrigerate.
5. Remove salmon from jellied broth. Remove skin. Put fish on serving plate. Top with Tarragon Mayonnaise. Garnish with lemon slices and parsley sprigs.

Salmon with Sorrel Butter

Linda Kosa-Postl
Never Enough Thyme
Granite Falls, WA

Makes 4-6 servings

2 lbs. salmon fillets
1 shallot, diced fine
1/3 cup dry white wine
1 1/2 cups chopped fresh sorrel leaves
1 1/2 tsp. chopped fresh tarragon
   (1/2 tsp. dried)
6 Tbsp. unsalted butter
salt to taste
pepper to taste

1. Grill fish over medium-hot charcoal fire, or broil in oven about 6 minutes per side.
2. In heavy saucepan, mix together shallot, wine, and a dash of salt and pepper. Cook until liquid is reduced to about 2 Tbsp.
3. Place sorrel in another saucepan. Cover. Wilt over low heat for 15 seconds. Remove and cool to room temperature.
4. Work the sorrel, wine/shallot mixture, and tarragon into the butter. Season lightly with salt and pepper.
5. Place salmon on platter. Spread with butter and serve.

Grilled Salmon

Harriette Johnson &
Dianna Johnson-Fiergola
Mustard Seed Herbs & Everlastings
Spring Valley, WI

Makes 6-8 servings

fresh fennel sprigs to cover salmon
3 lbs. salmon steaks or fillets
1 cup mayonnaise
1 cup plain yogurt
1 clove minced garlic
1/2 cup diced fresh dill
1 tsp. salt

1. Heat grill, then lay clean fennel leaves on grill rack. Place salmon on fennel.
2. Mix together mayonnaise, yogurt, garlic, dill, and salt. Spread on top of salmon.
3. Grill until done, 20-30 minutes.

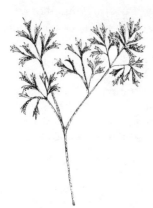

Salmon Loaf

Sue Floyd
Herb Herbert's Herbs
Tahlequah, OK

Makes 4-6 servings

15$1/2$-oz. can salmon
2 cups soft bread crumbs
$1/3$ cup finely chopped onion
$1/4$ cup milk
2 eggs
2 Tbsp. chopped fresh parsley
   (2 tsp. dried)
$1/4$ tsp. salt
1 Tbsp. chopped fresh dill
   (1 tsp. dried)
dash of pepper

1. Drain salmon. Reserve 2 Tbsp. of juice.
   Flake salmon and remove bones if
   desired.
2. Combine all ingredients, including
   salmon juice.
3. Place in well greased 8" x 4" loaf pan.
4. Bake at 350° for 45 minutes.
5. Let set for 10 minutes, remove from
   pan, slice, and serve.

Pesto Shrimp Over Pasta

Amy Hinman-Shade
Shady Side Herb Farm
Hungry Horse, MT

Makes 4-6 servings

1 lb. fresh or frozen shrimp
2 cups fresh basil leaves,
   washed and dried
2 cloves garlic, minced
$1/4$ tsp. salt
pepper to taste
1 cup grated Parmesan cheese
$1/4$ cup olive oil
12-16 dry oz. linguine or fettucine,
   cooked
1 cup pine nuts

1. Cook and drain shrimp in colander.
   Keep warm over steaming water.
2. Make pesto by placing basil, garlic, salt,
   pepper, and $1/4$ cup Parmesan cheese in
   food processor. Process for 10 seconds.
   Slowly add the oil while processing for
   another 10 seconds. Scrape sides and
   process again for 5 seconds.
3. Toss shrimp with pesto.
4. Spoon over hot linguine or fettucine
   and top with remaining Parmesan
   cheese and pine nuts.

Seafood Lasagna

Barbara Warren
Provincial Herbs
Folsom, PA

Makes 8 servings

2 Tbsp. butter
1 large onion, chopped
1¹/₂ cups cottage cheese
8 oz. cream cheese, softened
2 tsp. dried basil
¹/₈ tsp. pepper
1 egg, slightly beaten
2¹/₃ cups white sauce*
¹/₃ cup milk
1 clove garlic, minced
¹/₂ cup dry white wine
¹/₂ lb. bay scallops
¹/₂ lb. flounder fillets, cubed
¹/₂ lb. medium shrimp, peeled and
    deveined
1 lb. dry lasagna noodles, cooked and
    drained
6 oz. mozzarella cheese, shredded
2 Tbsp. grated Parmesan cheese

1. Saute onion in butter until translucent. Stir in cottage cheese, cream cheese, basil, and pepper. Remove from heat. Blend in egg. Set aside.
2. Mix together white sauce, milk, and garlic in large bowl. Stir in wine, scallops, flounder, and shrimp.
3. Cover bottom of greased 9" x 13" baking dish with one-third of the noodles. Alternate layers of cottage cheese mixture, mozzarella cheese, seafood mixture, and noodles, using one-third of each for each layer. Sprinkle top layer with Parmesan cheese.
4. Bake at 350° for 45 minutes, or until hot and bubbly. Let stand 10 minutes before cutting.

*Double the recipe for Sauce on page 187, substitute milk for heavy cream, and eliminate the tarragon.

Seafood Quiche

Alberta Wamsley
Thorn Tree Hill Herb Farm
Warsaw, IN

Makes 6 servings

1 pie shell
2 egg whites, slightly beaten
1 egg, beaten
1¹/₂ cups milk
¹/₃ cup chopped scallions
1 Tbsp. fresh oregano (1 tsp. dried)
¹/₄ cup chopped fresh basil
    (1 Tbsp. dried)
2 diced plum tomatoes
2 cloves garlic, minced
1³/₄ cups crabmeat
1¹/₄ cups shredded cheddar and Swiss
    cheeses, mixed
1 Tbsp. flour

1. Prick pie shell with fork. Line with foil and bake at 450° for 5 minutes. Remove foil and bake for 5 minutes, or until shell is nearly fully baked. Remove from oven.
2. Stir together egg whites, egg, milk, scallions, oregano, basil, tomatoes, and garlic. Stir until well blended. Add crabmeat.
3. Mix together cheeses and flour. Add to egg mixture. Mix well. Pour into pie shell.
4. Bake at 350° for 35-40 minutes. Let cool 10 minutes before cutting.

Desserts

Heavenly Fruit

Kelly Wisner
Herbal Heaven
Wernersville, PA

Makes 1 serving

1 cup fresh fruit (any variety)
1 Tbsp. coarsely chopped fresh basil
   (1 tsp. dried)
1/2 Tbsp. coarsely chopped fresh lemon
   balm or lemon verbena (1 tsp. dried)
fresh flower blooms

1. Cut fruit into bite-size pieces.
2. Stir in basil and lemon balm or lemon
   verbena. Blend well. Cover.
3. Place in freezer for at least 2 hours.
4. Before serving, garnish with a fresh
   pansy or sprinkle with miniature rose
   petals.

*A fat-free, healthy, and delicious dessert
on a hot humid day.*

Applemint Fruit Salad

Carol Vaughn
Healthy Horse Herb Farm
Onley, VA

Makes 6 servings

2 Tbsp. applemint vinegar (see page 56)
1/4 cup sugar or honey
5 cups cut-up fruit (3 apples, 2 bananas,
   and 2 oranges, mixed with 1/2 tsp.
   lemon juice, or your choice of fruits)
fresh mint sprigs

1. Mix together vinegar and sugar or
   honey. Fold mixture into fruit. Chill.
2. Garnish with a sprig of mint and serve.

Fresh Fruit Dip

Judy and Don Jensen
Fairlight Gardens
Auburn, WA

Makes 2 cups

8 oz. cream cheese, softened
2 Tbsp. orange juice concentrate
7-9-oz. jar marshmallow cream
1 tsp. chopped fresh tarragon

1. Mix together all ingredients.
2. Serve with fresh fruit.

Tarragon, Grape, Honey Sauce

Brandon Brown
Brown's Edgewood Gardens
Orlando, FL

Makes 1/2 cup

3 sprigs fresh tarragon, finely chopped
1/4 cup seedless red grapes, quartered
1/4 cup honey

1. In saucepan, heat together all ingredients until flavors blend, but herb and fruit do not lose their texture.
2. Serve over ice cream or frozen yogurt.

Lemon Balm Blueberry Cake

Wendy Harrington
Harvest Herb Company
Malone, NY

Makes 8-10 servings

3/4 cup milk
3 Tbsp. chopped fresh lemon balm leaves
2 eggs
1 cup sugar
6 Tbsp. butter, softened
2 cups flour
1 1/2 tsp. baking powder
2 Tbsp. grated lemon zest
1 1/2 cups blueberries, fresh or frozen
powdered sugar

1. In saucepan, combine milk and lemon balm. Heat until hot but not boiling. Allow to cool to room temperature.
2. In mixing bowl, cream together eggs, sugar, and butter. In separate bowl, stir together dry ingredients.
3. Add dry ingredients to the creamed batter, alternately with the lemon balm/milk mixture, stirring constantly until well blended and smooth.
4. Fold in fresh blueberries and lemon zest. (If using frozen berries, thaw, drain of all juice, and toss lightly with 2 Tbsp. flour, before adding to batter.)
5. Pour batter into greased 8" square cake pan.
6. Bake at 350° for 50-60 minutes, or until cake tester comes out clean.
7. Dust with powdered sugar.

Harmony Poppy Seed Cake

Donna Treloar
Harmony
Gaston, IN

Makes 1 full-sized loaf, or 4 mini-loaves

Cake:
2 cups flour
1¼ cups sugar
2 eggs
1 cup milk
1 tsp. salt
1 tsp. baking powder
¾ cup cooking oil
2 Tbsp. poppy seeds
1 tsp. butter flavoring
1 tsp. almond flavoring
1 tsp. vanilla
3 Tbsp. chopped fresh lemon balm
   (1 Tbsp. dried)

Glaze:
¼ cup freshly squeezed orange juice
¾ cup sugar
½ tsp. vanilla
½ tsp. butter flavoring
½ tsp. almond flavoring
1 Tbsp. chopped fresh lemon balm
   (1 tsp. dried)

1. In large mixer bowl, blend together all cake ingredients. Beat for 2 minutes, or until well mixed. Pour into greased 9" x 5" loaf pan or 4 mini-loaf pans.
2. Bake at 350° for 1 hour (less time for mini-loaves). Test with toothpick.
3. While cake is baking, mix together orange juice and sugar in saucepan. Stir frequently and cook slowly until sugar melts. Do not boil. Remove from heat.
4. Stir in vanilla, butter flavoring, almond flavoring, and lemon balm.
5. While cake is still hot and in pans, spoon glaze over cake. Let sit for 15 minutes before removing from pan. Cool.

Bay Leaf Pound Cake

Nancy J. Reppert
Sweet Remembrances
Mechanicsburg, PA

Makes 12 servings

4 bay leaves
½ cup milk
½ cup butter, softened
¾ cup sugar
2 eggs, room temperature
1½ cups cake flour
1 tsp. baking powder

1. Mix together milk and bay leaves in saucepan. Bring to simmer, stirring occasionally. Remove from heat and cool completely.
2. Beat butter until creamy. Add sugar. Beat until creamy. Add eggs, beating until fluffy.
3. Sift together flour and baking powder. Add to creamed mixture just until blended.
4. Strain milk and discard bay leaves. Mix cooled milk into batter just until blended.
5. Spread into greased and floured 8" x 4" loaf pan.
6. Bake at 350° for 40-50 minutes. Cool for 10 minutes before removing from pan.
7. Serve plain or topped with pureed strawberries or peaches.

Rosemary Pound Cake

Janet Piepel
The Herb Pantry
East Wenatchee, WA

Makes 2 loaves

1 cup butter, softened
1 cup sugar
1/4 cup honey
5 large eggs
2 cups cake flour
1 tsp. baking powder
1 Tbsp. fresh rosemary (1 tsp. dried)
1/4 tsp orange extract
1 1/4 tsp. grated orange peel
1 1/2 tsp. orange juice

1. Cream together butter and sugar until light and creamy. Beat in honey.
2. Add eggs, one at a time, beating 1 minute after adding each egg.
3. Sift together flour and baking powder. Gradually add flour mixture to sugar mixture, beating on low speed just until blended.
4. Gently stir in rosemary, orange extract, peel, and juice.
5. Pour into two greased and floured 8" x 4" pans.
6. Bake at 325° for 45 minutes. Cool in pans for 10 minutes. Remove from pans and cool on wire rack.

Quick Rosemary Pound Cake or Brownies

Elizabeth O'Toole
O'Toole's Herb Farm
Madison, FL

Add 2 Tbsp. of finely chopped fresh rosemary to any cake mix or brownie mix.

Cool Citrus Cheesecake

Elizabeth ('B') O'Toole
O'Toole's Herb Farm
Madison, FL

Makes 10 servings

4 oz. low-fat cream cheese
2 1/2 cups low-fat cottage cheese
3 egg whites
1/2 cup sugar
2/3 Tbsp. lemon juice
2 tsp. lemon zest
2 tsp. orange zest
2-3 Tbsp. fresh lemon thyme or lemon balm
1 cup ground almonds
10" graham cracker crust
fresh Johnny-jump-up blossoms

1. Process cream cheese and cottage cheese in blender or food processor until smooth.
2. Add remaining ingredients (except crust) and blend until well combined. Pour into crust.
3. Bake at 350° for 30 minutes. Turn oven off and leave cake in oven for another 5 minutes. Remove and cool.
4. Cover and chill. Top with fresh Johnny-jump-up blossoms to serve.

Lemon Thyme Cheesecake

Alberta Wamsley
Thorn Tree Hill Herb Farm
Warsaw, IN

Makes 6 servings

1 unbaked pie shell
12 oz. cream cheese
2 Tbsp. honey
2 Tbsp. butter
2 eggs
4-5 Tbsp. finely chopped lemon thyme

1. Prick pie shell with fork. Line with foil. Bake at 400° for 5 minutes. Remove foil. Bake 10 more minutes, or until shell is almost done. Remove from oven. Reduce oven temperature to 350°.
2. Beat together cream cheese, honey, and butter until soft and creamy. Beat in eggs and fold in lemon thyme. Pour into pie shell.
3. Bake at 350° for 45 minutes, or until knife inserted in center comes out clean.
4. Serve with mint herb sorbet.

Chocolate Mint Bran Brownies

Lucy Scanlon
Merrymount Herbs
Norris, TN

Makes 10-12 servings

1 Tbsp. water
3 Tbsp. baking cocoa powder
1 Tbsp. dry instant coffee
2 very ripe bananas
2 cups sugar
3/4 cup egg whites (about 6 egg whites)
1 tsp. vanilla
1 cup dry oat bran
1/4 tsp. salt
1 cup nuts and/or raisins (such as almonds and currants)
1/2 cup chopped fresh chocolate mint leaves (3 Tbsp. dried)

1. Blend water, cocoa, coffee, and bananas in food processor.
2. Add sugar, egg whites, and vanilla. Mix well.
3. Stir in by hand oat bran, salt, nuts, raisins, and mint.
4. Pour into greased 8" x 8" baking pan.
5. Bake at 350° for 45 minutes. Cool for at least 10 minutes. Cut into squares.

Sweet Remembrance Bars

Paula Winchester
Herb Gathering Inc.
Kansas City, MO

Makes 8-12 servings

2 eggs
1 cup packed brown sugar
1 cup flour
1 tsp. baking powder
$1/2$ tsp. salt
1 Tbsp. minced fresh rosemary
    (1 tsp. dried)
1 cup golden raisins
1 cup chopped pecans
2 Tbsp. grated fresh orange peel

1. Beat eggs. Stir in sugar and mix well.
2. Sift together flour, baking powder, and salt. Add gradually to egg mixture. Mix well.
3. Fold in rosemary, raisins, pecans, and orange peel.
4. Spread into greased 9" square pan.
5. Bake at 350° for 25 minutes, or until golden brown.
6. Cool before cutting into bars.

A heart-healthy dessert—no oil!

Herb Cookies and Cake

Lynn Halstead
The Kitchen Garden
Canadensis, PA

To spice up any plain baked goods like sugar cookies or pound cake, try adding 2 Tbsp. of fresh chopped mint, rosemary, basil, or lemon thyme to the batter.

Rosemary Dessert Squares

Martha Gummersall Paul
Martha's Herbary
Pomfret, CT

Makes 8 servings

2 eggs
1 cup brown sugar
2 tsp. vanilla
1 cup flour, sifted
$1/2$ tsp. salt
1 tsp. baking powder
1 Tbsp. chopped fresh rosemary
    (1 tsp. dried)
$2/3$ cup chopped pecans
1 cup raisins
$1/4$ cup chopped dried cranberries
$1/4$ cup chopped dried apricots

1. Beat eggs. Gradually add brown sugar, vanilla, flour, salt, baking powder, and rosemary. Mix well.
2. Fold in pecans, raisins, cranberries, and apricots.
3. Pour into greased and floured 8" x 8" pan.
4. Bake at 350° for 30 minutes. Cool before cutting into bars.

Chocolate Chip Mint Cookies

Elaine Seibel
Scents and Non-Scents
Hill, NH

Makes 8-9 dozen small cookies

1/2 cup butter or shortening, softened
1/2 cup firmly packed brown sugar
1/2 cup white sugar
1 tsp. vanilla
1 egg
1 1/4 cups sifted flour
3/4 tsp. baking soda
1/2 tsp. salt
1/4 cup dried mint, crumbled
10-oz. pkg. chocolate chips

1. Cream together butter and sugars. Stir in vanilla and egg. Mix well.
2. Combine flour, baking soda, salt, and mint. Add to creamed mixture and mix well. Stir in chocolate chips by hand.
3. Drop dough by teaspoonful on an ungreased cookie sheet.
4. Bake at 375° for 8-10 minutes.

Mint Cookies

Jeanette Page
The Backdoor Store, Herbs & More
Oak Ridge, TN

Makes 3 dozen cookies

1/2 cup butter, softened
1 cup sugar
2 eggs
1 Tbsp. chopped fresh mint (1 tsp. dried)
5 drops essence of peppermint oil
1 1/2 cups flour
2 tsp. baking powder
1/2 tsp. sea salt

1. Cream together butter and sugar. Add eggs, mint, and oil and mix well.
2. Stir in flour, baking powder, and sea salt. Mix well.
3. Drop by teaspoonful onto lightly greased cookie sheet.
4. Bake at 350° for 8-10 minutes.

Variations: Instead of mint and peppermint oil, use lemon balm and essence of lemon oil. Or substitute lavender or anise in place of mint.

Lavender or Mint Cookies

Lorraine Hamilton
Lorraine's Herb Garden
Neelyton, PA

Makes 2 dozen cookies

1/4 cup butter, softened
1/2 cup sugar
1 egg
1 Tbsp. chopped fresh lavender leaves (1 tsp. dried), or 1 Tbsp. chopped fresh mint (1 tsp. dried)
1 cup flour
1 tsp. baking soda
1/4 tsp. salt

1. Cream together butter and sugar.
2. Stir in egg and lavender or mint. Mix well.
3. Sift together flour, baking soda, and salt. Add to creamed mixture.
4. Drop by teaspoonful onto greased cookie sheet.
5. Bake at 375° for 7-10 minutes. (These cookies burn easily, so watch them carefully.)

Herb Tea Cookies

Timothy L. Newcomer
The Herb Merchant
Carlisle, PA

Makes 3 dozen cookies

1 cup butter, softened
1/2 cup sugar
1/2 (scant) tsp. peppermint or
   spearmint oil
2 Tbsp. chopped fresh peppermint or
   spearmint (2 tsp. dried)
2 cups flour
few grains salt
2-3 drops red, yellow, or green food
   coloring
granulated sugar

1. Cream together butter and sugar.
2. Stir in oil, mint, flour, and salt. Mix well.
   Chill.
3. Color sugar with food coloring.
4. Roll dough into 1" balls and roll in
   colored sugar. Gently press each ball
   with thumb to flatten slightly. Place on
   greased cookie sheets.
5. Bake at 350° for 10 minutes.

Lemon Thyme Cookies I

Madeline Wajda
Willow Pond Farm
Fairfield, PA

Makes 4 dozen cookies

1 cup butter, softened
1 1/2 cups sugar
2 eggs
3 cups unbleached flour
1 Tbsp. cream of tartar
1/2 tsp. salt
1/2 cup, rounded, chopped fresh lemon
   thyme (2 Tbsp. dried)

1. Cream together butter and sugar. Add
   eggs and mix well.
2. Sift together flour, cream of tartar, and
   salt. Add to creamed mixture.
3. Stir in lemon thyme. Chill overnight.
4. Roll into walnut-sized balls. Place on
   greased cookie sheet.
5. Bake at 350° for 12 minutes.

Candied Mint Leaves

Lorraine Hamilton
Lorraine's Herb Garden
Neelyton, PA

Mix egg white with 1 tsp. orange
juice until frothy. Paint fresh mint leaves
with mixture and sprinkle with
superfine sugar. Let dry on waxed
paper.

Jill's Lemon Thyme Cookies

Betty Leonard
Hampton Herbs
New Carlisle, OH

Makes 8 dozen small cookies

$^1/_2$ cup butter
2 eggs
8 oz. cream cheese
1$^1/_2$ cups sugar
2 Tbsp. lemon juice (or 1 Tbsp. lemon
   juice and 1 Tbsp. lemon vinegar)
1 tsp. grated lemon rind
2-3 Tbsp. chopped fresh lemon thyme
   (2-3 tsp. dried)
2$^1/_2$ cups flour
1 tsp. cream of tartar
$^1/_2$ tsp. salt

1. Cream together butter, eggs, cream
   cheese, and sugar.
2. Add juice, rind, and lemon thyme. Mix
   well.
3. Sift together flour, cream of tartar, and
   salt. Work into creamed mixture.
   Refrigerate until thoroughly chilled.
4. Roll into balls about 1-inch in diameter.
   Place on greased cookie sheet.
5. Bake at 350° for 10-15 minutes.

Lemon Thyme Cookies II

Nancy Ketner
Sweet Earth
West Reading, PA

Makes 3 dozen cookies

$^1/_2$ cup butter
$^1/_2$ cup shortening
1 cup sugar
1 tsp. lemon extract
1 egg
2 tsp. chopped fresh lemon thyme
   ($^2/_3$ tsp. dried)
2 cups flour
$^1/_2$ tsp. cream of tartar
$^1/_2$ tsp. baking soda

1. Cream together butter, shortening, and
   sugar. Add extract, egg, and lemon
   thyme. Mix well.
2. Sift together flour, cream of tartar, and
   baking soda. Add to creamed mixture.
   Mix well. Chill.
3. Roll into 1" balls. Place on greased
   cookie sheet and flatten.
4. Bake at 350° for 7-10 minutes.

Tip for Using Herbs

Shatoiya de la Tour
Dry Creek Herb Farm
Auburn, CA

When adding fresh herbs to cold
dishes, be sure to allow several hours
for the dish to marinate so that the full
flavor of the herbs comes through.

Stir-N-Drop Herbal Cookies

Sheryl Lozier
Summers Past Farms
El Cajon, CA

Makes about 2¹/₂ dozen cookies

2 eggs
²/₃ cup vegetable oil
2 tsp. vanilla
2 Tbsp. grated lemon rind
6 Tbsp. chopped fresh lemon thyme
   (2 Tbsp. dried)
³/₄ cup sugar
2 cups flour
2 tsp. baking powder
¹/₂ tsp. salt
1 Tbsp. sugar

1. Beat eggs with fork. Stir in oil, vanilla, lemon rind, and lemon thyme. Blend in ³/₄ cup sugar.
2. Sift together flour, baking powder, and salt. Add to egg mixture. Mix well.
3. Drop by tablespoonsful about 2 inches apart onto ungreased cookie sheet. Lightly oil the bottom of a glass and dip it in 1 Tbsp. sugar. Stamp each cookie flat with bottom of glass.
4. Bake at 400° for 8-10 minutes.

Rosemary Almond Cookies

Flo Stanley
Mililani Herbs
Mililani, HI

Makes 25-30 cookies

¹/₂ cup unsalted butter
¹/₄ cup sugar
1 Tbsp. Pernod (anise-flavored liqueur)
   or 2 tsp. vanilla
1¹/₄ cups flour
¹/₄ tsp. salt
1-2 Tbsp. chopped fresh rosemary
   (1-2 tsp. dried)
¹/₄ cup chopped almonds
¹/₄ cup sugar

1. Cream together butter and ¹/₄ cup sugar. Blend in Pernod or vanilla. Mix well.
2. Stir in flour, salt, rosemary, and almonds. Mix well. Dough should be soft but not sticky. Add more flour, 1 Tbsp. at a time, if needed.
3. Roll dough into walnut-size balls. Roll in ¹/₄ cup sugar. Flatten between palms of hand to about ¹/₄" thickness. Place on greased cookie sheet.
4. Bake at 350° for 15-20 minutes, or until golden. Keeps well in airtight container.

Note: *Dough may be rolled into logs, placed in plastic wrap, and frozen for future baking. Thaw slightly, slice ¹/₄" thick, dip in sugar, and bake.*

Blueberry Cobbler with Mint

Amy Hinman-Shade
Shady Side Herb Farm
Hungry Horse, MT

Makes 6 servings

1/3 cup sugar
1 Tbsp. cornstarch
1/4 cup water
4 cups blueberries
3 tsp. chopped fresh peppermint
   (1 tsp. dried)
1/2 tsp. vanilla
1 cup flour
1 Tbsp. sugar
1 tsp. baking powder
1/2 tsp. salt
1/4 cup butter
1/4 cup milk
1 egg, beaten
sprigs of fresh mint

1. In saucepan, combine 1/3 cup sugar, cornstarch, water, and blueberries. Heat on medium-high until hot and bubbly. Stir in peppermint and vanilla. Mix well. Keep hot.
2. In a separate bowl mix together flour, 1 Tbsp. sugar, baking powder, and salt. Cut in butter until mixture becomes the size of peas.
3. Stir in milk and egg. Blend well.
4. Pour hot blueberry filling in greased 8" x 8" pan. Spoon dough over fruit.
5. Bake at 400° for 20-25 minutes.
6. Serve warm with ice cream and garnish with sprigs of fresh mint.

Apple Crisp with Dill

Gene Banks
Catnip Acres
Oxford, CT

Makes 4 servings

2 cups peeled and finely sliced apples
1 tsp. dill seeds
1/4 cup butter, melted
1 egg
3/4 cup sugar
3/4 cup flour
2 tsp. baking powder
1/2 tsp. salt

1. Place apples in greased casserole. Sprinkle with dill seeds.
2. Mix together butter and egg. Sift in dry ingredients and stir just until mixed.
3. Drop by teaspoonful onto apples.
4. Bake at 350° for 40 minutes.
5. Serve warm with cream or vanilla ice cream.

Peppermint Whoop-Tee-Doo

Shatoiya de la Tour
Dry Creek Herb Farm
Auburn, CA

Makes 8 servings

3 egg whites
1 cup sugar
1 tsp. vanilla
1 Tbsp. chopped fresh peppermint
20 butter crackers rolled into crumbs
3/4 cup chopped pecans
1 cup whipping cream
1 Tbsp. sugar, or to taste
1 drop essence of peppermint oil

1. Beat egg whites until stiff.
2. Fold in 1 cup sugar, vanilla, peppermint, cracker crumbs, and pecans.
3. Pour into buttered 8" x 8" baking dish.
4. Bake at 350° until brown, about 20-25 minutes. Cool.
5. Whip cream with 1 Tbsp. sugar.
6. Fold in oil.
7. Chill before serving. Top baked dessert with whipped cream.

Bay Custard

Paula Winchester
Herb Gathering, Inc.
Kansas City, MO

Makes 6 servings

1½ cups milk
1 cup light cream
4 large fresh bay leaves (1 dried bay leaf)
4 beaten egg yolks
¼ cup honey
dash of salt

1. In saucepan, combine milk, cream, and bay leaves. Heat until scalded. Cool about 10 minutes. Remove bay leaves.
2. Stir about 1 cup of the hot mixture into egg yolks. Stir in honey and salt, and then add to remaining mixture in saucepan.
3. Pour into 9" quiche dish. Place in a 9" x 13" cake pan. Fill pan with 1" of hot water.
4. Bake at 350° for 35-40 minutes, or until just set. Remove dish from water. Cool, then chill before serving.

Variation: *Substitute peppermint, rosemary, or lemon thyme for bay.*

Rice Pudding

Maria Price-Nowakowski
Willow Oak Flower and Herb Farm
Severn, MN

Makes 6-8 servings

1 cup rice
6 cups milk
½ cup, plus 2 Tbsp. sugar
1 whole vanilla bean, slit
¼ cup chopped fresh lemon thyme
cinnamon for dusting

1. In Dutch oven, cover rice with 1 inch of water. Boil for 5 minutes. Let stand until water is absorbed.
2. Stir in milk, sugar, and vanilla bean. Simmer for 45-60 minutes, until rice is tender. Add lemon thyme 10 minutes before end of cooking time.
3. Remove vanilla bean, pour pudding into individual bowls, sprinkle with cinnamon, and serve.

Pineapple Mint Ice

Diane Clement
Clement Herb Farm
Rogers, AR

Makes 4 servings

1 cup cubed fresh pineapple,
    or 1 8¼-oz. can unsweetened
    pineapple chunks
½ cup grapefruit juice
¼ cup honey
15 fresh mint leaves (pineapple,
    peppermint, or spearmint)
½ tsp. grated fresh lemon peel
2 Tbsp. fresh lemon juice
fresh mint sprigs

1. Mix together all ingredients. Puree until
   pineapple is completely blended and
   mint leaves are finely chopped.
2. Place in freezer until mixture is firm but
   not solid, about 1-2 hours.
3. Scoop out into sherbet or tall parfait
   glasses. Garnish with mint sprigs and
   serve.

Mint Sorbet

Karen Ashworth
The Herb Shoppe
Duenweg, MO

Makes 1 quart sorbet

¼ cup large fresh sprigs applemint,
    orange mint, spearmint, or chocolate
    mint (5 tsp. dried)
5 cups water
1½ cups sugar
1 cup seltzer water without salt
juice of 4-5 lemons
1 egg white, stiffly beaten
fresh sprigs of mint

1. Chop mint leaves coarsely. In saucepan,
   mix together mint, water, and sugar.
   Bring to a boil. Stir to dissolve sugar.
   Reduce heat and simmer for 5 minutes.
   Cool. Refrigerate for at least 8 hours.
2. Strain out mint leaves.
3. Add seltzer and lemon juice to mint
   mixture. Freeze in ice cream freezer or
   in deep freeze. When mixture is semi-
   frozen, fold in egg white and freeze
   until frozen.
4. Serve in individual glasses with sprigs of
   mint.

Rosemary-Orange Sorbet

Danielle Vachow
Busha's Brae Herb Farm
Suttons Bay, MI

Makes 12 servings

1 cup sugar
1 Tbsp. grated orange zest
1 cup water
3 4-inch sprigs fresh rosemary
2 cups orange juice
2 Tbsp. lemon juice
1 egg white
fresh rosemary sprigs

1. Place sugar, orange zest, and water in
   saucepan. Bring to boil. Remove from
   heat when liquid is clear. Stir in
   rosemary sprigs. Steep for 10 minutes.
   Strain liquid through clean muslin
   cloth. Cool to room temperature.
2. Stir in orange and lemon juices. Freeze
   for 8 hours, until nearly solid.
   (However, if mixture becomes too hard,
   it is difficult to whip.)
3. Remove from freezer. Scrape mixture
   out of container and into a large bowl
   with a spoon, breaking up the mixture

into chunks. Whip with a wire whisk until frothy but not melted.

4. In small bowl, beat egg white until stiff but not dry. Gently fold into whipped frozen mixture.
5. Return sorbet to freezer until serving time. Scoop out with ice cream scoop. Garnish with sprigs of fresh rosemary.

Lemon Granita

Janette Petersen
Rose Herb Nursery
La Center, CO

Makes 10-12 servings

4 cups strong lemon tea made with
   lemon mint
1½ cups sugar
2½ cups fresh lemon juice
lemon herbs for garnish

1. Combine tea and sugar in large saucepan, stirring over medium heat just until liquid comes to a boil and the sugar is dissolved. Remove from heat and cool.
2. Stir in lemon juice. Pour into shallow glass dish and place in freezer for 5 hours, stirring thoroughly every hour. Pack in a bowl and refreeze.
3. Spoon into sherbet dishes and garnish with lemon mint, lemon balm, or lemon verbena.

Horehound Candy

Davy Dabney
Dabney Herbs
Louisville, KY

Makes 1 lb. candy

2 qts. water
1 cup chopped fresh horehound
   (⅓ cup dried)
1 cup chopped fresh lemon balm
   (⅓ cup dried)
2½ cups sugar
2 tsp. cream of tartar
lemon sugar (see recipe below)

1. Bring 2 quarts water to boil in large saucepan. Stir in horehound and lemon balm. Cover and steep 10 minutes. Strain into large pan.
2. Stir in sugar and cream of tartar. Boil, without stirring, until candy thermometer reaches 312°.
3. Pour mixture into greased 9" x 13" pan. Cool.
4. Cut into squares and roll in lemon sugar. (If mixture has become too hard to cut, break into pieces and roll in lemon sugar.) Pack in airtight container. Good for sore throats and coughs!

Lemon Sugar

½ cup chopped fresh lemon balm
1 cup superfine sugar

Mix together lemon balm and sugar. Store in closed glass jar, shaking every day for a week. Pour sugar through strainer to remove chopped leaves before using.

Basil

The Plant

Basil grows tall and bushy with large, deep green leaves and spikes of small white flowers.

Its Flavor

Basil is pungent and spicy, but not bitter. It has strength, but doesn't overpower.

Its Growing Needs

Basil is an annual that requires rich soil and full sun, but dislikes persistent scorching heat. Frost blackens it dramatically and destroys it quickly. Pinch off the flowers to keep the leaves sweetly pungent and to encourage fuller leafy growth of the bush.

Grow indoors in potting soil in a sunny window or under plant lights. Keep well watered and at room temperature.

How to Harvest It

Basil thrives when its leaves are picked, so harvest the leaves as soon as the bush has a good start. Keep a fresh bunch of basil on your kitchen counter in a glass of water. It will stay fresh for several days at moderate temperatures.

To dry, hang bunches upside down in a warm room with low humidity. Because of its high content of natural oils, basil loses much of its power when dried.

Preserve basil's fuller flavor by whirling fresh leaves with a trickle of oil or melted butter in a blender or food processor. Refrigerate until needed. Or make pesto (many recipes are in this cookbook!) and freeze it for wintertime use.

Tear basil leaves into small pieces, mix them with water, and place the mixture in ice cube trays. When frozen solid, move the cubes into plastic bags and keep them in the freezer. Add basil ice cubes to your sauces and stews.

How to Store It

If you wash the leaves, pat them dry since water tends to blacken them. To freeze, lay leaves on cookie sheets in a single layer. When frozen, transfer to plastic bags and store in freezer.

What to Eat It With and In

Basil brings gusto to tomatoes. Basil is one of several basic ingredients in pesto, which remarkably dresses up pastas, chicken, and fish.

Distinguishing Qualities

Basil comes in many varieties, each with its own subtly identifiable flavor— purple or dark opal, lemon, cinnamon, Genoa green, lemon, lettuce leaf, Thai, and anise.

Tips

Add basil to a cooked dish just before you serve it. When exposed to cooking heat, basil turns black and bitter.

Keep harvesting leaves, and the basil plant will keep producing them (providing, of course, that you are meeting the bush's growth needs otherwise).

Add whole or shredded leaves at the last minute to dishes that are cooked for a while. The basil will retain its aroma and flavor longer when treated that way.

Tear basil leaves rather than chop them.

Bay

The Plant

"Sweet bay" is a small evergreen tree. The most pleasing and commonly used variety is *Laurus nobilis.*

Its Flavor

Bay leaves' fragrance nearly matches their flavor in strength. Both are pungent, somewhat peppery, with barely a tinge of bitterness.

Its Growing Needs

These semi-hardy, little trees grow slowly and can be tricky to root; it's best to buy them as potted plants.

Grow them outdoors in filtered sun and in soil that drains well. Let the ground dry out a bit between waterings. Fertilize them occasionally.

Bring the plants in before frost and place them in a window with bright light, but with no direct, or with only minimal, sun.

How to Harvest It

Pull off a leaf whenever you need it. There's no reason to dry the leaves unless you cannot have access to a plant year-round.

How to Store it

These are hardy plants that do well in sunlight, whether indoors or out. Because of the leaves' heartiness, drying and storing them is less necessary than with many other herbs.

But if you choose to dry the leaves, clip the branches and hang them in a dark, dry place. When the leaves are fully dried, carefully pull them off the stems and store them in airtight containers.

What to Eat It With and In

Cook bay with meat and seafood; add it to stuffings, soups, and stews; stir crushed bay into bread doughs; drop whole leaves into puddings and custards.

Bay is usually a basic ingredient in bouquets garnis; when used in that way, the leaves are crumbled. Otherwise, the leaves are most often used whole.

Distinguishing Qualities

Bay's fragrance and flavor usually reach their peak three to six days after the leaves are picked. The natural oils concentrate during that time.

Bay stems can be shaped into decorative and functional wreaths. Hung in the kitchen, such a wreath offers the cook easy access to dried bay leaves.

Tips

Remove whole bay leaves from the cooking pot before serving the dish. The leaves do not soften with cooking and can catch in or scratch diners' throats. (It is safest to put crumbled bay leaves in a muslin bag before adding them to a roast or stew, for the same reason.)

Add bay leaves at the beginning of your cooking, baking, or roasting (in contrast to many other herbs which lose much of their flavor when heated).

Fresh leaves are beautiful as a garnish.

Place a dried bay leaf in your jar of dried rice to give flavor to the rice.

Chives

The Plant

Chive leaves are grassy green, long, thin, and tubular and grow in lush clumps. Chives shoot forth purple floral seedheads, lovely in a bouquet—or on a salad or steeped in vinegar.

A perennial, chives need a dormant period—during the winter if kept outdoors; in the refrigerator or a cold dark shed if kept indoors.

Divide the clumps as they get pot-bound, or as they begin to take over the neighboring herb or flower beds.

The Flavor

The leaves taste delicately onion-y; the flowers are crunchy and even more mildly onion-y.

Its Growing Needs

Chives thrive best in full sun but will grow in less than that, even in partial shade. They prefer well watered, but also well drained, soil.

How to Harvest It.

Cut off the leaves with a shears as close to the ground as you can, so when new shoots push up they'll have no yellowed tips.

Chives can be harvested all during the growing season.

Cut off some flowers to encourage leaf growth. Let a few flowers dry on the stalk and go to seed to insure a new crop of chives.

How to Store It

Snip fresh chives and freeze them immediately in plastic boxes or bags. Freeze them in whole lengths and cut off what you need throughout the winter, or cut them into snippets before freezing and break off pieces as you need them.

Although dried chives are considerably less flavorful than fresh, drying may be necessary or practical. Lay stalks inside a paper grocery bag, fold it shut, and refrigerate it. Within a few weeks the chives will be dried. Chop them and place them in airtight containers.

What to Eat It With and In

Mix chives into egg recipes and light sauces, fold into cooked vegetables, stir into salads or soups. Chives enliven any herb butter. They work well as a garnish.

Distinguishing Qualities

Chives are one of the easiest herbs to grow. They're a good beginner's herb.

Chives are one of the first herbs to reappear in the spring.

Starting chives from seeds is a long, slow wait. You will grow less impatient if you begin with a clump of stalks from a nursery or someone else's herb garden!

Tips

Trim your chives regularly. Because they grow up and out profusely, they will soon topple over and look wildly uncombed.

Add chives at the end of your cooking process if you want to enjoy their maximum flavor and color.

Chives brighten almost any hot dish or salad. Add them impromptu as you finish up your food preparations.

Cilantro and Coriander

The Plant

Cilantro grow to a foot in height. Its leaves are oval with deep cuts, resembling a flat-leafed parsley.

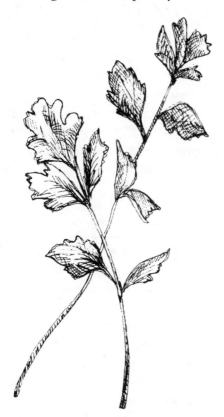

Its Flavor

The leaves of the plant—commonly known as cilantro—have an earthy, grassy taste with a tinge of anise.

The seeds—frequently called coriander—have a citrus-cumin flavor.

Its Growing Needs

Cilantro likes full sun to partial shade. Seed it directly into your garden where there is good drainage. Water frequently. Cilantro's life is relatively short. So re-seed or plant a new crop about every two weeks during the growing season to be assured of a continual supply.

If you grow cilantro indoors, use deep pots since the plants have long roots. Give them plenty of direct sun, water, and good drainage.

How to Harvest it

Cut the lower, flat leaves with a shears just before you're ready to use them. Begin harvesting when the plants have grown to be several inches tall.

Cut the stalks off when the seed pods begin to turn brown. Place the stalks in paper bags and hang them upside down. The drying seeds will fall conveniently into the bags. Rub the dried pods between your fingers to extract all the seeds.

How to Store It

Cilantro loses most of its flavor when it is dried, so use it fresh whenever possible. To keep cilantro fresh, place stalks in a plastic bag and refrigerate them, or place stalks, stem-end down, in a jar of water and refrigerate that.

You can also buzz the leaves in a blender, along with oil, to preserve their lively flavor.

Or chop the leaves finely, drop them into ice cube trays, fill the trays with water, and freeze them. Add a cube to your cooking pot whenever you choose.

Dry the coriander seeds, then store them in an airtight container in a cool, dark place. Crush the seeds just before you are ready to use them.

What to Eat It With and In

Historically the seeds, roots, and leaves of this plant have been ingredients in Indian curries; Chinese, Thai, and Cambodian sauces; and Mexican, Central and South American stews.

Not only does cilantro/coriander enhance those dishes, the leaves and seeds bring zip to salads, to stir-frys, to seafood, lentils, and pilafs made from a variety of grains.

Distinguishing Qualities

When cooked, cilantro leaves become somewhat blunted in their flavor. They will still add depth to a dish in that form. Used raw, however, the herb's flavor is sharper and more easily detected.

Tips

Use fresh leaves whenever you can. Dried cilantro has little flavor.

Use fresh seeds whenever possible for the greatest impact. Keep them in airtight containers and crush them just before you're ready to use them.

Dill

The Plant

Three parts of the plant are edible: the feathery leaves, often called dillweed; the seeds, which grow in the yellow flower heads at the tops of the tall, willowy stalks; and the golden flowers themselves.

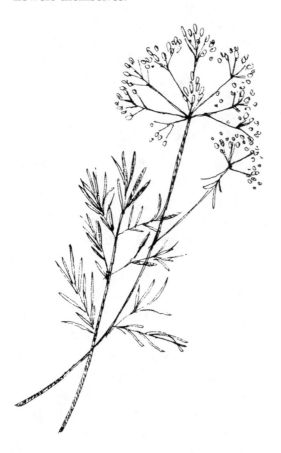

Its Flavor

Dillweed is pungent with a bit of a bite. Its flavor has echoes of celery and parsley. The seeds are similar in taste to anise and caraway.

Its Growing Needs

Dill has a very long taproot and so it does not do well indoors in an herb pot. Nor does it transplant well because its root is easily broken. It flourishes most when it is seeded directly into the bed in which it will grow.

Dill prefers a lot of sun and moist, but well drained, soil. It grows tall—from two to four feet in height—on somewhat weak stems that tend to become straggly.

Dill will not last the whole summer long, so plant new seeds about every two weeks to ensure a usable crop until frost.

Although dill is an annual, it does tend to re-seed itself. That means you will likely see dill sprouting in your garden next year, but not necessarily at the same place you first planted it!

How to Harvest It

With a scissors, clip the leaves close to the stem when the stalks have grown to be about four inches high. Flowers will appear about two months after you've planted the seed.

After the plant has flowered and the seeds in it have begun to brown, cut off the flowers with about one foot of stalk, and hang the flowers upside down. Place the flower heads in paper bags so the seeds drop into them.

What to Eat It With and In

Dill adds zip to pasta and tossed salads, to dips, egg dishes, cottage cheeses, and to fresh tomatoes. It gives similar character to white sauces and butters, to fish, chicken, and veal, and to steamed vegetables.

Dill seeds liven up breads and crackers, and, of course, dill pickles.

Distinguishing Qualities

Dried dill retains the power of its flavor. In fact, you may want to use only $1/4$ or $1/5$ as much dried dill you would fresh dill. While dill has a certain fragility of flavor, it also bears a cleanly distinctive taste.

Dill—either fresh or dried—is a favorite flavoring for vinegars.

Fresh dill sprigs are a graceful garnish.

Tips

While dried dill keeps its flavor, it does lose its aromatic strength, as compared to fresh dill.

Dill is most effective with more delicately flavored meats such as chicken and veal, rather than with cuts of beef.

Add dill at the end of the cooking process in order to keep its fresh flavor.

Dill is a good salt substitute with just-harvested vegetables.

Lemon Balm

The Plant

Lemon balm is a part of the mint family. It is a hardy perennial that becomes bushy and grows powerfully throughout its corner of the garden. Its leaves are gently triangular in shape with sawtoothed edges; its tiny white flowers draw bees.

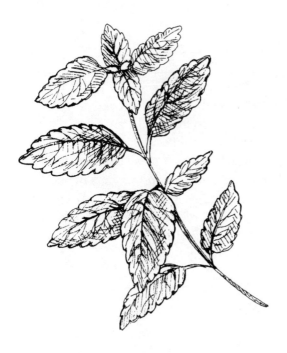

Its Flavor

Lemon-y mint. Decidedly citrus.

Its Growing Needs

A plant with few demands—light conditions can be from full sun to partial shade. Ideal soil conditions—fairly moist, well drained, moderately fertile.

Grow from seeds, from cuttings, or by dividing the plant's roots. Mulch the roots well and the plant should survive the winter.

Lemon balm will grow to a height of 2-2½ feet and to that width, as well.

Lemon balm will grow indoors if it gets sun for at least four hours daily, and if it is well watered and well drained.

How to Harvest It

Clip leaves with a scissors or knife whenever you are ready to use them. They are at their most piquant when they have just been cut.

The leaves do bruise, so handle them gently.

How to Store It

If you can't use them fresh from the bush, fresh leaves can be stored in a plastic bag in the refrigerator for several days. Or freeze chopped leaves in water in ice cube trays.

Dried leaves quickly lose their aroma and give up much of their flavor-rich oils, but they do retain some hint of lemon and mint.

Cut branches for drying just as the plant begins to bloom, hang them in a dry, airy place for about a week, and then crumble the dried leaves into airtight containers. Over time, the leaves will lose much of their flavor.

What to Eat It With and In

Lemon balm dresses up light, uncooked foods—green salads and fruit dishes. It makes a remarkable tea, served hot or cold. It gives a lift to cooked vegetables, fish, chicken, grains, desserts, and jellies.

Distinguishing Qualities

Lemon balm's hearty green growth belies its delicately subtle flavor.

It marries naturally with honey to produce a well balanced tea concentrate.

Tips

Heat destroys the oils in lemon balm's leaves. So add them at the end of your cooking process to retain the leaves' maximum flavor.

Lemon balm leaves infused with a cup of boiling water and the addition of honey produce much the same effect as old-fashioned lemon-honey cough drops.

Stir chopped lemon balm into any recipe that uses lemon juice. The lemon-y flavor will be enhanced, as will the color, and you will be adding a taste of springtime, also.

Lovage

The Plant

Lovage's leaves resemble celery—flat, deep cuts, and a rich green color. Its graceful stalks can reach a height of six feet and are an attractive backdrop to a flowerbed or herb patch, or a lush filler in an empty corner of the garden.

Its Flavor

Lovage's leaves not only look like celery, they have a deep, intense celery flavor. Its stems bear the same celery taste—raw and strong and unbleached. Lovage seeds are edible, too, and can be used as celery seeds are, although in smaller amounts since they carry a more concentrated flavor.

Its Growing Needs

The plant will flourish in rich soil; it will grow well in moist soil that drains well. Given full sun, the foliage becomes a deep green and equally flavorful; with less sun the leaves are paler and milder. It is an unfussy, hardy perennial.

Lovage will grow indoors in fertile potting soil.

It frequently re-seeds itself. It tolerates being transplanted, especially when it is young. Old plants can be divided; rootings with green shoots can be planted successfully in early spring.

How to Harvest It

Snip fresh leaves as you need them. If you like mild tasting stems, cut the lightly colored, young growth in the spring.

How to Store It

The leaves dry well and retain their robust pungency. Hang bunches of them in a warm, dry spot for a few weeks; then, when dried fully, crumble them into airtight containers.

The stems don't dry well—they're too tough and have too high a moisture content. Plan to use them only in their fresh state.

Catch the dried seeds by hanging the seed heads upside down in grocery bags.

What to Eat It With and In

Use lovage wherever you would use celery, but use it sparingly. It has a strong, robust character. Chopped fresh, mature leaves and stems brighten soups, stews, and hearty beef roasts.

A few chopped young leaves work well in tossed salads.

Add seeds to bread dough. Sprinkle them over potatoes or rice or garden salads.

The hollow stems make tasty straws. Serve them standing in tall glasses of tomato juice.

Distinguishing Qualities

Lovage announces its presence in whatever dish it is placed. It is savory, whether used fresh or dried.

Tips

Become acquainted with lovage before you use it in large amounts; then experiment. A few tender leaves bring springtime to a dish of creamed new potatoes and peas.

Use dried seeds or dried foliage in bouquets garnis.

Mint

The Plant

You'll know it's a mint (there are hundreds of varieties) when you smell or taste the leaves. Most stalks grow to be two to three feet tall and put forth broad, crinkled, veined leaves.

These are invasive plants that take over space both under—and above—ground. Contain them by growing them in large pots, by giving them a bed all by themselves away from other herbs, or by sinking 12-inch wide boards 10 inches into the earth in the shape of a square, and then planting the mint within the "fence."

If you want to grow a variety of mints, plant them in different areas of your garden because they readily cross-pollinate.

Its Flavor

Mints are spring-mountain fresh and tinged with whatever fruit taste they carry—from apple to orange to pineapple—or whatever medicinal flavor they offer—spearmint and peppermint among them.

Its Growing Needs

A hearty perennial, mint does best with a lot of water, moderately rich soil, morning sun, and afternoon shade.

Mint is a beautiful and functional houseplant, especially when grown in a hanging basket. Although it may not be as flavorful as those mints you grow outside, clip the runners and use them in cooking, or stick them in water, or back in the same pot, to root.

Start your mint crop with a plant or cuttings; then you will be assured you are getting the variety you want.

How to Harvest It

Snip off the larger leaves and the clusters of leaves at the top growth of the plant. In so doing you'll get strong flavor, and you'll encourage the plant to become more bushy.

If you plan to dry the leaves, cut off full stems and hang them up to dry in a dark airy place. When the leaves are completely dried, you'll be able to strip them right off the stems.

How to Store It

Mints survive well in the refrigerator if they are kept dry and stored in plastic bags.

Or put fresh mint leaves in small plastic bags or boxes and freeze them.

Place mint leaves, whole or chopped, in ice cube trays, cover with water, and freeze.

Store crumbled dried leaves in airtight containers.

What to Eat It With and In

Teas, jellies, and sauces, of course! Experiment with the multitudes of mint varieties, singly or in combinations, hot or cold.

Add mint leaves to cold fruits, ice creams, and salads.

Use in chicken dishes; stir into tabbouleh, potatoes, or peas; blend with yogurt or serve with cucumber slices or potato salad.

Distinguishing Qualities

Spearmint is one of the most aggressive mints in the garden, but it is one of the most delightful in teas and jellies!

Peppermint sweetens your breath and your hands. It can, however, overpower a pot of tea or a dish of steamed vegetables.

Mints are loaded with vitamins A and C.

Tips

Use only the leaves of the mint plant in salads, desserts, sauces, and cooked vegetables.

Use leaves and stems to make well flavored teas.

You can make a good cup of tea with dried mint leaves, but they may bring a somewhat dusty flavor to the drink. Fresh or frozen leaves have a clearer, purer taste.

Cut the plant off at the ground when the leaves start to yellow. That will allow it to lie dormant until it is ready to begin producing again.

Oregano and Marjoram

Oregano and marjoram are related—how closely is a subject of debate among botanists. For culinary purposes it is enough to know that they are similar in their growth and flavor. They are distinguishable in the way they look and taste, yet they are interchangeable in cooking.

The Plant

Oregano is a hardy perennial that tends to sprawl. Its dark green leaves are rounded; in late summer it blooms pinkish-purple flowers.

Marjoram is a smaller plant and more viny. Although it is a perennial, it behaves more like an annual since it cannot survive hard winters. Its leaves are oval, and it produces little knotty nodes along its stems, a telltale difference from oreganos.

The Flavor

Fresh oregano resembles thyme and balsam in its flavor. When dried it is sharper, full of zest, quite pungent, and even pine-y.

Marjoram has echoes of mint and an edge of sweetness, followed immediately by a slight bitterness.

Its Growing Needs

Neither oregano nor marjoram are fussy about soil makeup as long as it is well drained. They do prefer a lot of sun and a moderate amount of water.

They develop fuller stalks and lush growth when they are routinely trimmed back.

You can start the plants from seed. You will be less discouraged if you begin with a cutting or a stalk and a root that have been divided from a mature plant.

How to Harvest It

The flavors of both oregano and marjoram are the brightest when the leaves are cut just before the plants bloom. Use them fresh, or cut the branches at this stage for drying.

How to Store It

To preserve some of these herbs' fresh flavors, chop the leaves and stir them into olive oil. Refrigerate the mixture; then use it over pastas and pizzas.

Put fresh leaves in plastic bags and refrigerate or freeze them. Chop fresh leaves, place in ice cube trays with water, and freeze.

Hang stems of oregano and marjoram in bunches, upside down in a dry, well ventilated area. Or lay the branches on screens to dry.

When the leaves have fully dried, strip them off the stems into airtight containers.

What to Eat It With and In

Oregano zips up the taste of any tomato-based dish. Especially in its dry form, it can overtake a palate, so go lightly! Soups, stews, meats, and poultry can all benefit by the addition of oregano.

Add oregano or marjoram or both to salad dressings and to Italian, Mexican, and Greek dishes.

Marjoram complements bean recipes of almost any variety, as well as lamb and egg and stuffing dishes.

Distinguishing Qualities

Marjoram is milder, sweeter, and subtler than oregano. Yet both bring a pine-y, somewhat sharp twist to whatever dish they join.

Tips

Dried oregano carries more punch than fresh.

Dried marjoram offers a sweeter bouquet and flavor than fresh.

A marjoram branch bearing leaves and knots brings flavor—and visual interest—to a jar of vinegar.

If you want to add either herb in its fresh form to a cooked or baked dish, add it at or near the end of the heating process to maximize its fresh taste.

Parsley

The Plant

Two main types are readily available—the curly variety and Italian broad-leafed. The curly grows to be about a foot tall; the Italian passes it by a few inches. Both make a sort of elegant border to an herb garden with their full, bushy, dark green growth.

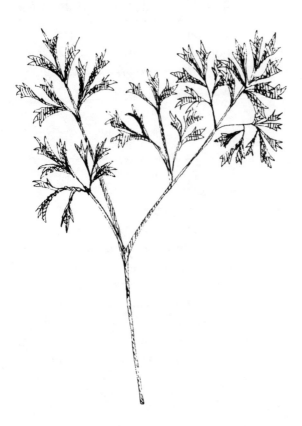

Its Flavor

Curly and Italian parsleys can be used interchangeably, although the Italian has a heartier flavor.

Both are somewhat pepper-y with a quiet but definite tang.

Its Growing Needs

Parsley likes full sun, but prefers shade when the sun is at its hottest. It likes a lot of water and benefits by some fertilization.

Parsley can frustrate a gardener who tries to start the plant from seeds. It is a slow and erratic germinator. Plant the seeds where you want the full plants to grow, since transplanting them risks damaging their long taproots.

Parsley can be grown indoors, although it becomes paler and ganglier than when it is exposed to full sun.

How to Harvest It

Cut off parsley's outer leaves at the base of the plant so the inner leaves can mature for the next cutting.

Keep clipping them off and bringing them in as long as they are richly green.

How to Store It

On the morning you plan to freeze parsley, hose the plants with fresh water to wash off the dirt. Let the sun dry the leaves. Then cut off the stems, clip them and the leaves (or just the leaves) into pieces, pack them in small plastic bags, and freeze.

Parsley also keeps for days in the refrigerator, especially if it has been washed, dried well, and placed in plastic.

Dry the leaves by hanging the stems upside down or by laying them out on screens in a dark, dry, well ventilated place. In contrast to some herbs, parsley loses much of its power when dried.

What to Eat It With and In

Parsley, in its sturdily green yet quiet way, seems to complement every herb its paired with, every pasta, salad, meat, vegetable, or main dish it's added to. It seems impossible to overdo parsley.

Parsley stems enrich soup stocks and stews. Stuff a chicken with parsley sprigs.

Distinguishing Qualities

All parsleys are loaded with vitamins (especially A and C), minerals (notably, potassium), and antiseptic chlorophyll.

Parsley can stand in for lettuce in sandwiches, for basil in pesto, and for nearly any other herb in a vegetable dip.

Tips

Mildly tempered as it is, fresh parsley can sweeten one's breath.

Italian varieties are a bit tougher to chew than the curly ones. They also have a more pronounced flavor. Cut them into small pieces before tossing them into your garden salad.

The less curly the parsley, the easier it is to wash it successfully.

Rosemary

The Plant

Rosemary is a bushy little evergreen-like shrub that grows to be about two feet tall during the warm months in a temperate climate. Although it is a perennial, rosemary needs special care and covering to survive frost, and it seldom weathers temperatures in the teens (F) or below.

Its needle leaves are silvery green; there are many varieties, with equally varied shades of gray and green.

Its Flavor

Rosemary is piney, pungent, and gently peppery. Its aroma spins together balsam, resin, and fresh sea breezes. Its flavor and smell have strength and persistence.

Its Growing Needs

Belying the power of its aroma and flavor, rosemary can be a finicky plant to grow. It thrives in full sun and well drained soil. In fact, it prefers drier soil, although if its roots and stalks become too dry, it is impossible to revive the plant. It grows best in an alkaline soil; fertilize sparingly.

You will likely be a happier herb gardener if you begin with a rosemary plant, rather than with seeds (which may seem reluctant to germinate and grow). But watch for bugs and mites if you bring a plant home from a nursery.

Mist the leaves regularly, and you'll dismay the bugs and encourage the plant.

How to Harvest It

Clip the stems before they get woody. Keep fresh sprigs in plastic bags in the refrigerator, or stand the stems in a jar of water.

How to Store It.

If you want to use fresh rosemary, lay an entire sprig over a roast or a dish of sliced potatoes as you put them into the oven to bake.

If you want fresh rosemary leaves to flavor a drink, tie them up in a cheesecloth bag and put that into the pot. That saves fishing out individual leaves later, or risking swallowing the tough, scratchy needles.

You can also finely chop the fresh leaves, or crush them with a mortar and pestle, just before you are ready to stir them into a dish.

Dry sprigs by hanging them up to dry in a warm, moist-free place. Or spread sprigs out on a screen to dry. Shake the dried needles into a bag, and then place them in an airtight container.

Crush the dried needles, also, or remove them from food before serving it.

What to Eat It With and In

Rosemary is not timid, so it needs a robust taste partner. It does wonderful things to hearty vegetables (beets, and cabbage), bland vegetables (potatoes and beans), stuffings for pork or poultry, and to strongly flavored fish, to meat you want to roast or grill, and especially to lamb. Stir into soups or jellies; steep it for tea.

Distinguishing Qualities

Keep your rosemary stems, even when they've grown woody. Toss them into the coals in your grill; they will add flavor and aroma to whatever is roasting above.

Strip the stems of all their leaves except for a plume at one end and then use the stems as skewers to hold vegetables and tender cuts of meat. Broil the kabobs.

Tips

This powerful herb can behave delicately. Add a pinch of crushed rosemary to bread dough. Lay a fresh branch of the plant on the top of whatever you're grilling. It will leave its piney flavor in whatever you cook.

Sage

The Plant

Sage becomes downright bushy, and even woody, in four or five years. The plants often grow to be two or more feet tall and about four feet in diameter. Its leaves are bumpy, grey-green, and gracefully broad and long.

Its Flavor

Sage carries traces of lemon and camphor and resin. Its distinct and somewhat intrusive flavor allows it to bring alive more mild-mannered dishes such as stuffing, potatoes, or pork. Or it can add zest to an already powerfully flavored cheese, wild game, sausage stew, or quiche.

Its Growing Needs

Sage is not finicky. It does best in full sun and well drained light soil.

Common sage can usually live through winter's cold temperatures. Prune it in the late summer or early spring to shape it and encourage new growth.

It will grow in a tub or window box and even indoors, although it won't be as luxuriant as when it grows in an outdoor garden.

After several years when the plant gets woody in the center, pull down some of its branches and cover them with dirt to encourage them to root and start a new plant. Or discard the old and begin with a new one.

How to Harvest It

Pull fresh sage leaves just when you are ready to use them. (Save the stems. Break them up and scatter them over your barbecue coals to flavor whatever is cooking.)

Clip sprigs for drying just before the sage flowers. Be sure to dry the leaves thoroughly before putting them in jars to prevent them from developing a musty flavor. Keep the leaves whole, and then crumble them (don't grind them) just as you are ready to add them to your dish.

How to Store It

Harvest the leaves year-round. If you want to dry them, keep the sprigs hanging. You avoid the risk of packaging the leaves before they're thoroughly dry; you avoid crushing the leaves, and thus loosing their more delicate, lemon-y taste.

What to Eat It With and In

Add sage to any meats (from roasted to pan-seared to broiled), hearty bread doughs, soups, omelets, marinades, and lentils.

Distinguishing Qualities

Sage, whether fresh or dried, has strength. Dried sage has a more powerful flavor than fresh. Experiment with your preferred amount before tossing in handfuls.

Some cooks eliminate salt when they use sage.

Tips

When you're making kabobs, thread a sage leaf on the skewer between each piece of meat and chunk of vegetable.

Tarragon

The Plant

There are two main varieties. Be sure to get only French tarragon. (Russian tarragon will not do. It is virtually tasteless, but is an aggressor in the garden.)

A full-grown plant becomes a willowy two-feet tall. Its dark green leaves are thin, long (about two inches), and pointy.

To avoid getting the imposter variety, buy a tarragon plant (not seeds) from a reputable and knowledgeable greenhouse. Crush a leave from the plant and sniff it. French tarragon is all licorice and anise. The Russian brand smells like hay or grass. And observe a mature plant. Avoid any with thick stems that look like a creepy, unkempt ground cover.

Its Flavor

Tarragon is delicate, yet it announces its presence. In its fresh form it will remind you of lemon and anise. Dried, it becomes sweeter.

Its Growing Needs

Don't try to start with seeds. They are too difficult for most gardeners to start. (Furthermore, you may not get the real McCoy.)

Buy rooted cuttings or small plants in the springtime and put them in your bed about 18 inches apart.

They will need uninhibited sun, plenty of water, but well drained and sandy soil.

Its leaves need moisture, too, especially if the sun is hot.

Growing tarragon indoors is tricky. Too much water can rot the roots; too little and the leaves dry up.

The plant needs a time of rest, so cut it back before frost, cover it with mulch, and give it a break. If you grow tarragon indoors, it also needs some time outdoors in the cold or in the refrigerator.

How to Harvest It

Pull the fresh leaves off the stems. Use them whole or chopped.

How to Store It

Place fresh leaves in plastic bags and refrigerate them for a few days. Or freeze them in ice cube trays covered with water. Or mix them into butter, which can be added to vegetables or meats. Or fill a glass jar loosely with fresh leaves; then pour in white wine vinegar until they are covered. Cover the jar, refrigerate it, and pull leaves from the jar as you need them.

Dry tarragon by spreading the stems on screens in a warm, dry, shaded area. Or hang the branches up to dry in an airy, shaded spot. Strip the leaves off the stems as soon as you can do so easily, and pack the leaves in airtight containers.

What to Eat It With and In

Chicken, fish, egg dishes, peas and potatoes, grilled meats, sauces for meats, and cooked vegetables. The French have memorialized the herb, making it a fixture in the classic combination known as fines herbes. There it partners with parsley, chervil, and chives and is customarily used with green salads, egg recipes, poached chicken and fish.

Tips

Make your own tarragon vinegar. If flavored vinegar is your intent (rather than preserving the fresh herb), bring the vinegar to a boil, pour it over several tarragon sprigs in a jar, seal the jar, and store it out of light for at least three weeks before using it.

Thyme and Lemon Thyme

The Plant

There are multitudes of varieties. Common thyme is a modest little bush (8-12 inches tall, and plumply rounded); others, such as lemon thyme, tend to creep over the garden, making them lovely, aromatic ground covers or border plants. They are hardy perennials.

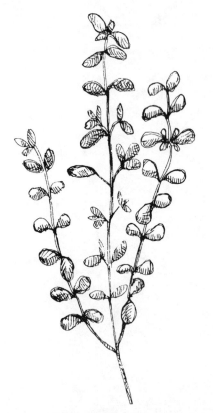

Thyme has a miniature quality—fine, dainty green leaves, each barely ¼ inch long. Flowers, also finely formed, range in color from pinks to lavenders, but also include some whites and reds.

Its Flavor

Hard to name, but definitely pungent and bite-y. Lemon thyme is, well, lemon-y and light.

Its Growing Needs

Thymes aren't fussy, as herbs go. They do best in sandy or light soil; good drainage is essential for their fine root system.

Thymes like a lot of sun.

For a well shaped plant, and for full growth, prune several times a year, ideally in early spring, when buds appear, and six to eight weeks after flowering.

Dry those trimmings for wintertime thyme.

Start new plants by dividing old ones. Or buy young starts at a nursery where you will be sure to get the variety you want.

How to Harvest It

Cut sprigs three to four inches in length. Run your fingers or fork tines down the stems and the leaves will pop off.

Cut sprigs of the same length for drying. Cut them just before the thyme flowers.

How to Store It

Fresh sprigs can be kept in plastic bags in the refrigerator for several days. Fresh leaves can be dropped into ice cube trays, the trays filled with water, and frozen until needed. Or mix fresh leaves into butter, or cover them with oil or vinegar.

Hang branches of thyme upside down in an airy, dark place. When the leaves turn crisp, slide your fingers down the stem and catch the leaves in an airtight container.

What to Eat It With and In

Thymes work with almost anything—add fresh or dried leaves to soups and stews, cooked grains, egg dishes, many yellow and orange cooked vegetables, marinades and stocks, roasted and broiled meats.

Place a sprig of fresh thyme in the cooking pot for stews, sauces, or fresh vegetables. Remove before serving.

Add fresh lemon thyme leaves at the end of cooking chicken or fish, vegetables, soups, or salad dressings.

Thyme adds life to bouquets garnis.

Distinguishing Qualities

Lemon thyme creates flavorful vinegars, teas, and jellies.

Don't discard thyme stems. Toss them into the stew (just remember to remove them before serving it) or over the barbecue coals.

A little thyme adds interesting flavor to a green salad.

Thyme dries well, but loses some of its zip in the process. Consequently, fresh thyme has more punch than dried. Adjust your seasoning accordingly.

Thyme is said to offset the greasiness of fatty foods. It brings a good balance to goose and duck, lamb and pork.

Tips

Mulch liberally around your outdoor thyme plants. That will keep the leaves from getting dirt-splattered when it rains. The leaves are so small they are hard to wash adequately. Good mulching helps avoid that problem.

Index of Herbs

Basil

Appetizers and Snacks
Basil Dip, 12
Basil Vinegar Mushrooms, 23
Basiled Cracker Bites, 29
Basil Tapenade, 17
Boursin-Style Cheese Spread, 7
Cheddar Crisps, 26
Fool's Boursin, 7
Goat Cheese and Tomato Flatbread, 13
Green Dip, 11
Herb Garden Dip, 11
Herb Melba, 15
Herb Toastettes, 15
Herbal Cream Cheese, 6
Herbal Cheese Spread, 6
Herbed Cheese Dip, 12
Herbs-Liscious Mushrooms, 23
Jeanette's Spring Rolls, 21
Layered Cheese Torte with Pesto, 16
Pesto Pizza Rounds, 14
Rosemary's Garlic Cheese Spread, 8
Tomato-Basil Tart, 19
Beverages
Basil Mint Tea, 30

Mulled Cinnamon Basil Punch, 35
Peach Basil Cooler, 36
Veggie Beverage with an Herbal Twist, 36
Breads, Rolls, and Muffins
Batter Bread with Sun-Dried Tomatoes, Cheese, and Herbs, 73
Heard's Easy Herb Bread, 80
Herb Beer Bread, 70
Herb Bread, 63-67, 80
Herb Peel-Away Bread, 65
Herb Whole Wheat Bread, 66
Pesto Bread, 68
Pizza Dough, 80
Quick Basil Beer Bread, 69
Whole Wheat Pesto Bread, 68
Breakfast Foods
Basiled Eggs, 84
Bruschetta, 82
Quick Rice and Egg Stir-Fry, 88
Tomato Egg Bake with Basil, 82
Tomatoed Eggs and Pesto, 84
Condiments
All Purpose Freezer Blend Pesto, 60
Basic Basil Pesto, 57
Basic Herb Vinegar, 53
Basil Butter, 41
Basil Cream, 46

Bay

Chives

Cilantro

Coriander

Appetizers and Snacks
Guacamole, 20
Spicy Peanut Dip, 28
Main Dishes
Low Calorie Beef Burritos, 159
Turkey Tenderloin au Poivre, 192
Soups
Mexican Black Bean Soup, 92
Quick Tomato Soup, 94
Tomato Soup with Lentils, 93

Dill

Appetizers and Snacks
Baked Herb Cheese Spread, 5
Boursin-Style Cheese Spread, 7
Chive-Dill Spread, 10
Crabmeat Nibblers, 25
Crabmeat Spread, 26
Cucumber Appetizers, 22
Dilled Green Beans, 22
Dill Dip, 9
Dill-Radish Dip, 9
Dip with Dill, 10
Fool's Boursin, 7
Garlic-Dill Dip, 9
Herbal Cream Cheese, 6
Herbal Cheese Spread, 6
Herbed Party Mix, 29
Homestyle Boursin, 7
Quick Salmon Mousse, 25
Rosemary's Garlic Cheese Spread, 8
Salmon-Stuffed Mushrooms, 24
Seasoned Oyster Crackers, 28
Sesame Dill Dip, 10
Veggie Dill Dip, 9
Beverages
Veggie Beverage with an Herbal Twist, 36

Breads, Rolls, and Muffins
Corn Dilly Bread, 78
Dark Herb Bread, 66
Dill Bread, 71
Dilly Cheese Bread, 78
Dilly Cheese Muffins, 74
Dilly Corn Muffins, 74
Dilly Cottage Bread, 70
Garlic Dill Bread, 71
Herb Beer Bread, 70
Herb Bread, 63-67, 80
Herb Peel-Away Bread, 65
Quick Basil Beer Bread, 69
Ready-for-Lunch Herb Bread, 64
Breakfast Foods
Breakfast Pizza, 87
Dilled Scrambled Eggs, 85
Quick Rice and Egg Stir-Fry, 88
Condiments
Betty's Herb Butter, 41
Broth Blend, 39
Creamy Dill Dressing, 51
Creole Herbal Mustard, 45
Dill Butter, 42
Dill Salad Dressing, 50
Dill Sauce, 46-47
Dill Sauce for Fish, 47
Dill Vinegar, 55, 125
Dilled Cucumber Salad Dressing, 51
Elaine's Dill Sauce, 46
Herbed Cream Cheese Salad Dressing, 49
Herbed Salad Dressing, 49
Parsley Herb Spread, 42
Roasted Garlic and Herb Butter, 42
Super Seasoning, 37
Desserts
Apple Crisp with Dill, 214
Main Dishes
Baked Herb Parmesan Roughy, 200
Fresh Dilled Fish, 194
Grilled Salmon, 201
Hamburger Stroganoff, 164
Hampton Herbs' Chicken Couscous, 191
Herb Baked Orange Roughy, 199

Lemon Balm

Lemon Thyme

Lovage

Marjoram

Mint

Oregano

Parsley

Rosemary

Sage

Tarragon

Thyme

Index of Recipes

Notes

Notes

About the Authors

For years, Dawn J. Ranck has been growing herbs, cooking with herbs, teaching about herbs, and generally spreading her contagion about the little plants and the way they enliven food. She is an advocate of bringing herbs to everyone's kitchens, not just to the cooking artists'.

Ranck lives in Harrisonburg, Virginia. She is also the co-author of *A Quilter's Christmas Cookbook.*

Phyllis Pellman Good has had her hand in many cookbooks, authoring *The Best of Amish Cooking* and *The Festival Cookbook,* and co-authoring *Recipes from Central Market, The Best of Mennonite Fellowship Meals,* and *From Amish and Mennonite Kitchens.*

Good and her husband Merle live in Lancaster, Pennsylvania, and are co-directors of The People's Place, a heritage interpretation center in the Lancaster County village of Intercourse, PA.